I0558315

Enoch Mast's Ballroom

Paul H Lepp

508 West 26th Street KEARNEY, NE 68848
402-819-3224
info@medialiteraryexcellence.com

TABLE OF CONTENTS

DEDICATION

This Book is Dedicated to

Robert Patrick Reid

March 17, 1948 ... May 3, 2023

Two Are Better Than One, For If Either Of Them Falls, One Can Help The Other UP...

Ecclesiastes IV: IX – X (RIP Bobby...Pauly)

CHAPTER I
FRAMEWORK

The lion's share of history consists of anonymous people and random events. Of these people and events, it is unavoidable fate the past surrenders its secrets to. It's only by chance we learn what took place and to whom.

On the last warm day of the year in Cleveland, Ohio, during the late Autumn of 1914 a stonemason entered Lake View Cemetery through the Mayfield Gate in search of Enoch Mast. He never forgot that day, it was exceptional in so many ways. He recalled how the bright morning sun made him roll up his sleeves and pull down the brim of his cap to shade his eyes. Three days earlier the temperature was in the low twenties with two inches of snow on the ground. The stonemason chuckled; it came as no surprise; he had lived in Cleveland long enough to know how fickle the weather could be. If anything, the atmospheric conditions of Autumn in Ohio taught one to expect the unexpected.

As he walked, he put his right hand into the pocket of his overalls and pulled out a clean white handkerchief. Wrapped in it was a vivid Burmese 'pigeon blood' ruby the size of a table grape. After he unwrapped it, he stood perfectly still, overtaken by the fortune he held in his hand. He closed his eyes at that moment and let the gem fill his senses with the incredible feeling of wealth.

In his grasp was at least ten years' wages, maybe more. The sunlight penetrated the gem to where it glowed like an ember. He briefly considered who or what could keep him from walking off with it. The temptation left as soon as it arrived with the awareness that he would rob himself and his family of all trust and honor. The impact of the reflection caused him to cover it back up and put it in the deepest part of his pocket until he needed it.

*****

As the stonemason reflected on the event, the day began no differently than any other with one or two exceptions. He and his wife ate breakfast before their children were awake. He'd drink a second cup of coffee, and they'd visit while she would pack a full-grain leather sack with his lunch. She filled it first with a ceramic bowl which held some black olives and next a bottle of red wine, both protected by a thick well-tooled leather cover. They always went in before any of the other items she would pack.

The full-grain leather sack and its accessories were a wedding gift from his uncle; it left the kitchen full in the morning and returned empty at the end of the day. Its constant use put a bronze-like patina on the supple leather that reflected the stability one seeks in one's life and that one day would make his uncle's gift a family heirloom.

Except for certain holidays, the routine hardly ever changed. Most mornings, a filled sack placed in the center of the table after the second cup was always up for grabs. For some unknown reason, they played a simple game to see who could snatch the lunch off the table. They were competitive, maybe four out of ten times, she gave back what she had won, but between two short kisses: the first to distract her and the second to thank her he'd take it six out of ten. The second kiss was always a bit longer, and it was hard at times to determine who legitimately won; each, at one time or another, had a reason to let the other win.

He remembered the morning he went to the cemetery they played hard, and in the end, he wound up with the sack and she wound up with the contents. He had the empty sack. She had what filled it. How they both stood silent for a few moments realizing it was the first time they had ever tied, or so it seemed, and it made them laugh. How he held the sack open, and she repacked it, how amused they were at each other's claim of victory.

After the contest, he took his lunch out the back door onto the porch, down the steps, and into the neighborhood. On his twenty-minute walk to the shop, he'd carry his sack lunch in a sea of lunch pails as if he were no different than the rest. He would politely nod to all he passed.

His destination was the two large red sliding doors of a substantial stone building in an alley off Superior Road. With the doors opened, the structure revealed twelve twenty-foot by twenty-foot bays, six on each side of the building, twenty feet above them; a skylight ran down the center of the roof the length of the shop. Each bay also had a four-foot by eight-foot window. The building took full advantage of all the natural light it could. A dozen Journeyman Stonemasons, a half dozen apprentices, four bookkeepers, and three bosses occupied the building.

The Company offices, storeroom, payroll window, and lavatory were in the rear of the building. There was plenty of floor space, workbenches, durable hand tools, jacks, chains, and hoists, along with a network of heavy-duty overhead tracks that held a variety of pulleys to lift and move the mass and weight of the work in progress. It was dangerous work; the load and tools were unforgiving, and accidents usually killed or maimed their victims. Most of all, the cost of such events devastated the company's bottom line and penalized all. One had to pay attention to their work and stay focused on everything surrounding them.

On the floor, there was one apprentice to every two stonemasons. Their job was to handle the scrap, maintain a safe area, sharpen the tools, and fetch them when told while observing the methods of their stonemason, each in competition for the first open bay.

Those who worked there came from the same country, even the bosses. They all had a part in creating a reputable and profitable business. It was a good setup for those who would give birth to first-generation Americans. Through their efforts, the next generation would find it easier to explore the possibilities of their new homeland to take full advantage of the opportunities that came their way.

The shop was almost perfect, except for the English rule. Immigration created the regulation. In 1907 one point two million immigrated to America. By 1910, thirteen and a half million immigrants were in the country, all wanting to speak their language. By 1914 the mandate issued by management in 1911 that all shop business was to be in English took hold. Spoken, written, and read at work at all times—those who wouldn't or couldn't-fired. The approach was essential for the growth of the company. The policy created a cross-pollinated language made up of domestic and imported words. Over time a vocabulary evolved, and a language most could follow, employees, bosses, and customers.

*****

The stonemason was first in and out of the shop the morning he went to the cemetery. It was unusual. He could count on one hand the number of times it had happened. As he put his sack lunch into his toolbox, what was more remarkable and unexpected was what he placed it next to - a set of instructions written by his boss and a clean, folded white handkerchief. In general, his directives stated the ruby found in the folded handkerchief was a birthstone, and he was to always refer to it as such. He was to take it to a specific place and, once there, permanently set it on top of a monument.

His boss wrote in English on the same level the stonemason read the language, which at best was weak in meaning but firm in the effort. Over the years, the two of them, and the others, created a language only spoken and understood by those in the shop. Their jargon consisted of mispronounced and misspelled English whose meanings were always the whispered words of a foreign language and always ended with, "*Capeesh*, understand?"

Fortunately, the instructions in the toolbox came through to where the stonemason had no questions. What he understood most was the destination was not far from the shop, and the work would be easy. He softly whistled parts of the aria 'Un bel di" from Puccini's *Madame Butterfly* as he lifted the leather strap attached to the toolbox over his left shoulder and headed out the door.

He first read the instructions in his bay at the shop. When he finished, and without looking, he put the handkerchief and what it held deep inside his right-hand pocket. He folded the instructions to where they'd fit in the upper pockets of his bib overalls and thought about them as he walked.

At the cemetery and after he put the ruby back in his pocket, he reread the instructions and began to carry them out. He double-checked the location by section and name. He was remarkably familiar with the section but not the name. He muttered, "Enoch Mast?" More than once, and nothing came back to him. All he knew about Enoch Mast didn't go beyond; he was the reason he was there that morning, and that was enough. The stonemason shrugged and gave it no more thought as he walked toward the familiar section in search of Enoch Mast, unaware of the historical disclosures that came with the name.

When he arrived at the site, a monument off in the distance caught his attention before he began his search. He stopped momentarily to observe, for the first time, from the ground up and in the sunlight, Bruno Balissaari's completed *Floating Cube*. It had become a much-talked-about recent masterpiece added to the cemetery by his good friend.

Balissaari's work always impressed the stonemason. Bruno lost the thumb and forefinger on his right hand when he was an apprentice. The stonemason knew how hard it was to hold the tools of the trade with all five fingers, let alone three. What had his interest in Balissaari; was the irony; the accident was the most critical part of his apprenticeship that made him the best in the shop.

Unwritten but understood, shop etiquette allowed the journeymen to critique another's work critically, but only within the shop's walls. The practice kept them sharp and was seen as good for business. Once a piece of work left the shop, continuing the evaluations was considered bad for business. It was also considered poor form to look for another's finished work specifically. However, to come across another's monument in the line of work was a different matter.

Balissaari's work was a composition of four pieces of granite. A base is made up of three slabs. The first two slabs are three inches thick. The third slab is two inches. The first slab is a grey four-foot square, centered on top of it, a grey three-and-half-foot square. The third grey slab is a significantly undersized square foot centered on top of the second slab. A pale red granite cube rests on the third slab, all six sides a three-foot square. Balissaari chose the cube because when the six sides are unfolded, they form a cross. His work could have just as easily been called the *Unseen Cross*.

The design gave the illusion of a large granite cube that mystically floats two inches above its six-inch base. At first sight and from a distance, a floating cube appears. The intent of the design works. However, up close and upon further inspection, the unseen undersized third slab comes into view, and the mystery is solved.

The monument illustrates that reality isn't always as it first appears. The stonemason recalled how his search ended before it began. He found Enoch Mast's name as he looked over Balissaari's work on the side of the cube that faced Lake Erie.

It was unexpected, the observation startled him. It shouldn't have; he walked by the name numerous times at the shop. The times Bruno worked on the monument, and they would visit. As they talked, he noticed how his friend moved his hands over the stone and how the letters he carved became symbols and the words they formed designs. It was Balissaari's style he admired. Over the years, the two had carved more names in stone than they could remember. Names and dates meant little to them, how they were carved everything.

*****

His gaze turned into a stare as he focused on the job. The focus sidetracked as the stare turned into a broad smile which gave way to a brief chuckle. He felt the irony of introducing a birthstone to a tombstone to make it one stone a humorous contradiction.

He began to ponder. There's always a line between the two. Birth and death can't occur at the same time. There is no death without birth. It didn't feel right to try and change the order. The stonemason felt the birthstone represents the beginning of life and the tombstone the ending. The two stones represent two separate events; neither complements the other; they contradict each other; they don't belong together as if they were the same.

He also knew what he thought didn't matter. What mattered was the job, which was to follow instructions and, for some reason, make these two stones one. He shrugged, slipped the leather strap off his left shoulder, bent over, and placed his toolbox on the ground. He straightened up, stretched, and stood motionless for a few moments, overwhelmed by the beauty of the day and how good he felt.

*****

In the warm light and gentle breeze of late Autumn, the stonemason fell under the spell of how it all came to be, him working outside in such a fine cemetery under such a clear blue sky, how at the end of the day, he would return to a comfortable home and good family. Conscious only of the fact it was Enoch Mast who brought him there that day and nothing more.

He began to reminisce; it was a little over two decades he left Italy to become an American. He liked being a citizen; his appearance was impressive. His family had enough to eat, suitable clothes, and a roof over their heads with heat, indoor plumbing, and electricity. He was comfortable.

He was satisfied with the stability, but his children weren't. They were interested in progress. Advancement was the power behind why they could read, write, and speak English beyond the capabilities of their parents. Where English was the parent's second language, it became their children's first. The Americanization of the 'Little Italy,' their parents had worked so hard to create for them, became one big paradox.

In America, he became a strong, healthy middle-aged tradesman with broad shoulders, a thick mustache, and a full head of hair. He lacked a formal education but was well-trained in a trade. He had a craft, which, in 1914, was in high demand. The customers for his skill were wealthy, and though they paid conservatively, the volume of work they provided offset the imbalance.

The stonemason was no stranger to the cemetery. It was like a second home to him and the others from the shop. Section 22 was an Italian stonemason's heaven. The tombstones and crypts in this section were large and expensive and called 'monuments' and 'mausoleums.'

Their size, as big as the wealth behind the names carved on them: Henry Chisholm, father of the Cleveland steel industry; Marcus Hanna, businessman, and Senator; Flora Stone Mather, philanthropist; Joseph Carabelli, noted stonemason and sculptor; and Enoch Mast, no idea.

The ground in the section was extremely exclusive. The joke at the shop was the section featured three types of people: the very ricco (rich), the highly affluente (affluent), and the incredibly Prospero (prosperous). As a source of work, with these three types of customers, Section 22 was the jackpot for an Italian stonemason.

The best feature of the section was the room it had for growth. There was not only Section 22 but also Section 22A and 22B. The consumption of these sections would increase the need for more Italian stonemasons and all the Italian merchants, bankers, and chefs who would follow. Section 22 provided all the potential needed to create and maintain the best of both worlds – an always evolving 'Little Italy' within America.

*****

The work at hand that Autumn morning was to be done on his dear friend's large, highly polished cube of pale red granite. The stonemason was there because of the company's tragic 1914 Independence Day picnic at Silver Lake, where Bruno Balissaari drowned while swimming with what some thought was a friend, he had run into that no one was introduced to or saw again.

His passing was a double loss. Not only did the stonemason lose a close friend, but an apprentice as well. The open bay Bruno left went to the stonemason's apprentice, yet to be replaced. The situation left him and a colleague with all the light and minor work.

The major work for him and his colleague would return when the company brought in a new apprentice. The new apprentice would go to the senior stonemason on the floor, and everyone moved a notch to where the two newest journeymen would get the most senior apprentice. It was a system all understood and the best fit for the company.

The composition of the floating cube monument was his friend's masterpiece and well received by the Client, who had paid for the gravesite, tombstone, and gem. The total cost of the Enoch Mast monument, paid by the Client, could be measured by how many times the stonemason's annual salary would go into the final bill. The Client paid twenty times the stonemason's annual salary in one afternoon as if it were nothing.

The positive reception and possibility of future projects from such a customer didn't go unnoticed or unrewarded by the company. "Well received by the customer" was how the stonemason made his money, and the company made its name.

Balissaari's six-sided cube provided four large vertical panels, nine square feet, for names, dates, and epitaphs. The top panel was the one to be worked on. The unseen bottom panel stayed the same. Twenty-seven cubic feet of pale red granite resting on a two-step, eight-inch-high platform of polished dark gray granite for contrast. To be embedded on top of the monument, in its center, the birthstone.

With the birthstone as its origin, a simple compass of true: North, East, West, and South rendered for all to see. For a moment, the stonemason thought, 'Why?' Eventually, the thought of 'why' was overpowered by the thought of 'how?' He had no control over all the answers to 'why' a compass. What he could control was the 'how.' He knew that when he had a chisel in hand, the 'how' would take over and in some way create a design the Client would appreciate.

Until a new apprentice arrived, he and his colleague would be the ones from the shop to update the monuments and carve the dates of birth and death on the work sold by the company. The chore at hand, for the stonemason, was the perfect job to consume a beautiful day and a pleasant change of pace. What was even better, there was no sketch with the instructions; he was in total control of the design.

He knew how deep to cut and turn what he removed into the powder and paste he'd need, how to use it to set and blend the birthstone into the top of the pale red granite cube. The stonemason knew every trick of the trade to accomplish the project.

He already had in mind the style of lines, arrowheads, and how he would carve the letters to define the four directions of the compass. It came to him after he glanced at the leather sack in his toolbox that one line would be longer than the other three to symbolize a cross.

The South would be the farthest from the origin. A mob lynched eleven Italians after a murder trial in New Orleans in 1891. It didn't matter to the rabble, six of the eleven had been acquitted, and three had mistrials declared. It became America's largest mass lynching. It happened the year he arrived; one victim was the uncle that gave him the sack. After twenty-three years, the South's position on his compass would be his reminder to all; the incident would never be forgotten nor forgiven. The compass he would carve as a cross would be in memory of those lynched. His answer should anyone ask about his design and the South's distance from the origin.

For one offbeat moment, he thought of carving a short message about what he'd once heard; the four letters on a compass can spell the word 'NEWS'- which comes from all directions and in two forms, good and bad. The thought left him as soon as it became apparent it went way beyond the scope of the conditions given in the instructions.

*****

The stonemason ended his gaze over the landscape of the cemetery. He sat down and took the fine leather sack from the toolbox. From it, he pulled out the large linen napkin wrapped around some prosciutto, provolone, and bread, followed by the leather-covered bowl of black olives and the leather-covered bottle of red wine. The food and wine were in good quantity for the early morning buffet he was about to have.

He recalled sitting on the ground with his back against a neighboring monument. At that moment, the only problem was fitting four hours of work into the newly accepted eight-hour day. He took out a large pocket knife, picked up a stick, and began to whittle as he thought about all the different compasses he had seen on land and at sea.

*****

He'd wait for the sun to rise slightly higher in the sky and use the idle time to find a design. On that day, instead of eating his lunch all at once in a brief time, he would graze through it over a more extended period, and as he did, he enjoyed every bite he took. Enough wine was left to compliment a cigar when the food was gone. He lit it up around one in the afternoon, and he and his cigar and wine shared the project and finished it as the sun faded in the western sky. Four hours of non-stop work that felt more like four minutes.

The birthstone was set on top of Enoch Mast's family monument. The stonemason reminisced how before he began to carve the cross, the gem looked insignificant compared to the area around it and wondered if it was by design. He muttered, "A grape in the middle of the table." It struck him as strange how something so desired could fall so fast in its appeal. What was the Client's intent? The gem seemed precious in his hand, set in a large field of pale red granite, insignificant, small, and out of place.

The lines ran from the birthstone in one of four ways, each ending with an arrowhead aimed at the letter of the direction. The letter 'N' on the compass pointed North towards Lake Erie. The carving was one of the best pieces of work the stonemason ever produced and overshadowed the beauty of the ruby. It was also the final phase of a project which, from start to finish, worked out well for both the Client and the company.

*****

The stonemason always looked back on that enchanted day; there wasn't anything about it he didn't love. It never left him how pleasantly surreal it felt. It wasn't too long after the job that the company rewarded him. The boss said his work was "Well received by the Client." They had a few glasses of red wine in the boss's office, an envelope filled with cash handed to him, along with the news of when the new apprentice would start. All that took place was good.

They lit cigars. In their shop language, they began as good a conversation as one can have about the Enoch Mast family monument in section 22. Neither thought, as it unfolded, the story of Enoch Mast's ballroom would be a dusk-to-dawn account of Enoch Mast's society and the changes he saw.

What the stonemason enjoyed most from the memory was the following Saturday morning when he returned home. How the wrath of his wife was subdued entirely, not so much by the envelope he handed her, but by the incredible story he told her that held him captive through the night, neither of them would ever forget it.

*****

As he looked back on all that took place, the reality was that had the stonemason and his boss's conversation been a hundred percent in Italian or English; it wouldn't have flowed as well as it did. The combination of the two languages used by them was easy to follow. The stonemason's boss joked, "I was *surpresso* – surprised - you returned that day." The stonemason replied, "così sono io" - so am I." His boss continued, "As of now, only three of us know about the 'ruby' you, me, and the Client." The stonemason laughed, correcting him, "You mean the *pietra portafortuna* - birthstone? Remember the instructions?" He recalled how small and unimpressive the gem looked after he set it. The stonemason added, "One would have to look hard to find it; it's a small grape on a big `table."

His boss laughed as if he understood and asked his opinion on how long he thought it would be before it disappeared. The stonemason shrugged and chuckled. "*Chissa* – who knows?" But the Client wouldn't steal it, leaving you and me. One of us will be disappointed in himself when we go to get it, and it's gone. On the other hand, one of us won't." The boss thought about the remark; it puzzled him for a moment, long enough to bring on some laughter as they thought about the situation. Each knew what the other knew; neither one would ever take the gem.

*****

When the laughter stopped, the stonemason was comfortable enough with the boss to make a request. "Tell me about who is out there, who the Client is, and why they wanted this done?" His boss replied. "I'll tell you who is out there; I'll give you the background and portrait of Enoch Mast from when he was born to when he died. But you don't need to know who the Client is or why they want something done."

*****

The stonemason recalled that what followed was fully understood by him but would always be challenging to explain to others. Enoch Mast was a person the stonemason's boss had never met or knew of until the Client showed up. Other than the boss, the Client was invisible to all in the shop but always a topic of conversation. The one fact that mattered the most was the Client's account was significant and always current.

From the moment the Client entered the boss's office, a stream of knowledge poured down on the boss to where he became an overflowing reservoir of all the details, great and small, of the life and times of Enoch Mast and his ballroom.

The Client gave the boss two dates, three additional names, and four epitaphs for the monument. The Client felt all the abundant information he gave the boss was necessary for the boss to put his best man on the project to provide a masterpiece, a stone worthy of the Mast name.

As his boss began to go on about Enoch Mast, the stonemason became aware he would be one of the very few to know about who was under the cube. The stonemason believed, outside of the Client and his boss, he would be the third person and part of the trinity to know the secret of 'who was out there' in section twenty-two of the Lake View Cemetery in Cleveland, Ohio.

He wasn't. The third person to know was Bruno Balissaari, who died soon after he found out. Bruno Balissaari never mentioned 'Enoch Mast' to the stonemason in any of their many conversations before he died. Had the stonemason known who was third, and in light of what happened to him and the stranger he was with, he wouldn't have asked, but he had no way of knowing there was someone in front of him, and the story continued to unfold.

The stonemason wanted to know who came up with the concept of the floating cube. However, he never asked about the concept. Instead, he asked about the epitaphs written on the four sides of the cube. It wasn't the question he wanted to ask, but for some reason, the one asked.

As his boss began to answer, the stonemason interrupted "Why do three of the four panels have "In Memory Of" and one doesn't? Those under the East, West, and South.' Why are three out of four dates of death the same and one isn't? Those under the North, South, and West," His boss answered, "The East is in memory of his wife, the West is in memory of his daughter, and then added, "She was forty-two at the time, but had the mind of a six-year-old." The South is in memory of neither brother nor son by blood, yet one who became part of the Mast family. Those with 'In Memory Of,' their locations, as they say, are known but to God. The North represents the only one buried there."

His boss pointed out each side had a direction and each direction an epitaph. "Before you ask why, Mary Irene in the West and Brooks Mast in the South have the same epitaph, which I believe goes…

May it be the last breath here is the first breath in paradise…

It is because they disappeared together, and on the same day, Enoch Mast died." The boss next told the stonemason, "Irene Kathleen Mast, in the East, died in 1889, swept away in the Johnstown flood when the dam at the South Fork Hunting and Fishing Club burst. Her epitaph is said to be what she always told her husband if she died before him.

I will be up the road with those who waited for me, waiting for you...

The Northern epitaph has to do with what one learns from life…

The past always surrenders its secrets to fate …

It belongs to the one buried there, Enoch Mast."

*****

The stonemason had read the epitaphs but couldn't recite them. If he had any questions about them, he forgot what they were. Overpowered by the recall, his boss demonstrated on each vertical panel of Balissaari's *Floating Cube*. The literature on the monument didn't hold his attention as much as the idea for the design. No Enoch Mast, no *Floating Cube* struck the stonemason the most. At the time, the stonemason was far more impressed with the monument than the man under it.

The stonemason wanted to know who came up with the concept from the boss. But epitaphs and directions sidetracked his effort to know, and it would remain a mystery who came up with the floating cube - Balissaari or the Client?

*****

His boss had an excellent office. It featured a door with his name on it, thick rugs, drapes, and in one corner, a small, well-built pantry of cupboards and drawers, primarily filled with bread, cheese, olives, anchovies, prosciutto, wine, candy, and tobacco. In the corner diagonally opposite the pantry sat a small wood-burning stove on a large well-manicured thick piece of slate. Surrounding the slate is an ornate stable brass rail to put one's feet on. The stove pipe through the outside wall was barely noticeable, making the corner even more inviting.

Between the pantry and the stove, against the wall with the office door, on top of a thick oriental rug, and under a large kerosene lamp that hung from the ceiling, a substantial rolltop desk with two pigeon holes for each month, stuffed with letters and envelopes, and open and shut drawers. In front of the desk was an ample well-made leather chair. A large clock hung on the wall opposite the desk; it was next to an extensive calendar and a sizable bulletin board with notes and drawings pinned to it. At a right angle to the desk, a large window, with an ample sill filled with scale models to show customers along with a clear view of the street. Pulling the cord to the heavy felt green drapes, the street view altered.

The stove, another leather chair, identical to the one in front of the desk. Next to the chair was a well-built large heavy-duty box filled with scrap wood from the crates used to protect the shipments of large pieces of granite and marble made to the building. When business was good, the box was full.

There was an ample supply of everything—an abundant number of cigars and bottles of wine to keep the mood mellow. There was plenty of wood for the fire to maintain a comfortable room temperature and contribute to the velvety light. The room filled with a soft glow and friendly shadows after the boss lit the lamp over the roll top. The stonemason and his boss put their feet up, the boss on the huge rolltop desk, and the stonemason on the brass rail in front of the stove.

The door to the stove was open, and the stonemason, with poker in hand, tended the fire; the embers reminded him of the ruby and the day. The boss pulled back the drapes to watch the snow coming in from the lake reflect the light from the street as it began to cover the ground. Both leaned back in their chairs and focused on what was before them.

At first, the two talked to each other, but there was no eye contact, each captivated by the fire and snow in front of them. When they did speak, they retreated into their native tongue, unaware of how much the English Rule had replaced it. They both got up a few times to refill their linen napkins with food from the pantry, grab a few cigars, fill their glasses, maybe empty an ashtray, or go to the lavatory.

*****

When they finally settled in, a most peculiar event took place. A single voice took over the room and told the story as late afternoon turned to evening and evening to dawn. The Client became the invisible ventriloquist in the room and spoke through the boss in a more feminine than masculine voice.

The boss, unaware he was speaking, heard the story of Enoch Mast and his ballroom no differently than the stonemason. Neither was aware of who was speaking as they listened to the life and times of Enoch Mast and those who surrounded him in all three tenses, past, present, and future.

It spoke to the stonemason and the boss through a trance the boss would go into whenever he put his feet up on the desk, which wasn't often. If he took them off the desk, the ventriloquist stopped. The boss and the stonemason had no idea how the voice came and went. Had they known, they could have avoided the intense periods experienced, the times the boss took his feet off the desk and broke the spell.

The voice told them all they knew were the names, dates, and epitaphs carved in stone on the monument. The voice advised the two to read between the lines and let the stone speak to them about where their names came from and their environment when they grew up. Let the cube explain to them the present can't exist without the past, and the future can't exist without the present—the present trapped between the two. The stone would tell both of them that nothing exists without a background; to be seen, every picture, person, and object has to have one.

*****

The voice demonstrated its knowledge of American history, and the stonemason, lost in the glow of the fire, didn't see his boss slowly move his feet on the desk, nodding his head up and down and slipping into a deep trance. The stonemason saw nothing but heard everything.

The trance brought on the voice of the past; it spoke of a bygone time; as the stonemason listened, he drifted away from the shores of the present and into the deep waters of the past. The voice then took on the many dialects and tones those on the stone would have heard daily.

It covered the span of time Enoch Mast was given, carved in stone below his name from July 8, 1839, to June 28, 1914. It spoke of paintings and how each has a 'center of interest' that draws our attention and how the 'center of interest' can't exist without a background.

To see the true picture of Enoch Mast, one has to view what was behind him and understand his upbringing and the time it took place. One has to see the shades of the *Antebellum Era* and the shadows of the *Gilded Age*, the two periods of time that gave color and contrast to Enoch Mast's life. He lived through the last half of the *Antebellum* Era and all of the *Gilded Age*. Antebellum is Latin for '*Before the War*.' The period between the end of the War of 1812 and the end of the Civil War in 1865. For Enoch Mast, the Civil War ended nearly two years earlier, when he was twenty-four, at Gettysburg in July of 1863.

*****

The Civil War ended the *Antebellum Era*. Around 1870 the era was followed by thirty years known as the *Gilded Age*. Enoch Mast was thirty-one at the start and sixty-one at the end of the Gilded Age. Over the thirty years he observed, the time turned out to be less than expected. Enoch was very aware of the differences between fantasy and the facts of the *Age*. At times it was every bit as difficult as the *Antebellum Era*, but in different ways.

*****

The tones and dialects of the voice came from a time between Enoch Mast's first to last breath, a period that lasted seventy-four years, eleven months, and twenty days. Both events took place in Cleveland, Ohio, where he was born under the seven stars found in the constellation astrologers call *The Crab* or *Cancer*. The sign that has a ruby for a birthstone. The first son of a teamster and seamstress named Uriah and Eve Mast. He was also the older brother of twins Ezra and Enos, born almost exactly one year later in 1840. He took his last breath, waiting to get paid at the Hardin Lasbrith estate in the ballroom he repossessed.

Throughout his life, he had the traits of the constellation he was born under. For the most part, he was an intuitive and caring individual. Fortunately, there were only a few times he became moody and vindictive. The times he became irritable and merciless were remembered by those who witnessed them.

His life was spent in an expanding country from his first to last breath. A country, like a child, that from time-to-time experienced growing pains, some mild but most extreme. A child born into an environment filled with pro-slavery apologists and anti-slavery abolitionists. He lived when the continual disagreement between slave states and free states about how territories would be given statehood and brought into the Union, free or slave, evolved into a full-blown war. The Gilded Age followed the Antebellum Era, where disagreements and conflicts between capitalists and progressives replaced those of the apologists and abolitionists. Throughout his life, there was never a shortage of disagreement and conflict throughout the land.

Enoch Mast existed in a country occupied by exceptionally reputable individuals and unbelievably ruthless people. A land where, at times, common ground didn't exist for its problems. A country where the laws made were to the advantage of some and the disadvantage of others.

The final tally shows Enoch Mast lived through the administrations of twenty presidents. Starting with the eighth president, Martin Van Buren, and ending with the twenty-eighth, Woodrow Wilson. The three he recalled the most were the sixteenth, the twentieth, and twenty-fifth, Abraham Lincoln, James A. Garfield, and William McKinley, who were shot. The other seventeen presidents all ran together in his mind.

Despite all the internal problems of democracy, the one feature Enoch Mast appreciated most was its stability. Stability other countries envied. The fact the interval between assassinations had grown was proof.

Enoch Mast was always a person of years, months, and days; he would be able to tell one in these terms of all the significant historical events that occurred during his life. He could tell one the time between the Lincoln and Garfield assassination was sixteen years, five months, and four days. The time between Garfield and McKinley was nineteen years, eleven months, and twenty-six days. To him, these intervals meant the majority of the time, the passage of power from one administration to the next was peaceful, and the length between assassinations was progress.

*****

The exception was the Civil War, which slowly percolated the year after Enoch Mast was born. Aside from all the compromises, publications, proclamations, and legislation concerning the significant issue of slavery, those born in 1839 were to endure; no single act did more damage to the country than the Census conducted a year after their birth in 1840. Its impact on the social fabric of the country was disastrous.

The 1840 Census was a ten-year enumeration. It was the sixth Census taken by the country; it laid the groundwork and developed the foundation for the credibility of all the stereotypes and myths about black people as an inferior race. The fables, created by the 1840 Census, were told to the white and black races from 1840 on. It defined an American society comprised of two components, a superior and an inferior race, as to who is what race, easily identifiable by skin color.

John C Calhoun was a senator from South Carolina. He was an influential person known to be intense and stern. He was a slave advocate and owner who believed in what his father had told him, to be successful, one should have the same investment in slaves as they have in the land. It was said he had a runaway slave that, when told of his capture, paid to have 'thirty good ones' put on the slave's back before he was returned as a prelude to his homecoming.

He's said to be the one who persuaded the administrators of the sixth Census that, for the first time, an attempt to count Americans who were insane should be made and included in the current Census and all the ones to follow—a seemingly legitimate request with no visible alternative or underlying motives.

The Census was a serious business. Marshalls, with the weight of the law, were responsible for distributing and collecting the questionnaires by a specific date. They turned the completed forms over to the government, which made the tabulations and measurements and published the findings. The information would be published in the *American Population in 1840* and made available to the public by purchase and libraries.

Broad questions were asked as to how many free white males and females, black males and females were in a defined area, and how many were insane. It was expected that the free insane population would reflect the same mix as the free general population. What the Census observed was not what was expected.

The data surprised everyone; it indicated slavery was suitable for black people. Contrary to popular opinion, it found that free blacks couldn't comprehend or handle the concepts of freedom, and succumbed to insanity at alarming rates, many times that of a slave. Slavery keeps blacks from going insane and is appropriate for them.

It didn't take long for the findings to come under fire. The numbers from the 1840 Census and methods used were often a complete departure from the procedures used and the number consistency shown in the previous five population measurements. A study of the sixth Census showed it was a severely flawed compared to the previous five and that some severe data manipulation may have occurred to arrive at certain conclusions.

In 1844 the *American Statistical Association* advised the steps to be taken to correct the errors in the Census and sent them to Congress in the form of a pamphlet with a written memorial, praying Congress to make the corrections. They were never made. At the time, John C Calhoun was no longer Senator; he was Secretary of State; he responded to all concerned parties the Census had been examined and its correctness substantiated. He concluded, "The relation now existing in the slaveholding States between the two [races] is, instead of an evil, a good—a positive good."

The American Statistical Association anticipated the type of response he made; *the* pamphlet they issued was a move to ensure any discussion of the 1840 Census would have to include them as to its accuracy.

It was the first measurement of the insanity issue; it would take another ten years, 1850, to see if the findings were fact or fiction. If the position presented in the 1840 Census was that slavery had benefits for blacks and freedom, its consequences were fact. Although questioned on several levels for many years, the myth became the gospel throughout the decade for pro-slavery advocates. It was preached to those born in 1839 continually throughout their formative years of development.

The attitudes it fostered took form to where, in 1845, Mississippi Senator Robert J. Walker advocated for the annexation of Texas, contacting all the major newspapers by letter. When the issue of future statehood, free or slave, came up, he cited the Census in his justification for 'slave,' stating, "In most cases, to live, to vegetate, is their only desire." 'Slave' would be in the black people's best interest.

*****

When those born in 1839 became adolescents, the 1850 Census showed the population had gone from seventeen to twenty-three million. What took center stage in 1850, in front of the Census, was the *Fugitive Slave Act*, which Congress passed that year into law. Escaped slaves caught in free states were to be returned to their masters. Officials and citizens of free states were to cooperate with all the laws found in the *Act*.

The law allowed slave catchers called 'Paddy Rollers' freedom to roam the country; they 'rolled' into towns on a wagon that carried a large iron cage. They worked for a fee and hunted with dogs. Bloodhounds are known to rip apart what they have caught if not called off. Those thrown into the cage on the 'Paddy Wagon' were sent back to their owners. Abolitionists mocked the law and called the 1850 Act the *Bloodhound Bill.*

The enforcement of the law by the free states in the North was poor. Local municipalities created ordinances to hinder the activity of the Paddy Rollers. They took every opportunity to make it time-consuming and expensive to return escaped slaves. Bribes were common and, in most cases, the only way around the rules. The Northern lack of cooperation angered the Southern slave states. From the start of the decade, the *Fugitive Slave Act of 1850* polarized the country.

*****

Those born in 1839 spent their first year as a teenager, listening to severe arguments, on a national level, over a book written by a woman. The book was written in Cincinnati, Ohio, by abolitionist Harriette Beecher Stowe. She composed a manuscript that had the same impact on the country as the 1840 Census. A novel that emboldened Northern Abolitionists and swayed away the support of some Southern sympathizers. Her work viewed slavery in a completely different light. It became one of the most influential books ever written by an American. Her work was published on March 20, 1852, by John P. Jewett and Company of Boston, Massachusetts. A two-volume set entitled *Uncle Tom's Cabin; or Life Among the Lowly.*

The novel started in serial form; The National Era, an abolitionist newspaper out of Washington, D.C. published a week's chapter. The weekly popularity grew to where the public wanted a

27

book. The book form sold three thousand copies the first day it went on sale. As fast as it went into print in America, it was quickly translated and in print throughout the European continent. It became an internationally known American work. An unforgettable episode of American history and also one of the first books Enoch Mast ever read, and it upset his father.

At the time, the Bible was the only book to outsell *Uncle Tom's Cabin*. The effect it had overwhelmed the moral aspects of society. It was loved by those who wanted the institution of slavery abolished, dead and gone, and hated by those who wanted the institution kept alive and well.

The Southern response to *Uncle Tom's Cabin* was quick with what became known as "Plantation Literature." A series of anti-abolitionist works such as *The Cabin and Parlor, or, Slaves and Masters* by Charles Jacobs Petersen, published in 1852 by T B Peterson Ltd. There was *Frank Freeman's Barber Shop* by Baynard Rush Hall and *The Planter's Northern Bride* by Caroline Lee Hentz. Plantation Literature failed; all the books combined didn't come close to the circulation and influence of Harriette Beecher Stowe's *Uncle Tom's Cabin; or life Among the Lowly.*

Abraham Lincoln, upon meeting Harriette Beecher Stowe, remarked, "So you are the little woman who wrote the book that started this great war." He made all aware of the author's sex and the instrument used to lay the groundwork for the war. It was an opportunity to place blame on someone other than a man and a government; he had a woman and a book. To him and many, the book's publication was still one of the major incendiary causes of the war. In reality, the book was a smoldering ember that took nine years after its publication to ignite the nation.

Throughout Enoch Mast's adolescent years, the country continued to expand. The Kansas-Nebraska Act of 1854 replaced the Missouri Compromise of 1820, where Missouri entered as a slave state and Maine entered as a free state. The Compromise balanced the equation but didn't solve the problem.

The 1854 Act established how new territories would enter the Union. They would be brought in, free or slave, by popular sovereignty. A vote would determine what they would be. At the time, even a fifteen-year-old could see what was on the horizon. The Act facilitated the influx of both pro-slavery advocates and abolitionists to swell their numbers inside the territories. From 1854 to 1859, pro-slavery 'Border Ruffians' and abolitionist' Free Soilers' fought over the land. The violence was pronounced and severe enough that the territory soon became known as 'Bleeding Kansas.'

What both sides of the issue in Congress eventually agreed on, from what was witnessed out west, perhaps the answer to expand or prohibit slavery in new territories and future states, be explored in the Supreme Court. The Court's decisions were the course to take. In 1857 the case of Dred Scott, a slave, who sued for freedom from his master, miraculously proceeded through the court system to the highest court in the land.

The case arrived at the Supreme Court to provide the definitive answer on the matter. In the end, the decision made by the Justices was that Dred Scott was 'property', not a person; as such, he had no legal rights or recognitions afforded a human being. Chief Justice Roger Taney went on to state blacks were "So far inferior that they had no rights which the white man was bound to respect." The direction from the Supreme Court, blacks were not persons, but property was not well received by many and created an ever more hostile environment and resistant attitude towards the Fugitive Slave Law.

In the last year of the decade, 1859, Enoch Mast turned twenty. It was the year radical abolitionist John Brown, a participant in the Pottawatomie Massacre and Bleeding Kansas veteran, raided the armory at Harper's Ferry, Virginia, to arm a slave rebellion in the South. He was stopped by a small force of U.S. Marines led by Colonel Robert E. Lee. Twelve of his supporters were killed. John Brown was captured, charged with the murder of five men and tried on October 27, and hanged on December 2. He became an abolitionist martyr. What has never been told, John Brown would never have known about the armory at Harper's Ferry had it not been for a conversation he once had with Enoch Mast.

At twenty-one, those born in 1839 were counted for the third time in the 1860 census. The Census in 1860 of thirty-three states, eighteen free, fifteen slave, and ten organized territories, put the population in the North at twenty-two million and in the South a total of nine million (five million free, four million slaves). Total United States Population in 1860 was thirty-one million.

The chain of unfortunate events that began to unfold fifteen months after John Brown's raid gathered momentum. On March 4,1861, Abraham Lincoln was inaugurated. It was a landslide victory in the North for Lincoln. In the South, a majority of states didn't put him on the ballot.

Close to forty days after the inauguration, on April 12, 1861, the Civil War took root. Fort Sumter in Charleston Harbor was fired on and captured by the South Carolina Militia. In Virginia, close to four years later, after the battle of Appomattox Court House, it ended, on April 9, 1865.

In the three years, eleven months, and twenty-eight days there were over one-hundred significant engagements and fifty major battles between the North and the South. Best estimate, a total of six-hundred-eighteen thousand perished in the conflict. A little over Three-hundred-sixty thousand Union and two-hundred-fifty-eight thousand Confederate.

The 1865 total war dead, as a percent of the 1860 census total population, is two percent. Taken as a percentage of the 1860 Southern population, the South lost two-point-nine percent of their populace, and the North, taken against their 1860 population, lost one-point-six percent of their populace. The two percent loss the country experienced was made up of males, twenty to forty-five years of age.

*****

The Confederate Constitution, created in 1861, primarily mirrored the U S Constitution. The exception: the alteration made to the fabric of the original Constitution, sewn on by the South, to protect the institution and practice of slavery. The Confederate alteration is found in

Article I, Section IX, Paragraph IV:

No bill of attainer, ex post facto law, or law denying or impairing the right of property in negro slaves shall be passed.

None of the major factors necessary to successfully wage a war favored the South. They didn't have the manpower and industrial strength of the North. These facts didn't matter to the South. The honorable and noble parts of their cause would overcome the North's powers and strengths. The Civil War had been called by those who were in it "A Rich man's war and a poor man's fight." Only a quarter of the free population in the South owned slaves. The *Planter Class* was able to get those who didn't, or three-quarters of the free population, to fight and die for a constitution that protected what few had and most didn't - slaves.

"The War of Northern Aggression," as the South called it, or "The War to Save The Union," as the North named it, were not without their cracks in solidarity. Volunteerism ended early; both sides had conscription; the South began to draft in April 1862, and the North in March of 1863.

On both sides, for some, there were ways the war could be avoided. The rich in the North could buy a substitute for three hundred dollars. In the South, those wealthy enough to own twenty or more slaves were exempt. Desertions were high on both sides. Richmond, the capital of the Confederacy, had food riots, and New York, the largest city in the North, had draft riots. For both sides, the romantic notions of noble conflict faded early. What followed was a long, harsh period of the realities of war.

There was no *Lost Cause*, as the South started to call the Civil War. There was, nonetheless, a *Lost Constitution* that tried to permit what the *U S Constitution* would not allow. Despite the claims of the best soldiers, leaders, and cause, the South's capitulation at Appomattox Courthouse, Virginia, was only three-hundred-twenty-two miles north of where the Civil War started in Charleston, South Carolina.

*****

Those born in 1839 lived a quarter of a century in a country made up of 'free' and 'slave' states. The departure of the institution of slavery began by executive order with Abraham Lincoln's January 1, 1863, Emancipation Proclamation. It only freed the slaves in the Confederacy. It did not free those in the four slaveholding states that remained in the Union: Delaware, Kentucky, Maryland, and Missouri.

It was to be seen as a humanitarian gesture. The Emancipation Proclamation's intent, however, was purely economic, not humanitarian. First, it changed the legal status of slaves from being property to being a person. Second, all the slaves in territory held by the Union Army were automatically freed. The proclamation was made to encourage slave's motivation to escape from the South in increased numbers. It was designed to attack the foundation of the labor-intensive Southern agrarian economy. The proclamation was to take away or severely weaken the one institution the South depended on the most - slavery.

The impact of Lincoln's executive order was felt from start to finish. By the end of the war. there were over two hundred thousand former slaves in the Union Army who had fought at such places as Milliken's Bend, Louisiana; Fort Wagner, South Carolina; Fort Pillow, Tennessee; Battle of the Crater, Petersburg, Virginia; Overton Hill, Battle of Nashville, Tennessee.

Two months before the Civil War ended and seven-hundred and sixty-one days after the Emancipation Proclamation, the institution of slavery was eradicated. It ended, on January 31, 1865, in the United States with the Thirteenth Amendment made to the *US Constitution*. It is what was won in the American Civil War. It takes as a fact there is a difference between a person and a property and that the two are mutually exclusive and can never be the same.

Two amendments followed the Thirteenth Amendment as a result of the Civil War; on July 9, 1868, the Fourteenth Amendment granted to all born or naturalized in the U S, including former slaves, citizenship, and equal protection under the law. On February 3, 1870, the Fifteenth Amendment was ratified and granted African American men the vote.

The postbellum period of Reconstruction, where the protection and rights of these amendments covered all, faded in the early eighteen-seventies; President Hayes ended Reconstruction and returned home rule to the South. A practice developed where equality and protection favored most but not all. Although the 'institution' of slavery was gone, the 'practice' wasn't. A financial system made up of land and debt created by the sharecropper. The 'practice' changed form and became 'peonage,' *involuntary servitude* or *debt slavery*. Part of the labor to work the land after the war came from chain gangs, mostly made up of those who couldn't afford to defend themselves in the legal system of the charges leveled against them by the authorities.

*****

The boss took his feet off the desk, and the room went silent. The two were stunned and looked at each other for an answer. None could be found. The stonemason nervously began to fidget with the fire while his boss got up and headed to the lavatory. When the boss returned, the stonemason went. Subconsciously they didn't want the 'voice' to return to an empty room.

In their travels from one location to the other, the stonemason and boss were very cordial with one another as they came and went. Both spoke in their own voice while they nervously resupplied themselves with what they wanted in the way of food, wine, and tobacco. They returned to the stove and the desk in the hope they could somehow continue where they left off with the voice. Both said nothing, and both wondered if it would be possible.

It was an unpleasant intermission full of apprehension; both felt they were left in the middle of nowhere with no closure in sight as to the life and times of Enoch Mast. They both yearned to hear the end of the story only the voice could give them. The stonemason sipped wine, and his boss lit a cigar; the stonemason put his feet back on the brass rail, and his boss put his on the desk. Soon after the boss slipped into another trance, the 'soul voice' returned in a cloud of smoke and went into the details of *the Gilded Age*.

*****

The voice set the stage for the *Gilded Age* against an economic background. How, in 1860, if the country's total wealth was one-hundred dollars, and the total population was one-hundred people, the distribution of wealth for ten people would be six dollars each; for ninety people, it would be between forty-four and forty-five cents each. In 1860, the richest ten percent of the population owned sixty percent of the wealth. By 1900 the distribution for ten people each would be nine dollars, and for ninety people, eleven cents each. in 1900, the richest ten percent owned ninety percent of the country's wealth.

The truth, from start to finish, throughout the *Gilded Age*, the rich got richer, and the poor get poorer. It was an Age that had serious problems when it came to the distribution of wealth and justice. The conflicts between Management and Labor over the distribution of both were as intense as any issue between the North and South during the *Antebellum Era.*

There were times management agreed with the attitude financier Jay Gould expressed, "I *can hire one half* of the working class to kill the other half." Labor answered with the attitude expressed by Eugene V. Debs, "The most heroic word in all languages is 'revolution.'" To let management know there was always the possibility. Throughout the *Gilded Age*, there were periods of unrest between the two that mirrored another civil war on the horizon, not over slavery but economics.

Both sides had their moments; Enoch Mast lost a brother in the coal fields of eastern Pennsylvania in one such moment of strife. The *Age*, despite all its class disagreements and conflicts, accomplished three incredible changes that gave growth to a shrinking middle class and secured its future.

*****

Mark Twain became America's first writer to gain wide respect and acceptance on the international stage. He wrote more than twenty novels. He co-authored only one. The co-author was Charles Dudley Warner, an American essayist. In 1873 Twain and Warner published *The Gilded Age: A Tale of Today.* Their book didn't have the impact of Harriette Beecher Stowe's novel but had some weight in the audience it created and the influence their audience had.

Twain and Warner saw an age in America where objects appeared to be solid when in fact, they were actually gilded or coated. The practice left the impression an object was pure when in fact it wasn't. They pointed out that what existed below the surface of the object was something quite different than what was shown. The two collaborated on a work that called out the difference between a perfect *Golden Age* and a less commendable *Gilded Age.* Their work expressed the American character of honesty; as much as a Golden Age for the country was desired, a *Gilded Age* was what, in truth, the country deserved and got.

Gilding wasn't just found in the objects of the time but also in the behaviors, values, and laws. Everything was different from what it appeared to be. It was a time when appearance overshadowed substance. What appeared to be pure throughout was a manufactured mirage. Many born in 1839 spent the major part of their life in the *Gilded Age* and were well aware of its illusions.

The time between the American Civil War and the First World War was a period where flaunting great wealth was the trademark of the age and the benchmark of success. For the ten out of a hundred who made eighty-one times what the remaining ninety made, at the turn of the century, there seemed to be no limits. A ballroom would be a perfect example. A standard feature found in their homes provided hard evidence of the owner's wealth and power. They were private auditoriums used to promote and secure the agendas of the advantaged.

Those born in 1839, like Enoch Mast, experienced a period in their lives from 1870 when the gap in wealth between the "haves and the have-nots" expanded at a rapid rate and grew from one year to the next.

The wider the gap and its rapid growth made for frequent unrest. What saved America from itself was the space it began to create between rich and poor. The space was filled with the American middle class through the development of three major innovations. A space that not only saved the middle class but also provided for its growth. The first innovation took place in 1862 when Congress passed the *Morrill Land Grant Act*. The second innovation happened in 1879 when Frank W Woolworth came up with the "Five and Dime" and mass merchandising. The final innovation occurred in 1883 when Congress passed the *Pendleton Act* and developed the Civil Service. These three innovations slowed the rate of conflict between the 'haves and the have-nots.' They allowed the middle class to expand and stabilize the times.

Although rooted in the Civil War, Congress had the presence of mind to pass the *Morrill Land Grant Act* in 1862. The effect it had on the *Gilded Age* is not to be overlooked. Federal lands were given to the states for higher education. Universities were to be built on them, and these universities were to be open to all.

The next four decades saw the number of state universities and colleges grow at a tremendous rate. Some of the nation's largest and best 'public' universities were established by the Act; a partial list would include Ohio State University, Perdue University, the University of Maryland, University of Wisconsin, Michigan State University, Rutgers, MIT, Cornell, Texas A&M, Nebraska, Washington as part of the sixty-five universities and colleges in operation at the turn of the century.

By 1900 more than a third of college graduates were women, the vast majority teachers. One of the first lessons learned by the country from the Act, the road to higher wages, was found in education.

Frank W Woolworth, in 1879, provided the arena where one's wages could be spent. He introduced Americans to 'mass merchandizing', giving the public both variety and volume on the general products used every day. The products were priced at a nickel and a dime. The 1890 steel mill worker's wage of a dollar fifty a day could buy thirty nickel items or fifteen dime items or any mix between the two with one day's pay. Woolworth provided variety, volume, and affordability at his *Five and Dime* Stores. They expanded the range of products to the consumer at a price most could afford, and the demand for the items stimulated production and job growth.

The jobs at the *Five and Dime* were in the private sector, and one's employment was left to the discretion of the employer. Government jobs were granted differently. At first American government jobs, up to 1883, was granted by the 'Spoils System.' The one who won a high-level election gave the jobs of their office to those who helped them win. It was a system, for the most part, infected by corruption, driven by the inexperienced, and fueled by bribes, kickbacks, and payoffs.

The *Pendleton Act* Congress passed replaced the Spoils System with the Civil Service. The *Act* stated access to Federal Government jobs required government employees to be selected by competitive exams and jobs awarded based on the exam results. A system built on 'Merit.' Many times, the higher-level jobs were filled in the same manner by university graduates. Also, the *Act* made it unlawful to demote or fire someone based on political reasons. The Act reduced government corruption and increased efficiency.

Those born in 1839 saw these three events take place. Each is like a trimester in the birth of the American middle class. The Expansion of education, the availability of merchandise, and the development of a competent government worked to the benefit of most but not all, although this has always been the goal. The features and benefits of these events were not all-inclusive. They worked for roughly ninety percent of the population, a high percentage but not a perfect percentage, and part of the reason the *Age* was 'gilded' not 'golden.'

*****

The 'voice' went silent for the third time. Neither the stonemason nor his boss spoke. In an act of faith, both sat patiently and silently for it to return. Their hope was tested only for a few moments. The short test gave the boss enough time to settle in for the long haul as he put his feet back on the desk. The moment it happened, the silence was broken, and the voice began, "You've seen the background and know the shades and shadows of the *era* and *age* behind Enoch Mast. Time for the portrait of the man to be fleshed out."

Both sighed in relief as the voice resumed from where it left off. The stonemason found the atmosphere too comfortable to abandon, the voice too enlightening to ignore. All they would want was within easy reach. The wine, food, and cigars were all there and part of the story of Enoch Mast as it unfolded in the comfort of the boss's office. The whole situation the stonemason found himself in was an experience he would never forget.

The boss lit a cigar and went into the final trance. In a cloud of fresh smoke, a sandstone road seventy-five blocks long, where the mansions sat back two to three acres from the boulevard, came into view. The place was Euclid Avenue, Cleveland, Ohio. At the time, the American boulevard was equal to any of the wealthiest avenues found in such European capitals as Berlin, London, or Paris.

Neither man moved from what was in front of them until dawn. By sunrise, the glow of the fire had died, the snow had stopped, and the 'voice' was gone. Through the final trance, it was told how it came to be; Enoch Mast was counted eight times in the country's Census. How Cleveland, Ohio, and Euclid Avenue, at the time of the *Antebellum Era* and the *Gilded Age*, became Enoch Mast's environment.

The times he transported items for customers and the times he built the staircases, halls, and ballrooms for some of the wealthiest men in the world. No different than Bruno Balissaari's *Floating Cube*, the portrait of Enoch Mast isn't always as it first appears. His life shows the debt owed by great people to the unknown people who filled their life.

CHAPTER II
THE BALLROOM

In the final trance, the voice went on uninterrupted till dawn. It continued in the dialects and tones of the time and told of how the thoughts churning in Enoch Mast's head wouldn't allow sleep.

Shortly before daybreak one morning he struck a match, lit a kerosene lamp, and stared at himself in the mirror on his dresser. So far, he was the only one who knew the Lasbriths were behind. Two weeks, to be exact, in paying him for his work. It was just a matter of time before the subject would come up with his friends, and he would have to explain how what never happened before had happened. It was a well-known fact he got paid on time, and everyone knew it.

Dressed before daybreak, he looked down on the dresser at an old cigar box half-filled with business cards on the left side of the mirror while combing his hair. There were three on the surface that intrigued him. He picked the cards up, studied them briefly, and put them in his vest pocket as if he were arming himself. For what, he didn't know. He just felt he should have them on him. Next, he took the invitation to a wedding reception he had ignored for weeks that took place the previous day, folded it to the size of the business cards, and also put it in his vest pocket as if it was the map to where he was going.

It was strange; the things he never did in the morning caused him to forget the first thing he did every morning, grab a handful of cigars from a box he always kept by the right side of the mirror. He had too much on his mind and forgot what he never forgot. He realized this soon after he left, and it upset him.

As he arrived in the kitchen, the new day's light slipped unnoticed through the windows and gently filled the rooms of the house he had lived in for the past forty-nine years. One could see the clear sky's reflection in Lake Erie's calm blue waters.

While he ate, he penciled a note on some butcher paper. A third of the way through, Enoch looked up and gazed out the window for an unknown reason. For a second, he felt the calmness of that morning overtake him, and his note about what he wanted to be done by the end of the day, where he went, and when he expected to be back, never added. Only the first part of the note, what he wanted done, got put down. The other two parts, where he went and when he'd be back, didn't. He was unaware of the omission when his moment of serenity ended. He returned to the note only to place a salt and pepper shaker on it as a guarantee to himself Brooks Mast would see it when he came down.

He put his dishes in the sink, grabbed an apple, and went out the kitchen door to a stable amid a rapid transformation to a garage. He fed the apple, out of guilt, to Emmett, the gelding, who shared the stable/garage with a 1912 Ford Model T' Runabout,' a horseless buckboard.

Enoch was at the age where he tried to avoid technology whenever he could, but it had a way of forcing itself on him at times. He had a young friend who was an electrician. A young man named Jesse O'Dell patiently took the time to instruct an older man all he knew about wiring and working with electricity, including its history. Jess had an excellent work ethic and a better sense of humor and was the best to spend a day with on any job.

He was the previous owner of the Runabout. When he first showed up with the Runabout, all Enoch did was make fun of it; he always referred to it as a "toy." He would ask Jess, "Know what the laziest part of your toy is? Jess would smirk and wait for the answer.

"The wheels, they're always tired." One day, in the middle of a round of laughter over a remarkable comeback to Enoch's comment about the truck, his friend started coughing up blood. Less than a year later, he died. He left a widow and three kids under the age of twelve.

In 1913 Enoch bought Jesse O'dell's 1912 Ford Model T Open Body *Runabout Roadster* with a pick-up box, or 'bed'. It was unique; it wasn't black; it was red. Red with a black button-tufted bench seat, adjustable windshield, and a black cloth drop-top. It had a speedometer, clock, and a brass dog bone motor meter (a radiator cap with a thermometer). It also had a brass Ford script step plate on the running board. The running boards had a mounted toolbox for repairs, and a battery and magneto box for easy crank starts. The Runabout Roadster had E&J Brass acetylene headlamps, side lamps, tail lamps, and an electric red STOP lamp. The powertrain was a one-hundred-seventy-seven cubic inch displacement, four-cylinder twenty horsepower engine with a two-speed planetary transmission.

He gave her more than her husband paid for the new truck to show his gratitude for her husband. After he bought it, he often stopped by and took her kids for a ride. He would tell them it would always be their dad's truck, even to him. That maybe one day it might make its way back to them.

The acquisition led Enoch and Brooks to an obsession they'd have for the rest of their lives. Brooks preferred the horse and buggy for the open road, but he marveled at how the truck was built and engineered to perform. He liked to study the ignition, gearbox, and drive train systems. The integration of all the moving parts when the machine wasn't moving, always walking around it, or crawling under it with a manual in his hand and reading up on the place he was visiting like a tourist.

Enoch was the opposite. He liked to study it in motion. He was mystified by the twenty horses held in the suitcase-size four-cylinder engine. He wanted to know how much the truck could hold and pull at a decent speed. How fast it could move without a load and how far it could travel before it needed a few gallons of ethanol or gasoline. Everything about it intrigued him. He felt the fuel for the twenty horses under the hood was cheaper than the oats they fed Emmet.

The recent technology captured both of them and dominated their conversations. They completely surrendered their spare time to read everything they could on the truck and perform the required maintenance like clockwork when it arrived. All they wanted to do was pour over the truck and figure out ways to get the maximum torque, speed, load, and range from the vehicle. Both wanted to know and do more with the motor and the suspension. They began to call it the 'pick-up' since all they did with it was pick up things and throw them in the box or take them out. The Runabout became a 'pick-up' As they pursued their desires, they became the early ancestors of the American backyard garage mechanic.

On the second turn of the crank, the engine turned over. Enoch jumped in, put the two-speed transmission in gear, and motored down the road at twenty-five miles per hour. The Stewart Speedometer went as high as sixty miles per hour. Still, forty-two was the best Enoch and Brooks ever got, and they had every intention of finding the missing eighteen miles per hour.

Twenty-five was the right speed to bring on his thoughts about the day ahead, the objective he needed to take, and the cards he had to play. He started by recalling how the predicament he found himself in came about and all that took place where he was going.

As he motored on, he imagined a third party narrating to him and the world how the representatives of the Lasbrith family approached him to discuss a project.

At a January tenth, 1914, meeting, Enoch Mast agreed to a second meeting concerning a construction contract with the Hardin G Lasbrith family to renovate a ballroom. The renovation was to be completed two weeks before the June twenty-seventh, 1914, wedding of Florence Lasbrith Benton to Chalmers Saxbee.

Enoch got the days (150) and money he wanted ($4,000). The agreement also included material costs plus lunch and dinner, Monday through Friday. On the twelfth, both parties signed the contract at the second meeting. Three days after the signing, the renovation began on January fifteenth.

It was the only time Enoch Mast and Hardin Lasbrith ever laid eyes on each other. As they waited for the Lasbrith envoy, Hardin asked Enoch if he was in the Civil War. Enoch answered with a nod. Hardin mentioned he was at Gettysburg and got another nod. The staff arrived, and Enoch moved to the business at hand. Neither impressed the other.

*****

The scenery for the Runabout as it traveled down the road was the trees, buildings, and pedestrians it passed. The background for Enoch's thoughts as they traveled through his mind were the people, places, and events. As he moved down the road, he thought about who put him in the driver's seat that morning; another followed H.E. Lasbrith, and that thought, how he would make him pay

The Lasbriths had a history of consistently awarding contracts to the highest bidder and always paying what the lowest bidder had put on the table. The bids provided the range, and the payment method gave them the highest quality at the lowest price. They found the cost of an army of lawyers on retainer to stall payment, on the complaints they made on the work done, more cost-effective than to pay in full. The practice was good for cash flow. Their lawyers were always busy. They made the courts their friend to where, after a while, the contractor willingly took a lower payment. Finally, accepting the fact some money was better than no money. That was their strategy, and it was known to many locally.

The signing of the contract put Enoch in a situation that could easily make him look like a fool to his peers, that he didn't know what was common knowledge. That he ignored the fact no one local would work for the Lasbriths. Significant projects at their estate were done by people from out of town, who were unaware of but about to find out how the Lasbriths operated.

As Enoch headed to their estate, he felt he was in an unpleasant situation that had to change. He thought about a coming luncheon, and the first question asked. He always liked to give 'answers' instead of 'explanations.' Answers can be short, but explanations are always long because solutions deal with 'facts' and explanations ' reasons.'

To take his mind off the gravity of the situation, he began to think of Jesse O'Dell and all the history he told him about electricity and how he passed on to him what he learned in school when they worked together: about Ben Franklin's May tenth, 1752, kite, and key experiment. Which proved lightning and electricity are the same. Jesse pointed out that what Franklin did was not lost on those who paid attention. A little over a century later, the secret world of how electrical charges, currents, conductors, capacitors, and circuits work was exposed. The age of electronics came upon us, bringing a *Second Industrial Revolution*, and electricians gave birth to a new trade.

Ohioans showed up to the dance early when it came to harnessing the potential of electricity. Outside the home, Charles Brush, born in Euclid, Ohio, provided cities with a cost-effective way to light their streets at night in 1879 when he invented arc lighting. One light had the power of four thousand candles. Brush's efforts made Cleveland the first city in the United States to have electric streetlights. That same year Thomas Edison from Milan, Ohio, came up with the first high-resistance, incandescent electric light bulb for inside buildings and homes. In his lifetime Benjamin Lamme, born in Springfield, Ohio, had one-hundred-sixty-two patents, the majority advancing electricity's use. These men and their discoveries helped Ohio emerge as a leader in industrialization during the late 1800s.

In 1907, Cleveland Public Power was founded to generate, distribute, and maintain electricity and supply city-wide service to business and residential areas. During the early 1900s, all the large cities across the state could offer electrical services for public and private use.

As Enoch recalled the first meeting about the ballroom, the emphasis was on what Hardin Lasbrith thought was innovation with installing electric chandeliers. What Hardin Lasbrith wanted followed a trend; it wasn't anything new or innovative. Enoch remembered he kept the thought to himself.

There were four tasks Hardin Lasbrith wanted to be completed by June fourteenth, 1914.

Five large crystal chandeliers installed on the ceiling.

At the ballroom entrance two five-by-fifteen-foot mirrors installed, framed, and gilded with gold leaf.

Build off the back wall of the ballroom a one-thousand-square-foot stage.

Between the two new mirrors stencil on the inside of the ballroom, a coat of arms in a sixty-four square foot area over the doors.

The time limit, Enoch figured five months or one-hundred-fifty days. Close to five weeks for each job.

The four tasks were nothing new; he could do them in less time if he had to, but getting more time made it comfortable. He didn't need the work; if he got a contract time of one-hundred-fifty days to complete the renovation, he'd be halfway home signing a deal.

The large mirrors and chandeliers were already on site. They weren't what they seemed. The mirrors were the reciprocal or two-way mirrors patented in 1903 by a Russian, Emil Bloch, who lived in Cincinnati. Guests, outside the ballroom, at the entrance would see those inside the ballroom through a window, while those in the ballroom saw themselves in a mirror. Less light in one room and more in the other causes the effect.

When Hardin found out about these types of mirrors, and before they were installed in the ballroom, smaller versions were strategically placed in every well-lit bathroom, bedroom, and dressing room, providing the opportunity to put a hidden viewing area behind the mirrors.

The chandeliers had been there a half a year. They were shipped from Vienna, Austria, and were from J & L Lobmeyr. The company and Thomas Edison had a partnership and co-developed the first electric chandelier in 1880, and the market evolved. The five on-site were well-crated Regency-style crystal chandeliers.

Enoch sat in Hardin Lambirth's bookless library, the shelves filled with marble reproductions of Roman antiquities, loosely calculating the project's material costs. He put each task at a thousand dollars, knowing some cost more and others less; it made it easier to calculate just as more days made him comfortable. His time and labor would cost the same as the materials, four-thousand dollars. To make such an amount in less than half a year was making money at a rate of a little more than three times what a Ford factory worker made in a year, and they made good money. Getting the time and the money into the contract would make it an exceptional deal.

It would be the perfect last job. Enoch's friends knew he was looking for such a project but were extremely surprised and put out by what they found he was considering.

Enoch Mast had a rhythm to his work that others couldn't help but observe and admire. The methods he employed made his work exceptional when completed. Nothing he did escaped Charles Schweinfurth, an architect who left New York City to come to a better market in Cleveland. Between 1885 and 1912, he built eighteen mansions on Euclid Avenue. For twenty-seven years, he'd finish one and start another each year. He tried to employ Enoch Mast on every one of them. He did on most, but other architects knew what Schweinfurth knew, and it usually came down to who got to Enoch First with the most.

Enoch Mast was a high-end tradesman seventeen years older than Schweinfurth. Clients who had seen a conversation between the two always felt Enoch was in charge. Even though they knew the actual relationship and Schweinfurth was the one they paid. Mostly, they would tell one they were usually humorous discussions similar to a father and son relationship only in reverse, where the practical one was the son and the audacious one the father.

At a monthly luncheon before he signed the contract, four friends, who were architects, had gotten wind of what Enoch was contemplating and recommended that he not take on the job. Stanford White, Richard Morris Hunt, George Post, and his sons, along with the most influential and opposed Charles Schweinfurth, who warned Enoch that Hardin E. Lasbrith was neither a reputable nor reliable client, that he was like dealing with a venomous snake.

At the following luncheon, all were surprised that he ignored their advice. At that time, Enoch told them he liked the setup and asked them to name a time a client didn't pay him in full and on time. It was a question that didn't need to be asked; everyone knew the answer. But as they thought about the situation and Enoch's nature, their reply was in-unison laughter. Each agreed it was his decision and, in a good-natured way, told Enoch they looked forward to watching every episode of what was about to unfold, thanking him in advance for the coming month's entertainment. Ending by telling Enoch how each looked forward to the luncheons.

*****

The gate to the Lasbrith estate was in view and appeared to be open. Enoch glided past it and onto the long gentle 's' curved driveway to where it forked, and the choices were the portico or service entrance. Enoch turned toward the service entrance and drove to the back of the mansion.

He parked the pick-up by the kitchen. He stopped and sat in the truck for a minute, listening to how the engine purred. Its sound temporarily erased all the deliberations going through his mind about what he would do. As soon as he turned it off, all his thoughts flooded back in with greater intensity than when they left as he began his walk toward the kitchen.

From the moment he got up that morning, Enoch's subconscious knew "what" to do, and it began working to the surface as the day progressed. "How" to do it was another matter. It was during the short walk from the pick-up to the kitchen that it came to him. The Lasbriths would always want him to be on the outside and off the property; he needed to be on the property and inside. Subconsciously he checked his vest pocket, holding the cards and invitation as one would check for a gun. He decided, at that moment, his objective would be the ballroom. He'd take it over and occupy it until he got paid or thrown in jail. Whichever came first. Enoch knew the Lasbriths were banking on a long-drawn-out war fought by their army of lawyers in the courts. Enoch wanted a quick deciding battle fought in the ballroom with whoever he had to, mentally or physically or both, demolish.

He'd capture the Lasbrith ballroom and let the psychological impact play out. Let the weight from the fact that the most significant room inside their mansion, their private auditorium, was occupied and no longer under their control bear down on them. The Lasbriths would never have expected such an event. It would be new terrain for them.

Enoch took out his pocket watch; the time was seven forty-five. He stood outside the kitchen door, took a deep breath, and knocked. His back was to the sun, and the morning mist covered his feet. He listened to the commotion going on inside. When they opened the door, the image he gave was of one who came out of the light that stood on a cloud with a vest pocket full of scripture, and at that very moment, the commotion stopped. The unexpected image caught the staff packed in the kitchen totally off guard. They were mesmerized by what they saw for a few moments and invited Enoch to squeeze into the kitchen with them.

Enoch became a permanent fixture in the Lasbrith household during the months that led up to the wedding reception. Over the days covering winter and spring of that year, he became familiar with the staff of about fifteen men and twenty-five women who worked inside the household and on the estate grounds. He talked to all he came in contact with, even if it was a passing 'hello.' From the scullery maids and chambermaids to the footmen and gardeners, along with all those in between, he made it a point to acknowledge everyone who worked there. All except the head butler.

He knew most, not all, but it seemed all knew him. Enoch was gifted in many ways; he was very fluid in his work, spoke in gentle tones, stepped aside in hallways, and held doors open for those whose hands were full. In passing, he complimented those around him whenever he could.

He followed a simple rule of getting along with everyone until they gave him a reason not to; when that happened, he became a formidable foe. It was an excellent rule to follow, and because of it, he had far more friends than enemies.

Enoch also had a quick wit. He knew when to make fun of himself and when to make fun of others. Like energy, he followed the path of least resistance. And it produced a more positive than negative charge with those around him.

The day after five hundred or so guests finally left the wedding reception, with the last remnants clearing out around six or so in the morning, the staff began the cleanup. The size of the kitchen could only hold half of what needed to be brought down from the ballroom. All that was brought down had several steps to go through before they opened up any space. Every item had to be washed, dried, sorted, inventoried, and stored.

All the gold and silver candelabra, gold, and silver-plated platters, serving bowls, serving utensils, silverware, fine porcelain plates, cups, and saucers were stacked here and there. Parts of the kitchen began to look more like the inside of a vault holding an immense treasure plundered from some unknown realm. Space was at a premium.

The semi-chaotic conditions caused by the first significant event after the ballroom renovation showed the kitchen should have been part of the restoration - the first part. The morning's breakage forced plans to enlarge the kitchen to be made at once.

"Where's the kitchen?" Enoch would joke as he passed through it every night when he left work. He enjoyed teasing the head butler Alden Sinclair about the situation after he pointed out that the kitchen floor space wasn't even close to a quarter of the ballroom floor space. He enjoyed informing Sinclair a quarter was the absolute minimum ratio the worst restaurants operate under.

Enoch took a vengeful pleasure in putting Sinclair in the position that he was responsible for telling the Lasbriths something they didn't want to hear. Every night before he left, he would ask Sinclair in front of whoever was present, "Have you told them yet?" He crowded Sinclair on the issue so much that Sinclair eventually avoided the kitchen at the end of the day, to where the staff thought either Enoch had no idea how dangerous Sinclair was or knew but didn't care.

Enoch listened intently to the kitchen staff's situation before speaking. It came to him he had walked in on the problem he had predicted. All there knew it, too, and thought, what could be better? He was right; it all began to drift into place with little effort on his part.

Enoch let their assumptions pass for facts in their minds. Everyone involved with clearing the ballroom and working in the kitchen believed he showed up to be the solution to their problems. They thought Sinclair wasn't around because he was with the Lasbriths updating them on the situation. All were surprised by how fast the Lasbriths reacted and got Enoch Mast to show up. Unaware of what they thought was wrong.

It was the perfect situation to get to the ballroom. All Enoch said was six words "I will wait in the ballroom." Letting all know he wouldn't add to the cramped conditions in the kitchen. There wasn't one among them who didn't believe this was why he showed up. Enoch was to meet with a Lasbrith family member or representative about enlarging the kitchen. None in the kitchen saw it for what it was, a takeover.

Before Enoch headed toward the objective, he began to mingle with staff. He left just as the debate to bring items down as space opened up in the kitchen. Or get the first half completely put away. Then bring down the other half. Enoch headed to the ballroom and was told someone would bring him a piece of wedding cake and some coffee.

*****

Enoch stood below the coat of arms inside the ballroom and gazed first at the cleared tables on the left and then the cluttered tables on the right.

The cleared side showed twenty highly polished, substantial four-foot by ten-foot, black walnut tables, end to end, with five chairs running the ballroom length on each side of a table. At the ends of the ballroom three sets of tables and chairs, spaced five feet apart, running the width, both ends, one set on the floor and the other on the stage. The cleared hardwood tables and chairs had a stark austere forsaken appearance. It wasn't hard to fall victim to the illusion where the cleared tables appear to be coffins, and the chairs on their sides, pallbearers.

Across from them, the battlefield, the same number of tables and chairs covered in fine white linen with gold and silver candle labra, at each end of a table, fine porcelain vases filled with fresh cut flowers between them. There were:

Silver-plated gravy boats.

Condiment trays.

Dishes of nuts.

Bowls of fruit.

Baskets of bread and rolls.

Platters of cheese.

Saucers of butter.

Every table had three sets of crystal and silver salt and pepper shakers. Each table had three large serving plates, one for fish, poultry, and meat.

The fine China for all on the table sat atop gold-plated platters that had a fine array of silverware on each side. The unconsumed food and drink, on and around the expensive clutter, supplied a full view of the excesses of the prosperous.

Enoch dragged an oversized stuffed leather winged back chair into the ballroom from the entrance and set up shop in the northwest corner. With the chairs back facing the corner, he had two large windows to look out of; to the north, Lake Erie was just visible on the horizon, and to the west, the emerging skyline of Cleveland. He pulled a table as close to the chair as he could

When he sat down, he began observing everything before him. He was on the uncleared side, and the tables' settings had various amounts of food left on the plates that had long grown cold. The crystal goblets and porcelain cups held various amounts of champagne, wine, bourbon, coffee, and tea; few were empty. Silver knives, forks, and spoons were in a random pattern by the plates and platters, like weapons dropped by retreating soldiers who could no longer continue their crusade to consume everything before them.

The gravy, wine, and coffee stains on the white linen between the plates and utensils looked like the fresh and dried blood on a snow-covered battlefield.

He glimpsed at a silver-plated ashtray with a half-smoked *Por Larranaga* premium Cuban cigar. It wasn't the brand but the length that impressed him when he plucked it out of the ashtray. It was a well-known fact Enoch Mast would smoke anything. He pulled a box of matches from his pocket and thought, "What a break!" The one thing he left behind when he left home. He lit the cigar and leaned back in the chair.

Enoch saw a familiar figure enter the ballroom through a smoke cloud. She walked between the cleared and uncleared tables and stopped in the center of the room. Like a needle on a compass, she turned in his direction and looked right at him. Their magnetism for each other was unchanged; they could always sense where the other was. Her name was Jenny, and she marched in a straight-line carrying cake and coffee on a silver tray right to him.

Without trying, she could give off a soft erotic glow that was hard to ignore. She was twenty years younger than Enoch and had evolved from a very striking to an attractive dark-eyed, dark-haired, smooth skin woman. When they met, their attraction for the other took them by surprise.

From the second Enoch entered the Lasbrith mansion, till the moment he left, on all one hundred fifty days he worked there, before the day would end, the two would always find time to briefly sneak off someplace to have a few words or at the very least to catch a glimpse of one another. There was a magnetism neither could overcome. They felt they were cautious enough to be able to carry on like this without drawing the attention of the staff or family members. They were the only ones who understood what was happening between them. Or so they thought.

It was hard to camouflage her in the pick-up when the few short rides he gave her at lunch around the estate turned into driving lessons that covered a lot of ground in more ways than one. A few times after work, they left the Lasbrith Estate to Osstill's pond or Enoch's. The only time they stopped on these trips was when they switched seats. The slide across Enoch's lap grew to be a slow and enjoyable process for both and often led to other versions of affection.

Jenny took right to the pick-up; her driving impressed Enoch, to where he felt safe enough to be a passenger and let her drive back from both places. At the same time, he researched the ride from a passenger's perspective. At first, she listened as Enoch passed on what he experienced to where she couldn't listen any longer. Eventually, she would be able to change the conversation from the pick-up to them. They learned a lot about each other when they switched seats.

She had served the families on *Millionaires Row* since she was fifteen. She was dependable, respectable but most of all likable. Her experience included employment for two well-known families before the Lasbriths. Under her terms of employment, Jenny was a pioneer and one of the first who was able to marry and have children while in service. She had a girl and two boys. Her husband had been a maritime worker; Lake Erie took him a year after the birth of their last child, who was named after him.

Her husband's name was Amos Amspoker, a pilot on a large cargo ship named the *Balltara*. There wasn't a current or channel in Lake Erie he didn't know. The ship and crew tested the shallow lake late in November when all had dropped their anchors for the winter.

The crew of the *Balltara* took the job because of the large bonus. They couldn't pass up the opportunity to make two months' wages in two days. All felt the bonus was greater than the risk. Even though it was a short voyage, they also knew better. They thought of themselves as the best on the Great Lakes. They gambled, and they lost.

Enoch recalled how she told him, "He did this with three young children at home." There was no sympathy or understanding in her voice when she said it. Enoch was more than familiar with her frigid tone and how it felt. There was a time, he had done the same as her husband to his wife, only he gambled and won.

Enoch was unaware he was being compared to her husband with all Jenny Amspoker said. Amos Amspoker was a much-loved man with many friends who would find him hard to forget, but he was also an unforgiven soul. The way he left her, he would remain as such. He left her with a deep love and no one to give it to. The second she learned Amos Amspoker left her, she always carried the burden of his loss in her heart. The moment Enoch Mast entered her life, the weight was lifted.

She smiled, "I see you found the cigars." Enoch replied with a grin, "Found this one in an ashtray." His honesty made Jenny chuckle, shake her head, and shrug her shoulders. She complimented him on his find and laughed, "You have the eyes of a hawk," she said it in such a pleasant tone the sarcasm was well masked. She next informed him, "If you open the doors of the large cabinet in the entrance, in one of the drawers, there's a large box of *Por Larranagas*, and on the top shelf, there's a couple of fifths of *Old Forester*. Help yourself."

She put the tray on the table by him and started to leave. Enoch said, "Wait," and she did. He knew she was upset, he never made contact with her after he left. It was a thin attempt at best as Enoch tried to tell her it was because of problems he was having with the truck, but that wasn't the reason. The real reason was his fear of commitment at his age; he didn't want to turn a wife into a nurse. He felt that would be the direction they were headed in if they kept it up. However, what he felt wasn't strong enough to overcome the desire he had for her.

It was her eyes that pulled the trigger. Right after she put the tray down, Enoch's lips formed around her name, and she heard "Jenny" as soft as she had ever heard it. A "Thank you" followed it, but not for what she had brought, but for the times they had talked, ridden in the pick-up, or just caught a glimpse of each other. She smiled and said nothing. Her eyes told him, "You're welcome, Enoch Mast." She was gifted in changing the formal to the informal and could make those around her feel comfortable and at ease if she wanted to.

As she took the coffee off the tray, both looked for ways to expand their conversation any way they could. She began, "You should hear what they say about you in the kitchen." But before she could continue, Enoch told her he didn't care what they were saying.

Instead, the two talked about the colossal wedding reception in the ballroom the day before. They both laughed at the paradox such events provide. Knowing not everyone at the previous day's extravaganza was on the level they pretended to be. They both agreed such events were similar to the different animals that gather around a watering hole; some are predators, others prey.

The environment was always attractive, but one would have to be aware of their surroundings and know it was as deadly as beautiful. Both Enoch and Jenny knew many careers and fortunes were made and lost in ballrooms. Both mutually agreed that those who worked for the wealthy knew the fact.

Enoch asked if Sir Carl was still around, and Jenny told him it was strange; she had just caught glimpses of him. The two began to talk about Sir Carl, the family dog, and the irony that Sir Carl was a bitch. She was a Pyrenean Mastiff, a large breed, and stood about three feet tall. Sir Carl was one of the most overweight dogs (close to 220 pounds) in Cleveland and likely in Ohio. She had a shabby long white coat and was allowed to wander the mansion at will. The Lasbriths treated her like some ancient and primitive cultures treated their sacred animals.

The dog ate better than most people in Cleveland and was not completely housebroken. With forty rooms to roam, she rarely went out. The dog was another Lasbrith family member the staff worked for. It was never her fault when she relieved herself in the house, but that of the closest staff member. What she left behind was viewed as if the staff member was the one who had just relieved themselves.

If they did not hate the dog, everyone employed in the household resented it, a massive stubborn animal with many unpleasant habits. All the Lasbriths spoiled the dog and spoke to it better than they did to the staff. To make the point, the family dog was more important than the family staff.

All one had to do to get a stern lecture from a family member was get caught yelling at her or calling her a bitch. The staff knew what sex the dog was, unlike the family. Enoch jokes to Jenny, "If she turned up dead, and they asked 'who would want to see her dead?' The only true and inescapable answer would be 'everyone!'" Jenny remembered how she laughed and repeated, "Everyone!" nodding in total agreement.

Enoch talked about how the dog loved to crawl all over the scaffolding knocking over the paint cans onto the floor and defecating on the planking. The loads she left behind didn't start to stink and didn't become slick until after he had stepped in them. He then confessed to Jenny several times he thought about poisoning the bitch. He had often set out to do it, but somehow fate always stepped in and favored the dog.

They talked about how Enoch took time to comment on a company founded in Cleveland, the Sherwin-Williams Company, and their re-sealable paint cans that cut his losses from the dog in half. It was as if the company personally knew the problems he was having with the dog. He told Jenny they were having a big sales conference at the Hotel Statler starting the following day. He half-heartedly suggested maybe the two of them should stop by the hotel.

The two laughed and shared stories about Sir Carl and other mishaps during the months Enoch shared the Lasbrith mansion with her and the staff. They talked about the dog, other people, the Lasbrith family, and themselves. Jenny subtly complimented Enoch more on the shape he was in than the ballroom renovations he made. She was good at this and did not stop until Enoch blushed.

Just as he gained his poise, Jenny brought up a time Enoch lost complete control of their conversation. She asked if he remembered telling her, "Your dress becomes you. But I don't know if it wouldn't look better hanging on some hook in the cloakroom over there and you and me being here without it." She told him of the look on his face when he realized what he had said, how he at once tried to apologize. She reminded him of how she stopped him in his tracks. She looked at the cloakroom, raised her eyebrows, turned her head, looked deep into Enoch's eyes, and said, "Someday, that just might happen. However, I would certainly prefer a hotel room to a cloakroom."

She produced a napkin and some silverware, picked up the tray, and returned to the kitchen; her hips moved subtly up and down as she went through the ballroom doors and disappeared. The last thing she said was, "Don't forget what's in the cabinet. I'll be back."

All Enoch wished for at that moment was another encounter with Jenny and for it to be soon and last long.

*****

Enoch thought of the good start he was off to; he had captured his objective in what had to be considered a minimum amount of time and effort. He felt ahead of schedule and had plenty of time to relax and plan the next move, but all he could think about was Jenny to the point he wanted to stop. To take his mind off her, he began to think of his family: father, mother, brothers, wife, and children, and the times they shared. During their time together, his family and Jenny's surfaced more than once, but in passing. Enoch gathered his thoughts about his family to tell Jenny about them. He gazed out the window and whispered, "My mother's name was Eve, my father's Uriah."

*****

Alden Sinclair had just arrived in the kitchen before Jenny returned. When asked how to continue, he informed the staff that the kitchen was to be cleared of all items before bringing down what remained in the ballroom. The household staff assumed he had told the Lasbriths of their situation, and they knew Enoch Mast had arrived.

The only Lasbrith he was with the morning after the reception was Olivia. He spent all his mornings with her, by her bed or in it, depending on the whereabouts of Hardin Lasbrith, who was often gone. He thought nothing of the chaos he saw in the early morning and felt the situation would be under control when he returned from what he called his morning' rounds.' To him, the morning after the considerable reception was just another morning. Hardin Lasbrith would be the last person Sinclair would bring up the issue; he wouldn't understand anything and was gifted at making bad situations worse.

Sinclair didn't show it, but he was surprised and upset when he put together from the surrounding conversations Enoch Mast was in the ballroom with cake and coffee—listening to how the staff was impressed with how he and the Lasbriths got Enoch to respond so fast. Sinclair, for a moment, hoped it was a bad dream. Conscious of the irony found in getting credit for something he didn't do or want. Cognizant Enoch Mast had come to get paid, and the fundamental policy to never be allowed on the property was no longer in effect.

To show the staff his awareness of what they were saying in their conversations, he asked Jenny, "How long were you with Enoch Mast?" She answered, "Not long enough." Those in the kitchen chuckled at her reply, knowing she was the female equivalent of Sinclair and the only one there in the position to give such an answer. Sinclair casually ignored her remark and left the kitchen no different than any other day.

Alden Sinclair did not share the admiration others had for Enoch. Over the days, weeks, and months Enoch worked in the ballroom, all on staff at one time or another, they all felt the dangerous undercurrents created by the interaction of Enoch Mast and Alden Sinclair. Their exchanges were intense and mysterious. From what the staff observed, it was a safe bet Sinclair and Enoch knew each other from the past. The fact it was true was never brought up by either of them in front of the staff.

They said little to each other when others were present. Those who saw the two interact would say they consistently sized each other up. They were more cautious than respectful of each other. The personalities that surfaced when they did talk were more dangerous and threatening in nature. It became apparent neither feared the other.

There was an edge to the few words they spoke to one another that left any audience wondering if the two weren't headed towards an epic conflict due to their past. Whatever had happened made their words seethe with venom. It made the staff wonder who would be standing in the aftermath.

The staff always felt they were in the wake of two storm fronts of equal force heading toward each other. They didn't know who to take refuge in, the one they liked or the one they feared.

Alden Sinclair was a man of sharp features. He had high cheekbones that set his almost black eyes deep into his face and were like looking into the eyes of a skull. He had a thin nose and lips, thinning black hair combed straight back, and large ears. He was a skinny, six feet three inches tall, a deceptively strong ectomorph. In his younger days, no one was better with a set of brass knuckles in Cleveland than Alden Sinclair; he could put them to sleep or crush their skull, whatever one wanted. After the Civil War, he changed; he used chloroform for the type of work he did. The only one who knew what he was, was the person who hired him.

Sinclair was the only person who understood a takeover was happening. As he walked, he thought about the predicament he was in. First and foremost, the situation was unfolding on his watch. It was a situation with different circumstances he and the Lasbriths had never dealt with before. If he didn't do something fast, it could spin out of control rapidly.

It was apparent threats and intimidation wouldn't work, and too many witnesses knew the last whereabouts of Enoch Mast to kill him. Even so, there might not be another way. All he knew was Enoch Mast had to be removed from the property one way or another before Hardin Lasbrith found out.

He hadn't been as upset as he was in quite some time and was thinking fast and walking slow. Thoughts raced through his mind at such a fast rate he began to wonder if he was experiencing the onset of a stroke or heart attack. It didn't matter; his sheer anger remedied the condition as he headed toward Enoch.

As Sinclair moved on, Enoch made his way back from the cabinet with a box of cigars and a fifth of bourbon; he sat down after finding an empty crystal water tumbler and poured himself a drink. The morning sun filled the ballroom, and without taking a sip, he got right up after he sat down and walked to one of the large mirrors.

As he walked, he lit a cigar, stopped, and stood about four to five feet from it. He faced the mirror and saw white hair, eyebrows, mustache, blue eyes, a ruddy complexion with weathered features on top, a six-foot one-inch, two-hundred twenty-five-pound frame, with above-average posture considering the age. He wore a light rust-colored shirt and a dark forest green leather vest. The tan pant legs were outside a fine pair of well-worn and maintained reddish brown leather boots, exposing not much more than their toe and heel.

On his way back to the overstuffed chair, for the second time, he picked up a basket of assorted dinner rolls and a platter of butter, along with a half-filled bowl of fresh fruit. He placed them on the table and went exploring again. The best finds of all were a fair size dish of shelled pistachios and cashews, a full bottle of Riesling wine, and a platter of assorted cheese. He laid out all the confiscated leftovers within arm's reach. Enoch leaned back, relit his cigar, and began to sip the bourbon, pleased with all he had and where he sat.

*****

For a second time a figure he knew well entered the ballroom. Enoch locked on to Sinclair like a sharpshooter the moment he walked in. He too went to the center of the ballroom. He stopped and began a three-hundred-and-sixty-degree scan. Two-thirds through he was somewhat startled when he spotted Enoch's raised tumbler of bourbon in a cloud of smoke, toasting his arrival. Sinclair barked, "You have no appointment! "Why are you here?" Enoch answered, "Quit playing dumb - you know why!"

Enoch's response angered Sinclair. He began to walk, in a hostile manner, towards Enoch to where one couldn't rule out a full-frontal assault. Enoch reacted by positioning himself to throw, with all his might, the heavy glass tumbler and bourbon into the center of Sinclair's face when he got into optimum range. Sinclair wasn't willing to gamble on whether or not he'd do it, and the idea that he wouldn't miss slowed down his hostile pace.

The two got to terms about two feet from each other, within striking distance. Enoch told Sinclair to sit down; Sinclair answered, "I'll stand," Enoch ignored Sinclair and pointed to a chair. Sinclair moved in its direction but stopped halfway. They looked at each other in silence for a few moments. Enoch spoke, "Tell whoever you need to the largest room in this house has been captured and that I'm not on the outside anymore. I'm on the inside until I get paid - in cash. Until that happens, I will own this ballroom." Sinclair had no problem seeing and believing he meant what he said.

The acids in Sinclair's stomach began to churn as the thought of two-hundred or so conference delegates and representatives of the *Bergoff Brothers Strike Service and Labor Adjusters* came to mind. They were due in the ballroom on Wednesday. To discuss the concept of Jay Gould's remark, "I can hire one half of the working class to kill the other half," and perhaps test it.

His second thought was he had two full days, and that was it, to get rid of Enoch Mast. Enoch stepped over the line this time, and Sinclair decided he had to disappear. Almost a full second after he made the decision, he began to look forward to carrying it out.

He didn't show his concerns, kept his stoic expression, reacted to Enoch's instructions, and told him, "I will do something about it." The 'something' would be murder. In his mind, something Enoch Mast so richly deserved.

Enoch initially had no idea why he selected them, pulled the three business cards and folded invitation from his vest pocket, and spread them on the table, more than willing to show his hand. In the event, Sinclair might call the authorities. He pointed to William S Rowe's card, Cleveland's Chief of Police, and told Sinclair, "He's expecting your call."

The next card he pointed out was the owner of the *Cleveland Plain Dealer* newspaper, Liberty Holden, and asked. "What if a couple of his boys are trying to dig up some news at the police station when you make that call? What if someone tips them off about the 'stolen' ballroom?" The last card Enoch showed was a card for a Pinkerton agent with their motto, "We never sleep." adding, "Neither do I." He unfolded the wedding invitation and tapped his finger on it. "Oh! And tell the Lasbrith's not to pretend they don't know me. Let's not go down that road."

It wasn't long after the telephone took root that business cards began to grow like the leaves on trees as soon as a name was married with a telephone number. Enoch was at a small social gathering after Rowe became chief. Their conversation was pleasant enough for Rowe to give Enoch his card. That was it; Chief Rowe wasn't expecting a call. He got Liberty Holden's card several years back when he was offered a maintenance contract for the Hollenden Hotel. Even though it was one of the best hotels in Cleveland, Enoch didn't appreciate the offer. He was, in a way, offended by it. Holden should have known he built rooms; he didn't maintain them. The last card was when he engaged the Pinkertons about his brother Enos. He played its easy-to-read motto, "We Never Sleep," to implant the idea he wasn't going away.

Enoch inhaled a cloud of smoke, took a long pull from the water tumbler, and exhaled the smoke in Sinclair's face. Through the smoke, all Sinclair could see was a big smile. He didn't return the smile and left seething with no idea of 'when' he would do it but an unmistakable picture of 'what' he would do. Sinclair spoke out loud and in Latin to himself, "Ego te interficiam" (I will kill you). Enoch surprised and shocked Sinclair when he replied, "Non nolueritis" (No you won't).

The stakes were high; Sinclair lived in the Lasbrith mansion more as a resident than an employee and had a very comfortable lifestyle. It would end if he didn't make the right moves. He had to change the situation he was in, and he had to move fast. It had been a while since he experienced the pressure he was under, and it bothered him.

Enoch held the terrain he wanted. As far as he was concerned, half the battle was over early. The other half would occur when a family member, lawyer, or accountant would show up with the money.

His memories and thoughts were turning out to be better company than he had thought. He could let his mind wander; he was comfortable in his command post. An animal instinct told him it was an excellent time to get some sleep. It could be hours, and it could be days before he got paid. It was safe to rest, but it would change. He knew the Lasbriths would send Sinclair again before any family members or representatives with cash would show up. Enoch took advantage of the situation and put out his cigar, leaned back, slid down some in the overstuffed chair, and closed his eyes.

CHAPTER III
A DECIMATION

Had Hardin Lasbrith known who was sleeping in his ballroom, what followed would have been different and perhaps not as bizarre. Had Enoch Mast known where Hardin Lasbrith kept four thousand dollars in his forty-room mansion, his takeover would end when the cash was in his pocket.

Enoch Mast put his cigar out to get some sleep in the ballroom; at almost the same time, Hardin Ellsworth Lasbrith awoke and lit a cigar in his bedroom. He got up and found his pants fetched a twenty-dollar gold piece and slapped it on the dresser by the door, then smacked the ass of his overnight guest and grinned. The guest was part of the wedding party and fell victim to Hardin's continual advances. She over-imbibes, to where his conduct eventually became acceptable.

She could not restrain her anxiety and disgust when she realized what part of the watering hole she woke up in and what had happened there. With her head pounding from the oncoming hangover, she forced herself to snatch what clothes she could, grabbed the gold piece off the dresser, and headed for the door. She soared through it like a small bird fleeing a massive and grotesque predator,

Hardin enjoyed watching her panic. He thought her sudden movements were out of fear of being caught by his wife, Olivia. He thought if she was escaping from anyone, it was not him, but her. Hardin never saw himself as a predator. He saw himself more as a planet who's gravitational pull no woman could resist. That the center of their universe was him, he believed all women were jealous of any woman in his company and wanted to be that woman.

Hardin could never escape his self-inflicted delusions that the attraction women had for him was genuine because of what he had to offer them physically and mentally. Blind to the fact he was a six-foot-three-inch bowling pin with slender shoulders and wide hips. All his hair resided on the left side of his head and combed over to where it touched his right ear. It was the source of a lot of behind-the-back and inside jokes. He refused to grasp that his great wealth held the attention of attractive women who loved money. That they were held in place by his vast fortune; without it, no self-respecting woman in her right mind would go to his bedroom.

He never let facts get in the way of his beliefs. His overnight guest is a perfect example. The truth is, his overnight guest wanted to escape him as soon as possible, and his current wife could have cared less if she had spent the night with him. She was like the guest; she also wanted to escape.

Hardin Ellsworth Lasbrith always chose to ignore the significant causes behind his many problems in life, and that was his absolute certainty that his thoughts and conclusions on any subject were truths. He was perceived by others the same way as his granddaughter's wedding cake. He boasted it was the largest ever made in Cleveland. Many agreed it was a giant cake, but truth be told, they'd seen larger ones at some of the grand openings and conventions held in the city.

Hardin Lasbrith and Enoch Mast were the same age. Both were, in comparison, twenty-seven years older than Hardin's current wife, Olivia. Hardin's first and second wives died of natural causes at a young age. There were always questions about their deaths. The first, Cora, gave him a son, Horace Bilton Lasbrith. His second wife, Elinor, delivered a daughter, Ophelia Lasbrith Benton; Ophelia's daughter, Florence Lasbrith Benton, was Hardin's granddaughter, who had married the previous day.

His current wife was the most attractive of the three, a former showgirl; she had a son from one of her previous liaisons, Blanton, who Hardin immediately sent to Ohio University after boarding school. While there, he committed suicide in his early twenties. Like Hardin's two wives, his death was sudden, unexpected, and discussed by many.

There were just as many questions surrounding Blanton's death as Hardin's two wives. There were always questions but never any answers or proof beyond hearsay. Horace's name appeared more than once in the paperwork behind the investigation into Blanton's untimely passing. The wealth of the Lasbrith family had a way of keeping those asking questions at bay. They were happy with the rumors that began to surface in the community. Gossip was far better than the facts. The family could live with the stories but not the truths behind the deaths.

An only child, Hardin, was raised by governesses and tutors. His behavior made them appreciate the holiday seasons more than anyone on the household staff. Often after the holidays, Hardin found himself in the company of a new governess or tutors, sometimes both. Word had gotten out, and those in the field charged the Lasbriths more than the average fee for their services. However, after a steady dose of Hardin's behavior, the money was insufficient to hold most.

Hardin Ellsworth Lasbrith was taught at home because no boarding school would have him. By more than one governess and tutor that migrated to such schools, they advised them to forgo the money due to his behavior. Except for the holiday seasons, he spent little time with his parents, Malcomb Sidney Lasbrith and Loretta Chance Lasbrith.

When he did spend time with them, their times together were awkward. His parents gave him a steady diet of strange and cutting conversations. The discussions generally followed a pattern where his parents would mock him and get Hardin to poke back. It was almost always two against one, with his parents dominating, but there were times when it became each against the other. These were the times Hardin won.

There was more resentment towards each other than love. They gave their devotion to their wealth. His parents loved what they had, and Hardin loved what one day would be his. As time went on, they became a family that mostly coexisted with each other, enjoying one's absence far more than their presence.

As he got older, Hardin always considered himself a well-educated person based on the number of teachers he had had. However, test results showed the exact opposite. His large allowance, not intelligence, kept him afloat during these times. His funding came from a family accountant who released it religiously on the first of every month; it was an amount twice the accountant's salary and a sum his parents had utterly forgotten they had set up. Even if they had, they probably would have still had the excessive amount sent to keep Hardin's exposure to them at a minimum. They didn't want to be annoyed by his requests for money.

Hardin learned from it all that he had a gift for finding those who could be bought and sold and those who couldn't. One was a group to be cultivated and exploited, the other to be avoided and exterminated. Hardin Lasbrith was from the school one doesn't 'work' their way to the top; one 'buys' their way.

He believed if one had an endless stream of money, like his parents and one day him, knowing who was on the take was all one needed to know to become powerful. He believed power and success were the same. To him, the concept of 'working' was a fairy tale; it took too long. If one had the money, the idea of' buying' was far more efficient. From a very early age, Hardin knew he had a price and thought if he had one, so did everyone else. Those who didn't have a price, who didn't know their worth, weren't worth knowing.

When he learned who and how to bribe most of his tutors, he kept appearing to be a student. But in reality, he abandoned his education, pursuing all forms of pleasure instead. All the paperwork behind his education, with his name on it, was bought, not earned. He became a gifted hedonist. Encounters with him turned into a game of charades; one had to constantly guess what he was trying to say through his gestures, not words. He was never clear on any topic he talked about. All Hardin knew was how to dress and act like a student. He never learned to think like one. His education was gilded, and over time, it became very apparent and exposed him for what he was, uneducated.

His approach to education was a mistake. Later, he found his lack of it kept him from the acceptance he desired and the circles of influence he longed to be in. He found wealth was one entity, education another, entities that should not be mutually exclusive. He was always able to say who had educated him. Still, he was never able to demonstrate the results of their efforts. Over time, the people he conducted business with never considered Hardin, an educated person; no, he was considered a ruthless person who confused wealth with knowledge. One with limited thoughts and primitive reasoning. One who spoke the most and knew the least.

When Hardin turned twenty-four, it was in the middle of the Civil War; for his birthday, his parents gifted him the required three-hundred-dollar commutation fee allowed under the Enrollment Act of 1863. Also, they hired someone to take Hardin's place in the Union army; he was double-covered from the draft.

The way they did this was to offer a young single man employed by AHP&D (American Hardware Production and Distribution), which the Lasbriths owned, a big promotion and salary upon his return from the war. It would be three to four times his salary. The corporation found a replacement and quietly sent him off.

It was his only gift that year and the last present his parents ever gave him, and it turned out to be the most important gift of his life. It allowed him to avoid the war and continue to learn and work in the family business. As a result, he and his father had a brief honeymoon period. They got along better once Hardin entered the family business.

When it happened, the two began seeing how much they were alike and had in common. Malcomb liked to think he taught Hardin everything he knew about how to succeed in business. Unaware, Hardin came by being deceitful and underhanded naturally. Both of their lives revolved around taking advantage of the mistakes and misfortune of others in different ways, and each had their style.

*****

The young man, who took Hardin's place, soldiered up with the Ohio 7th Infantry. In July of that year, in the first three days, he found himself in a small Pennsylvania town called Gettysburg. A battle took place there that started on July first and ended on July third, 1863.

The following day, Independence Day, became the most significant Fourth of July in the nation's history. The South's high watermark had reached Gettysburg; from there, it began to recede to where it came from. Hardin Lasbriths' replacement never saw that

July fourth or knew the outcome of the conflict, having been killed on the last day of the battle at Culp's Hill.

When the Lasbriths got word of this, they saw where they could use his death to their advantage. They would have a wake. Malcomb and Hardin would use the news of the young man's death to have a small service with a few of their privileged friends who they knew would speak of the event correctly to the right circles.

Not once was the substitute's name mentioned. Throughout the service, Hardin Lasbrith's name took its place, and he and his father presented to the guests as a war hero and a father who had made the ultimate sacrifice for the cause. What was made clear and emphasized several times was that what happened to his replacement could have happened to Hardin. Somehow, this made Hardin and his father heroes. The young man's name should have been spoken during the wake; Hardin's name was substituted instead, as if he had been at Culp's Hill.

The Lasbriths were persuasive enough to make it seem Hardin was there. Gettysburg was one of the major reasons that Malcolm Lasbrith hired Alden Sinclair as the head butler of the estate. He was in the battle. Sinclair was to manage the staff and coach Hardin on everything he knew about Gettysburg, among other things. As the years rolled on, many believed Hardin had been at Gettysburg when he hadn't. The Lasbrith family did nothing to change this perception of Hardin's service in the community, but those who had been at Gettysburg after talking to Hardin knew.

The Lasbriths were good at painting Hardin's service record and wealthy enough to have the documents they could access changed to support the myth. Anyone who questioned it made an example of; they punished one veteran in court and the newspapers to where he killed himself. He became an example of what could happen to those who doubted. As the years passed, those who stated their reservations about Hardin's service were the ones made out to be liars.

On top of this, no Lasbrith or anyone else could tell one the substitute's name. Which pointed to the fact there never was any substitute if no one could name him. It was not a fact but treated as one after a while. As it turned out, the Civil War worked out well for Hardin and the family business, he benefited from his artificial veteran status, and the corporation profited from it.

Four years later, when Hardin Ellsworth Lasbriyh was twenty-eight, Malcolm Sidney Lasbrith died. Hardin inherited the American Hardware Production and Distribution Corporation (AHP&D). AHP&D was founded by Hardin's paternal grandfather (Sidney Kaleb Lasbrith). Under Malcomb Sidney Lasbrith, the corporation profited immensely during the American Civil War, having sold vast quantities of all types of pulleys, ropes, chains, and telegraph wire to the Union Army for the movement of their wagons, artillery, and the development of their lines of communication. The telegraph wire was an essential product in that the Union took full advantage of the telegraph's capabilities to a far greater degree than the Confederates. The Lasbriths priced it accordingly and to their advantage. Although never said but wholly understood, profit took precedence over patriotism.

The increasing profits of their corporation allowed the Lasbriths to expand beyond Cleveland and into Cincinnati, Pittsburgh, and Philadelphia. As soon as the war ended, his father brought on board four new locations in the South: Savannah, Charleston, Atlanta, and New Orleans. To get the southern business, he staffed them with ex-Confederate officers. It took a toll on him. It wasn't too long after they were up and running, he died. Many say the South killed him before he saw a penny from their locations.

The American West opened up when the Civil War ended. As luck would have it, the corporation was ground floor when the demand for barbed wire went through the ceiling. Just as supply began to meet demand domestically, the Spanish American and Boer Wars broke out. For the first time, barbwire showed up on the battlefield. It became an international product with militaries across the globe driving demand. Potential sales were an ever-expanding universe of profit.

The war that would provide an almost never-ending international non-stop demand for barbed wire for the next four years was on the horizon. Sitting in the middle of all this activity were AHP&D and Hardin Ellsworth Lasbrith.

Eight profitable locations were in operation by 1870. The company ran almost by osmosis, with little effort from Hardin. Business was good in all areas of the corporation, and there didn't seem to be an end in sight. After a while, it appeared Hardin Ellsworth Lasbrith's real job was not making money but spending money on whatever he wanted, such as political influence, the demolition of labor unions, the total resistance to woman's suffrage, and the building of more lavish mansions, in cities like New York, Cleveland and places like the Hamptons and the South Fork Hunting and Fishing Club.

*****

Hardin moved about his bedroom, getting dressed. His movements were above average for his age, considering the abuse he put his body through over the years. He was a chain smoker, borderline alcoholic, obese, and seemed to successfully defy the laws of good health and not have to pay a heavy price. The only drawback was his physical appearance; he looked like someone who denied himself nothing and had the physique to prove it.

There was some poetic justice, though. The unexplainable longevity wasn't without various bouts of long periods of chronic pain. Gout was a contributor. However, the major provider of his aches and pains came from a disease he developed in his late twenties that he could only contain, not cure.

The condition robbed him of sleep and increased his appetite, making him irritable and mean-spirited. One who would laugh at a person's misfortune if one was to laugh at all. The few times Hardin did laugh, he always laughed alone at someone and the name he called them, never with them or at something or a shared joke. It became apparent to many that Hardin Lasbrith didn't get what others did; he often missed that many gags were at his expense. He never told any jokes or joked around; his strong suit was name-calling, and it held him back in the minds of most as someone of limited talent.

*****

A long piece, perhaps five feet, of dark red silk, no wider than two inches, with a gold-colored tassel at its end, hung from the wall by his bed. Hardin walked over to it and gave it a yank; a bell rang just outside the kitchen, notifying the staff his breakfast had to be made and delivered within twenty minutes or someone would pay the price; he used the failure of not meeting his first expectation of the day to fire staff members before sunset if he remembered. These firings took on informal and formal proceedings. He did it enough to where the staff was well aware of the consequences of a late breakfast.

A late breakfast meant a work day with an interruption, usually occurring at the most inopportune time. Sinclair would have to gather the staff, get rid of four, and then have replacements by the following day, which he always did. The subs were the same people dismissed the previous day. It was a strange game everyone was used to playing, and for most, it was an inconvenience, but it did have its benefits.

The day after the wedding reception, the pressure to perform was beyond a typical morning. To prepare a plate of four scrambled eggs, bacon, home fries, a stack of pancakes, a pitcher of maple syrup, a saucer of butter and jelly, rye toast, a glass of buttermilk, and a cup of coffee was beyond a tall order. It had to be prepared and delivered right during the staff's first clean-up operation after the renovation—a ballroom that was filled to capacity the previous day. It all had to be moved to a kitchen with severely limited space.

Hardin's expectations of the time required to prepare and deliver the perfect breakfast were always the staff's first burden of the day. To offset the pressure, those responsible for getting it to him on time would joke about what type of poison or human or animal waste they wished they could add to the meal. Then they would argue over whose turn it was to deliver the breakfast. Preparation was complex every morning. The morning after the reception, it seemed it would be almost impossible.

*****

While he waited for his breakfast, Hardin prepared a syringe. He filled it with an antitoxin of killed gonococci to control his persistent case of 'gleet' (gonorrhea). Over the years, Hardin developed a lingering condition maintained by continually visiting the best brothels in the eight cities AHP&D had a facility. He injected it into his right buttock, pulled it out, pulled up his pants, buckled his belt, and relit his cigar. Next, he took the syringe apart, cleaned it, and put it back in its silver case. The case was put away in the false bottom of the mahogany jewelry box on the dresser.

The vile that held the antitoxin didn't go in the box, it was empty, which angered Hardin, and he dropped it on the floor and crushed it with his foot, leaving it for the staff to clean up. It was the third vile he had exhausted that month, and he could not figure out why it was going so fast. The antitoxin was expensive. He had a right to be upset, but why he ran out prematurely went unnoticed by him.

What was occurring was the solid black ceramic vile stayed the same size as did the price, but the amount in it was reduced by a tenth each time Hardin ordered. Hardin had the impression he was using more, and it was doing less. The doctor treating Hardin's condition for the last three years had no problem taking advantage of him because he had no respect for Hardin. They traveled in the same social circles, and the doctor had witnessed firsthand how crude and vulgar Hardin could be. He made Hardin pay a high price for his professional confidence concerning his condition.

He charged Hardin the highest prices while at the same time experimenting on him with his remedies and the new and untested remedies of his colleagues, to who he charged a fee. As soon as one concoction seemed to reduce the effect of the disease, he'd raise the price, reduce the supply, confirm its success, and market it. Eventually, he'd replace it with a new remedy, repeating this process. Sometimes there were side effects; sometimes, there weren't. Either way, it didn't matter because he and his colleagues didn't care about the patient.

*****

Hardin took out his Patek Philippe pocket watch to see the time; it read eight-twenty. There should have been a knock at his door that very moment. It didn't happen. He wouldn't forget. However, he did forget that he didn't ring for breakfast at eight as he thought but at eight-ten.

He closed the watch and went to his desk. He opened a finely tooled leather satchel, took out some papers, threw them on the desk, and began to search for his spectacles. He was swearing under his breath the whole time about breakfast being late and his inability to immediately find what he was looking for.

*****

At eight-thirty, Jenny knocked on Hardin's door. There was no answer. She stood outside and dreaded the voice she would eventually hear; he liked to play what he thought was a guessing game—trying to get whoever was outside to open the door to see if he was there so he could punish them for an unauthorized entry. As she waited for the inevitable, she began to think how this was her second tray of the morning, how much she enjoyed serving the first tray, and how much she hated doing the second.

Hardin finally barked, "Come in!" She entered wearing her thickest skin. He was verbally abusive, and she knew what to ignore and what to pay attention to when he spoke. She always kept both eyes on him and made it a point always to be more than arm's distance from him. If he tried to close the distance, she slid to the right or left like a boxer trying to stay off the ropes, only in her case to stay away from the walls. The door appeared closed, but she always left it a little ajar for a quick escape. She was the best on staff in handling Hardin; she worked this routine religiously and shared her technique with all the women on staff.

*****

Jenny could tell by how he acted that he couldn't find something, probably his glasses. She put down the tray and joined the search. They were nowhere in sight, and it occurred to her to check the pockets of his silk robe resting on the back of the chair by Hardin's bed. She slipped unnoticed towards the robe as Hardin swore under his breath and scattered all that was on his desk in his futile search. Some documents remained on the desktop, while some were found on the floor.

Within a second or two, she had them in her hand, returned to the desk, and stood saying nothing. When Hardin looked up and saw his glasses in her hand, he quickly grabbed them. "Give me!" He exploded and then abruptly sat down at the desk, rapidly tapping his fingers on its surface, glaring at Jenny.

As she cleared a space on his desk for the tray, Hardin began to tell her a story about the Romans. Either he was never aware, or he didn't care, that he told this particular story perhaps two or three times a year, every year, for what seemed like forever. And when he told it, he always acted like he was enlightening the unfortunate listener for the first time. There was not a person on staff who had not heard it at one time or another. It made everyone feel he was going senile.

Hardin Lasbrith always considered himself the American Caesar. It was his favorite story about the Romans, and he thought his presentation made him sound educated instead of deranged. The sigh Jenny wished she could let out was like an oncoming sneeze, only easier to control. All she could do was roll her eyes when he wasn't looking and hope she would get the short version of what she had heard so many times.

Hardin always began the story by asking about "decimation," what it meant, and how the word came to be. In its shortest form, the story is about a Roman general who lost a battle he felt he should have won. The General thought about it and concluded it was not him but his soldiers who did not perform. To make sure this never happened again and to force them to accomplish what they would be called upon to do in the future, he ordered the survivors to count off by tens. Within every group of ten, lots were drawn for life, nine would win, but one would lose and be killed by the others. He killed one-tenth of his remaining troops to make his point. The practice became known as 'Decimation,' and it became a feared punishment. Like this Roman General, Hardin believed that fear was what motivated people.

Over the years, the mornings his breakfast was late, Hardin would threaten decimation. Once or twice a year, he would carry one out. Four people would pay with their jobs. The times when Hardin would carry out his threat, Sinclair would release four, only to rehire them the following morning. The practice had an ironic and reverse effect on the staff; the four chosen were punished by getting the day off with pay.

Sinclair knew Hardin had no idea who was and was not on the staff, except for him and Jenny. He wasn't about to compete for domestic help when the demand for labor in the industrial arena was drying up the domestic pool.

It worked this way. If Hardin got word back to Sinclair, it went ignored, and Hardin was told the decimation had been carried out when it hadn't. If Hardin were upset enough to tell Sinclair or Jenny to have the staff form up in the grand dining hall, he would personally choose the four in front of everyone; Sinclair would release them on the spot with the understanding they were to stay out of sight until the following morning.

The morning after the wedding reception, a dining hall formation seemed as inevitable as it was unwanted. If anything, the pressure the staff was under following the reception was something Hardin didn't care about. If anything, it was a situation that brought out his true nature to make people suffer in their job.

The dining hall decimations were sometimes considered a pleasant surprise when they didn't follow a significant event. When they did, the luster of their silver lining considerably faded for everyone but four. Hardin was utterly unaware that they were acceptable at times and aware, for the most part, they accomplished the dread he wanted to inflict. The decimations were a much talked about practice unique to the Lasbrith family and known about by domestics at other estates.

When Jenny returned to the kitchen from delivering her second breakfast, she informed Sinclair that Hardin was summoning him. Sinclair knew what was to come and shook his head in anger. He would have to form up the staff and have them wait in the grand dining hall for a decimation.

Next, he'd have to go to Hardin and lead him to the dining hall after Hardin told him about the Romans and 'decimation' for the millionth time. After their arrival, Hardin would then gleefully listen to each pretend to turn on one another to keep their job viciously, unaware the one viciously chosen stood in well with the others and would be back in the morning.

*****

The household staff was formed up in the grand dining hall and began waiting for Sinclair and Hardin's arrival. As Hardin waited for Sinclair, he gathered the papers scattered on the desk and floor while searching for his spectacles. He opened the center drawer and retrieved a black satin ribbon; he rolled the papers up, bound them with the ribbon, and tossed them back into the satchel.

He leaned back in his overstuffed chair and started thinking about his schedule for the next few days. Picturing the amount of time, he wanted to spend with his clients, making sure he had more than enough time to find out what he needed to know from his attorneys. He was thinking about where to spend the night downtown, at the club or the bordello. He was uncertain. Would he be gone one night or two? If he had to go to Kent, a trip he wanted to avoid, it would be two.

Mostly, the satchel held legal documents about patents and royalties, correspondence from attorneys, filed briefs, and court dates. It had all been prepared by an elaborate staff of high-paid employees who had recently been put under Horace Lasbrith's control that Hardin knew nothing about other than he had documents to waive in people's faces.

*****

Hardin's executives were like his doctor; they charged the maximum fees and provided the minimum effort. They could string out legal situations Hardin brought on AHP&D indefinitely. Once Hardin demonstrated he knew virtually next to nothing about AHP&D, all they had to do to keep the gravy train rolling was to continually flatter him on what he didn't possess - business skills. In reality, he was impressive in his ignorance of how the business operated. Anyone involved in the upper management that ran the day-to-day operations was quick to grasp this fact and take advantage of it.

The only thing they had to keep in the back of their mind was Hardin owned AHP&D and took in one year what would take them five years to earn. In turn, they were also well aware they made in one year what would take most people a lifetime. It was wise not to get too carried away with their interactions with Hardin and forget he was a very wealthy man and could afford to be ignorant, whereas they couldn't. Most of all, they always had to be aware that he was as vindictive as he was ignorant.

That he owned the company and could be as malicious as he wanted was all anyone who worked for Hardin needed to understand. For example, the attorneys at AHP&D encouraged clients, competitors, and customers to pursue legal actions if they were upset. They were aware with Hardin at the helm, there would always be a steady flow of work for them in the legal realm. If there was one thing Hardin excelled at, it was upsetting clients, competitors, customers, and, in general, people.

*****

The same year Hardin's father died (1867), Lucien B Smith of Kent, Ohio, was given a patent for barbed wire. He called his product an 'artificial thorn hedge.' Malcomb Lasbrith pursued Smith to obtain patent rights for AHP&D, which he never got but said he did. AHP&D went into the production of barbwire without a patent. Enough money was made from the move to indefinitely fight the issue in the courts. It wasn't too long after Malcomb's death Hardin began to claim barbed wire was his idea. Those who questioned him were released from the company or taken to court. Hardin took total credit for introducing this product line and its positive effect on the bottom line of AHP&D.

Seven years later, AHP&D was perusing and trying to obtain rights from Joseph F. Glidden's 1874 patent on the 'modern version' of barbed wire. Glidden was from Dekalb, Illinois, and had modified the previous version and created new product lines by introducing zinc-coated steel wire, double strand, double barb, conventional, and reverse twist types of barb wire.

By the end of 1875, AHP&D didn't have any rights to the product but had stolen enough technology, tooling, and machines to produce all types of modern barb wire at six of AHP&D's eight locations. Demand for the product was so great AHP&D's two most western locations were converted from production facilities to warehouse and distribution centers. The conversion was necessary to handle the demand from all developing regions in the western United States.

The years following the Civil War immediately saw the West offer new settings and opportunities; for both sides, Northerners and Southerners took advantage of what the West offered. They went off and became what is known as 'cowboys.' The migration created the need for new products. One of the first was revolvers, then lever action rifles and cartridges that fit both, which became high-demand products to secure land.

Next, the railroads moved west, and so did the telegraph, which depended on wire. However, the wire that had the same impact on the West as the rifle, six-shooter, trains, and telegraph was Lucien Smith's 'artificial thorn hedge' and John Glidden's 'modern' barb wire. Its swift emergence provided a dirt-cheap easy method of fencing that ended the open range.

Free grazing and open water rights disappeared whenever it showed up.

Large tracts of land could be taken and closed in with the minimum effort and cost. It seemed to be the ideal solution when one wanted to grab the most, fast. But the growth of barbed wire created as many problems as it solved. The 'Devil's rope' was what the latter settlers came to call it, and Hardin became fond of this name to the point of considering selling it as such. All his executives could do was stop him from taking the approach.

AHP&D had no rights to produce the modern version but made the product, anyway, bringing on suits by Glidden and others who had legally obtained the rights. Hardin didn't care. His approach was as long as the demand was greater than AHP&D's capacity, with the money pouring in; all he had to do was find the right politicians and judges to buy off, and this problem would be solved. It was quickly becoming a fact AHP&D was making the kind of money where they could buy a politician from the top shelf when the time came.

Hardin was so disinterested in the legal proceedings that he put his son Horace in charge of all the corporation's legal matters. He placed his son in this position to show that legal issues were essential to AHP&D, and their solutions were in the hands of the owner's son, who was next in line. It was an utterly cosmetic move on Hardin's part, a move that would prove later on to have been a colossal mistake.

His trip to the Cleveland offices would be Hardin's first introduction to the results of Horace's work. Another first, the headquarters office of AHP&D would hear the initial new direction Hardin would take the corporation. He believed introducing the new path there would be comfortable. Unaware of the future home office meetings over the new approach and Horace's unreliable work would be the perfect ingredients for nightmares.

*****

Horace's childhood was almost like Hardin's, except for the lasting effect the disappearance of his mother, stepmother, and stepbrother had on him. Some believed he was involved in the stepbrother's disappearance. There were always stories about Horace, and none of them were good.

The facts about him were worse. For example, Horace was a bed wetter, a condition he never overcame, which, when Hardin would overhear one of the staff mention or joke about, he would immediately send for Horace and severely beat him; this happened often.

When Hardin became part of the business, his relationship with his father improved somewhat; it improved to the point where each could see what they had in common. Hardin hoped this to be the case with his son. It was not the case. Horace's treatment at the hands of his father and then by others eventually drove him to alcohol. Then morphine, and then heroin to get off the morphine. Where Hardin developed into an exceptional hedonist, his son grew into an excellent addict. The only thing they had in common was each had a silver case with a syringe.

A perfect example of Horace's work would be the papers in Hardin's satchel. Horace prepared them. He prepared them by visiting the Cleveland headquarters late one night and prying open a few roll-top desks and randomly taking whatever papers were on and in them until he had an impressive stack of documents that looked presentable and filled the satchel.

There was just enough current related work; that would get conversations started, but most documents were not related in any form. Most topics and dates didn't line up, so no correct timeline could be made on any topics. Most documents in Hardin's satchel were random new and old information bound together by a black ribbon.

Eventually, they would lead to conversations on how the documents fit in with the corporation's current position and the future direction AHP&D wanted to take. What was in Hardin's satchel would confound the simplest of issues. What was taken from the departments Horace raided went unreported. Those in charge eventually put together what must have happened. In the coming meetings, what was in Hardin's satchel would produce scenes similar to a thief unloading his bag and putting the jewels of those he had just robbed back on the table for them to take.

*****

The legal aspects affecting AHP&D would camouflage the primary cause behind Hardin's trip. What it appeared to be was not the case. What was the point of the visit? To put the legal issues on the back burner and to introduce a new corporate direction and goal, the acquisition of the technology and equipment necessary to produce 'razor' wire. A wire that could be coiled flat and, when uncoiled, did not require posts. It became like a giant spring laying on its side stretched over the terrain requiring the bottom of a few coils to be attached to the ground to keep it in place. It was quick to set up and very effective; the flat barbs cut through clothing and flesh like a razor.

A major European war was on the near horizon. The development and production of a razor wire which could outperform the impressive results of modern barb wire would create a massive fortune for AHP&D. To replace Barb wire or 'war wire' with razor wire would put AHP&D on the international map with considerable deposits in the international banks.

The concept of producing razor wire didn't come from Hardin. It came from an employee, a draftsman. He submitted a drawing of what he had seen in some ancient book. The rendering moved through the proper channels. The employee believed he would be handsomely rewarded for the finding he had made. Once the concept was unanimously accepted and became an approved corporate project, all the previous work was correctly traced back to the employee to ensure others were not involved, and the employee was fired. Soon afterward, Hardin began to claim the employee's idea and work as his, and everyone knew not to question it. Hardin's reputation as both an innovator and businessman undeservedly began to flourish in business circles.

*****

Thirty-nine of the staff stood in the grand dining hall, waiting for the arrival of Hardin and Sinclair. The one missing was the stable groom. He was busy hitching a gray filly to a sleek custom-made shiny black buggy made by the Ohio Carriage Company out of Cincinnati. Hardin bought it in 1912 for close to one hundred dollars. It had a soft black leather tucked and rolled bench that sat two under a snug black canvas canopy trimmed in short gold fringe. Behind the seat was a small, highly varnished bed with a six-inch, highly polished brass rail that could carry a large trunk or tie down several pieces of luggage.

When finished, the stable groom was to take the handsome rig to the portico and wait for Mr. Lasbrith and his luggage. He was the only one excused from the formation but not the decimation.

As they milled about cursing the timing of the event and waiting for a signal from a lookout to find their wall, they eventually talked about the last decimation and a few stand-out decimations of the past. They spoke of those last decimated and what they remembered from their unexpected day off.

One was either a painting' or a 'mirror' person. To explain, one had to understand the layout of the grand dining hall. There were two walls covered with paintings and two walls covered with mirrors. The mirrored walls faced each other, making the dining hall appear much larger than it was. The walls of pictures covered with landscapes and portraits also faced each other. All were said to be originals, and when reflected in the mirrored walls, they created the illusion of an art collection that seemed to be much larger than it was.

It was the same with the dinner guests. Most remembered occasions as having more people than attended by their reflections in the mirrors. Independent of one another, one could gaze at a painting on a wall, while another could stare at the same picture in a mirror. The grand dining hall replicated the gilded attitude of the age, to take something and make it be what it wasn't, as being more prominent and holding more than it could.

Ten on each wall as a rule, and some stayed on one type of wall all the time, while a few mixed it up but had to find one willing to trade. In a year, one's affiliation with a wall might be brought up whenever one makes a mistake. Mirror and Painting People were true to their walls. Often when a person made a mistake of one affiliation, it was brought to everyone's attention by one from the other affiliation.

The dining hall was a microcosm of the society they lived in. Those who stood in front of the mirrors were joked about as being 'populists' in nature, while those who stood in front of the landscapes and portraits were 'elitists.' What was interesting about the whole setup was how the decimation unknowingly functioned to form a pseudo-two-party system made up of 'mirror people' and 'painting people' among the staff. As it turned out, 'mirror people' attitudes were the more liberal, and 'painting people' were the more conservative.

What was even more fascinating about the decimations over the years was the selection of candidates. Two candidates were chosen from each party. They were determined during the milling around when some shopped themselves while the more popular quietly waited. Jenny always got selected. After the candidates were chosen, they were sent to their wall. The rest continued to mill about, discussing what was to be said about each. All the candidates could hear was the laughter over what was about to be told about them to Hardin and Sinclair. There were a lot of staff rituals attached to decimations.

However, just because one might receive the most comments from the others, this was no guarantee of being selected by Hardin. One could make some negative comments about a candidate that Hardin admired and still be unchosen.

Most in the room understood the dynamics of Hardin's narcissism. Most times, comments such as "Sir, this person took a rather radical view on the necktie you had on the other day, that they took time away from not only their work, but mine as well to tell me as much" would be the type of remark Hardin looked for. Hardin loved it when it appeared his staff were fighting with one another; it was a behavior he encouraged. He enjoyed conflict as long as he didn't have to participate.

*****

Of all the decimations, this was the one Jenny hoped for, and if it happened, she knew where and who she wanted to spend it with when she was released. She wanted to go to the ballroom, leave her dress in the cloakroom, and find Enoch Mast. All that ran through her mind was a romantic fantasy of total surrender, to the point where for the first time, she began to shop herself on the floor. As degrading as she found it to be, she could not stop.

Fortunately, she was not very skilled at what she was attempting, and her efforts went unnoticed by most. The few that did pick up on her actions were able to put two and two together and come up with Enoch Mast. It wasn't until she overheard his name being mentioned by a few that she finally found the strength to stop what she was doing. Her emotions were mixed; on one hand, all she felt was the desire to see him. On the other hand, she was finding this desire made her feel uneasy and unsure about everything.

The fact of the matter was the odds of her being selected by Hardin almost didn't exist. They were along the lines of being killed in New York City by an elephant. Not that this couldn't happen, one could have an unfortunate day at the circus when it came to town or at the zoo if they went, but no one could recall if such an event ever, in fact, happened. If she were selected, then there would be no reporting back in the morning. If there was one person on the household staff of forty whose return would not go unnoticed by Hardin, it would be Jenny.

She knew if the fantasy running through her head came to be, it would come at a very high price. Even so, the facts surrounding the matter were not enough to kill the fantasy, only wound it. As hard as she fought the feeling, the possibility of committing employment suicide was always there.

A loaded pistol on the table; all one had to do was pick it up, place it on their temple, and pull the trigger. An outburst of profanity, fired directly at Sinclair, would give her the desired release. Heaven would be the ballroom and Enoch Mast. All she had to do was pull the trigger to make it happen. She was torn and uncomfortable, knowing an unfortunate event was just as likely to occur as not. Her immediate future attracted and frightened her at the same time.

*****

The lookout signaled, and each began to find their wall. Their conversations were reduced to short whispers, followed by complete silence when Hardin and Sinclair entered the grand dining hall. As in the past, Sinclair was a step and a half behind Hardin, who talked over his shoulder at him to give the impression it was Sinclair's idea that the decimation was needed and had come to him as the authority to carry it out.

Following tradition, the decimation always began with one word, "Romans." It was spoken by Hardin every single time one took place, so many times that some on the staff could time when he would say it and it became a background chorus. The timing of the choir was almost perfect to where one hardly noticed who joined in;

what went noticed was there was more volume behind the word "Romans" than normal.

He would say this one word when he arrived at the center of the grand dining hall, pause, and then wander into the most inaccurate history of the Romans and their empire possibly ever given. He spoke to those in front of the mirrored walls more than those who stood before the paintings, believing they were the larger audience. There were times he would rattle on for three-quarters of an hour and times he would go on for a quarter of an hour. One always hoped for the shortest version. He had the Romans conquering every known people, including the major tribes of the American Indians; he was hard to follow and became more mind-numbing as he went on.

Some could not hold back a sigh of relief when he finished. Hardin believed it to be a sign of gratitude in recognition of all he had informed them of, not the sigh of thanks that this phase of the decimation had ended.

The candidate selection was next. In the first three groups of ten, the choices went as planned. There was no fourth selection. Before he could make it, Hardin saw an enormous smudge on a mirror; this was bad, but not as bad as what he saw next, a massive cobweb on the uppermost painting on the entrance wall. The fact it was visible from such a distance terrified and infuriated Hardin, and he flew into what would be a memorable tirade. It went on for what seemed forever, hissing venom behind every word.

Cobwebs and spider webs were the most toxic items in Hardin's world. At around nine or ten years of age, Hardin was at the Lake View cemetery with a cousin from his mother's side. His aunt and uncle visited a family mausoleum to air it out. They then visited some other mausoleums. Hardin's cousin got him to go into the family mausoleum on a dare and locked him in it for almost a whole afternoon. When his cousin was asked where Hardin was, he told his parents Hardin was still at the mausoleum, not in it.

When Hardin was discovered, his cousin denied Hardin's account of being tricked. Hardin was told by his aunt and uncle, according to their son, he brought on what had happened by his own hand. His cousin's version was he warned Hardin not to go in and that Hardin went in and closed the door to keep him out; somehow, the lock caught. It was believable that everyone knew Hardin had a reputation that preceded him when it came to not listening to advice and heeding warnings.

He spent his afternoon in the dark. In a place filled with cobwebs and spider webs that he felt but could not see. He was eventually bitten by a 'fiddle back,' a brown recluse spider that crawled up inside his pant leg. He didn't feel it until it bit him high on his left leg, right by his left testicle. It was a mentally and physically terrifying experience that never left him. The bite took the rest of the summer and part of the fall to heal. It left a significant divot on his leg that he was very self-conscious of, the primary reason why he became unhinged whenever he came across a web of any type.

*****

No one missed, and all fully understood, the part of his tirade and the edict he issued about how their time would be spent. Every painting in the room was to be taken down, their front and back washed. They were to be put back in the same order, taken down again, and washed, front and back, ten more times. Every mirror was also to be washed ten times over.

His instructions became known as 'Hardin's ten phases.' The staff was to work on nothing but the grand dining room, day, and night, until the phases were completed, or he returned to dismiss them, whichever came first. Many knew it would be a considerable amount of time if the rumor he was going on a business trip proved true.

*****

Jenny was in the fourth group. No one had a chance to say anything about her after Hardin's tirade. She stood perfectly still, wondering if she should fire on Sinclair with a profanity-filled broadside of her acid opinion of both after Hardin's departure—the incredible stupidity of the whole episode.

Just as she was about to pull the trigger, Sinclair jumped in and tried to remind Hardin of the condition the ballroom was in from the recent reception. The leftover food and spirits evolving into garbage presented a more immediate problem.

Sinclair suggests taking care of the ballroom before the dining room would be more prudent. Hardin completely ignored him and stormed off, muttering how he wouldn't want to be Sinclair or any of them when he returned and found he and the others weren't working on the grand dining hall. With this final threat made to all, he headed for the portico, got in his sleek buggy, and trotted toward downtown Cleveland.

Hardin left, unaware Enoch Mast was in his ballroom. After the smudge and cobweb, Sinclair was not about to bring Enoch Mast into view. He would take care of Enoch; in his way, and Hardin would never know. As he thought about it, Sinclair believed his way would be the best way to handle the situation.

*****

As Sinclair and Olivia watched Hardin pass through the main gate, Sinclair asked, "Any idea?" She answered, "He stopped telling, and I stopped asking long ago." They watched until he was out of view. The large wrought iron gate, with its enormous old English style "L" welded to its center, was closed behind Hardin, and he was gone. How long, no one knew.

They watched from Olivia's bedroom window. Sinclair headed there after instructing the staff to get started in the dining hall. He spent every morning in Hardin's wife's bedroom. This behavior began when Enoch started work in the ballroom. The two events began at the same time. They were coincidences and nothing more. It was just Sinclair and Olivia's way of measuring the amount of time that had passed since they became involved with one another and how the last six months passed in no time.

The ballroom was their starting point; they liked to compare the start of the ballroom to the beginning of their Garden of Eden. As they went along, knowing the story of Eden, they began to wonder not 'if' but 'when' they'd be expelled, how would it all end. To counteract the feeling, they both started to live in the moment, making no plans, and the future became like a foreign land with a language they didn't understand.

Olivia had become like a piece of fruit in the stage of being over-ripe, perhaps one or two days from beginning to rot on the vine. Only in her case, maybe one or two years. Her hair was still as long and thick as it had always been, but the luster and shine were beginning to fade. Hairline cracks about her eyes and the corners of her mouth were getting deeper. Wrinkles were starting to evolve on her forehead. All her features were in a state of change.

However, the changes were, for the time, moving at a slow pace, and she still had a firmness in all the places that caught her eye. If she watched what she ate. Each day this became more and more difficult. And she wished she could give in to what she desired. But her beauty had one more task to complete before she could live as she wanted.

Sinclair was way over his head with Olivia. Where she was rotting on the vine, he was like a stump of a once large tree that took advantage of every plant surrounding it, always trying to suck up all the nutrients and water away from them. The tree had to come down if they were to survive. It did, but the shoots that covered the stump showed the tree was down but not dead and made the surrounding plants paranoid.

Sinclair was gifted at making people feel nervous and uncomfortable, it was how he made his living, but he had no effect on Olivia, a disadvantage for him from the start. She controlled everything in the relationship; it wasn't that he let her; it was that he couldn't stop her.

All Sinclair could do was lust over her. He knew she was a former showgirl and a very worldly woman. Who was still very much in that realm but, at the same time, very concerned about the next dimension? She went all in for heaven but got off on the wrong foot. How she searched for her salvation made her fall prey to those who knew how to take advantage of the situation.

She fell victim to those who read, carried, and claimed to know all about the Bible, who was in it, and what they said. The ones that say salvation comes from seeds. They talk about planting seeds that grow one's faith and the seed money necessary to provide a good crop—the ones who preach - no seed money - no faith - no salvation. The ones who taught one proved their faith by giving the rent money to God, in reality, them, instead of the landlord.

To her, going to a church was unnecessary to find salvation. She was attracted to the evangelists who could draw huge crowds, built prominent temples, and had more contributors. She was attracted to them because they lived as she did, were well off, and lived the gospel of wealth as proof of their great faith. She understood the benefits of having the gift to take advantage of others by testing their faith. Her theory was one does not find salvation; one buys it like everything else one wants. Because of this, she developed some bizarre beliefs and practices.

There was no way to explain the attraction other than Olivia wanted Sinclair to commit a murder for her. In return, she was willing to satisfy or fulfill any sexual fantasy he had in payment for the risk she wanted him to take. The way she set Sinclair up left him holding all the risk. In the end, if her plans did not work out, her story would be he forced himself on her. Even if Sinclair knew what she was doing, he had no power to break her spell. He was her prisoner. Killing someone to keep what they had going was not a problem; he'd killed people before for much less. He didn't feel he was being used.

Without a doubt, it was an extraordinary situation. In 'over his head' was putting it mildly. He was attracted to her as one might be to a venomous snake, the fascination of its flickering tongue, color, and undulating body overshadowing any awareness of its bite. It was as if Olivia subconsciously tapped into Alden Sinclair's fascination and fear of these reptiles.

Like a poisonous snake, he always had a wide toxic streak of evil running through him. It was a streak that helped him overcome most fears, in that most people feared him, but when it came to Olivia, this streak wasn't quite wide enough to cover all his fears of her. As it turned out, what this evil streak ignored the most was any sane thought to avoid her altogether. Such a thought was provoking enough to change itself into an obsession he could not overcome. An addiction to be around Olivia continually, no matter how dangerous she was.

In a short time, it came to pass that the two were continually at the other's side. The household staff noticed but did not talk about it right away. Nevertheless, rumors were not far behind, they would start, and when they did, he knew they would surface at the most inopportune time. It wasn't what Sinclair expected.

He expected cooperation in his requests, which he got. Olivia satisfied every one of them with the letter. What he didn't expect was behind every episode he conjured up with her, there was an ever-increasing amount of insanity that went with it. Which in turn offset any satisfaction. The situation brought on by their obsession with each other is a perfect example of life's two biggest disappointments: getting what one wants, in this case, cooperation, and not getting what one wants, in this case, satisfaction.

A case in point concerning the surfacing insanity would be George Went Hensley. Sinclair had never heard of the man, but Olivia certainly had. She told Sinclair that she wanted him to come to her at the first opportunity, or she would go to him. Either way, they were to meet. She gave her reason in an evangelical account of what she was and what she wanted to become, and Hensley was the one who could guide her on this journey.

She believed in his work. A discussion about this man went on for a whole morning during the filling of a request. When it ended, Sinclair, of all that was said and done, was most taken by the amount of money she said she had given a disciple of Hensley's in hopes of arranging a meeting. It never took place, and she never saw the man again. What dawned on Sinclair, more than her favors, was the small fortune she'd given up for nothing; he was astounded by the amount.

After hearing about her first attempt at a meeting, Sinclair thought Olivia to be an incredibly stupid woman. Thoughts turned to ideas, and ideas to plans. The first plan was to charge Olivia twice the amount and guarantee a meeting. For the first time, there would be a change in payment; payment for such a meeting would be in cash instead of favors, perhaps a mixture of the two, but not all favors. The method was becoming a somewhat boring payment system; he was running out of fantasies.

He believed he could make one of the first two of these conditions stick. Sinclair felt capable and connected enough to track down one George Went Hensley to set up a meeting. It never crossed his mind to question whether such a disciple of Hensley's ever existed. Or that the story and the amount of money was made up. All Sinclair thought was where others had failed; he would succeed in getting a meeting between the two. Unaware George Hensley would change everything between Olivia and him.

*****

From the outset, Sinclair was always aware Olivia wanted him to murder someone. He never asked who, and, in the beginning, she never said. The situation was acceptable with Sinclair. He certainly wasn't in any hurry to commit one. He wanted to put this deed so far out in the future that it would never take place, and he wouldn't ever have to know who the victim would be. His concentration was on the money for the meeting, not murder.

He believed one way to accomplish Olivia staying off the topic of murder was to keep her thoughts occupied with the idea of meeting George Went Hensley. Such a meeting was a ticket to a very handsome payday, almost equal to the new ballroom's cost. His plan seemed to have promise; Olivia was always interested in what Sinclair had on Hensley.

In the beginning, his reports were made up, but Sinclair had every intention of tracking Hensley down. He always kept the emphasis on Hensley.

On his days off, he began to investigate Hensley. Olivia always mentioned he was an evangelical, but never what type, a tent-show gypsy, or an in-town shepherd with a flock. He began to ask acquaintances in the saloons and pool halls he frequented if there was any 'angle' to becoming an evangelical. He was surprised by who his associates could put him in contact with and what these contacts told him.

In true fashion, he found the very first thing the evangelical contacts asked for was money, and Sinclair was good at knowing who to pay and who not to pay. One, who he spent a fair amount on, told him about the 'seed' and how it worked. The 'seed' was good for street corners, tents, and temples, and it all revolved around the sower of the seed getting paid before anyone else and more than anyone else. He found out not anyone could pull off being a 'sower.' One had to be ruthless to do it well.

Essentially one tells the people how many times the word "seed" is mentioned in the Bible; it can be any significant number; if you are talking to the right group of people, no one will know, and no one will check. Next, you mention all the other words that mean 'seed', like 'kernel,' 'pits,' and so on, to construct metaphors about flourishing growth from the seed, kernel, or pit—followed by what kind of ground the seed falls on the rocky ground covered with choking weeds, good soil, and so on.

According to the evangelical sower, growth comes from the seed of faith, which one must continually water with cash. There will be times when the faith from the seed will be tested. It may come down to watering the seed of faith or paying the rent. Through the seed of faith, you have sown, God will tell you what to do and who to pay. Sinclair was told if one played the seed analogy right, God would tell the victim to pay the sower before the landlord. All his contacts told Sinclair it was a good racket, but not everyone could pull it off.

Those ruthless enough to instruct watering the faith at all costs and who are good at this will always be wealthy at the expense of others who cannot or are unwilling to figure out what is happening to them. Simply put, the ones who benefit the most are those who tell those who fail the most; they didn't have enough faith, were unable to water the seed of faith, didn't give enough, and needed to give more.

The more Sinclair listened, the more attracted he became to all the possibilities of becoming an evangelical for all the wrong reasons. He was a few steps behind Olivia in his fascination. She was far beyond Sinclair's captivation, as he soon found out.

Before Olivia became a showgirl, she worked at an early age for a snake oil salesman in western Pennsylvania, who she knew by one name and most knew by another.

Although she never consumed any of the oil, she did believe it would do all the salesman claimed. She never questioned any of it, which is perhaps why she was so accepting of some who seemed to be in a similar artificial line of work claiming to help people. She was taught a faith that replaced any desire to become educated or use the brain God gave her.

*****

Each drew on the other in unusual ways during their unexplainable relationship. The mansion had forty rooms and was large enough to hold plenty of intrigue. There was enough household staff to have more than one rumor of what was going on; there would be no shortage of gossip to confuse any issue. Hardin was not much of a factor; his relationship with Olivia was no different than a female acquaintance he encountered in any hallway where he was staying. Something that did not happen that often but was to be taken advantage of when it did occur.

Mostly, mornings were always available to Sinclair, as were most nights with minor risk. Hardin rarely caught Olivia in the hallway, maybe once every three months. After Sinclair developed some thoughts on the so-called evangelicals, coupled with Olivia's desire to support them rather than learn about them, he earnestly began to work towards finding George Went Hensley.

His persistence paid off, and by the end of the second month of his search, he was put in contact with one who knew all about the man. For a fraction of what he planned to charge Olivia for a meeting, Sinclair found his first reliable source concerning Hensley and took some time off to travel to Cincinnati to set up a deal.

When he arrived in Cincinnati, he discovered Hensley came from a large poor family. He was born in Tennessee in 1880. He was 34 and wandered the South. He'd been married more than once, had many kids, and had a drinking problem. From Cincinnati, he was led on horseback by a contact to the small farm of a sharecropper in Kentucky said to be one of George Went Hensley's brothers.

The contact left, no, abandoned, Sinclair at the farm, having no desire to spend any more time there than he had to. It aggravated Sinclair to where he accepted the fact, he should have never given the contact a partial payment upfront and that he should have known better.

The place was as desolate as it was isolated. Hensley's brother was imposing in size, had a minimal vocabulary, and an unpleasant attitude. The whole setup made Sinclair apprehensive and, in turn, volatile. As they began to walk, Sinclair briefly padded himself down as one does when looking for a pack of smokes and reassuring himself where his pistols and knives were. Every weapon he carried was neatly concealed under his fine coat, tailored with each in mind. The brass knuckles, which he always liked to take, were hidden in the coat's side pockets, within an arm's reach, and didn't require any other tailoring. He always had the knuckles at work and play; they went in his coat like a pocket watch every morning.

They walked to a small outbuilding one windstorm away from total collapse. Inside was a skinny unhealthy-looking man in tattered bib overalls and a dingy white shirt, pulling on a jug of shine, oblivious to their arrival and staring at a child-size coffin. Coming from the closed box, a very faint, almost inaudible sound of hissing and rattling could hardly be heard but not ignored. Sinclair was at a loss as to what it could be. But aware he had heard such sounds in the past. If he were to guess, he would have said the sounds were like a small child wrestling with their last breath.

He stood and joined Hensley in staring at the box, fully expecting a body to be inside. He prepared himself for the possibility. Thinking Hensley had a lot of children, and one was probably in the box. That was the closest situation Sinclair could come up with to explain Hensley's drinking and staring.

Eventually, George Went Hensley looked at the two, stood up, and walked to the coffin. It sat on two saw horses and was four to five feet from them. He turned, faced his brother and Sinclair, and shouted scripture at them, the seventeenth through the eighteenth verse of the sixteenth chapter of the gospel of Mark. "And those who believe shall use my authority to cast out demons, and they shall speak new languages. They will be able even to handle snakes with safety."

At that exact moment, he shoved the lid off the coffin, reached into it, and pulled out two handfuls of copperheads. He began to wave them in front of the two, tempting the snakes to bite and frightening his audience. He did this for a while, talking in tongues to the point of almost yelling while waving the venomous snakes around.

He walked towards the two, and they retreated to the outside of the building. He then stopped in the doorway, turned around, and put the snakes back in the coffin. Through all the commotion and agitation, not one snake bit him.

It was not at all what Sinclair expected. It took him totally by surprise. When Hensley walked toward him with the snakes, Sinclair went inside his coat and had his hand on a gun, trying to decide how to shoot Hensley so he wouldn't let go of the snakes when he hit the ground. They both retreated to the door. Once they were outside, Hensley stopped at the door. Sinclair brought his hand outside the coat empty-handed but kept it where it would take no time to return to the gun.

While Hensley's back was turned going to the coffin, his brother grabbed Sinclair's arm and spoke for one of the few times they had been together. Learned from experience, in a concerned and anxious voice, said, "He's been bit over a hundred times; he gets crazy around the snakes; we got to git!"

He continued to talk as he led Sinclair to his horse.

Only part of what he was saying came through. The part that did left Sinclair with a vision of George Went Hensley holding back a snake, provoking it, and letting it bite him repeatedly to build up his immunity to the venom. That was the trick.

He got on the horse and returned to Cincinnati and then Cleveland; he never saw George Went Hensley or his brother again. Not once did she ever mention the man was a snake handler—this upset Sinclair. During the search, Sinclair assumed George Went Hensley was a con man behind a pulpit, not a madman with poisonous snakes.

Olivia never lost interest in Hensley. Sinclair believed she wanted to know how the snake handler survived the venom. She believed him to be selling the tickets to immortality. She wanted to know how such a faith works and where one buys a ticket. But after a while, the lack of results in trying to set up a meeting put any talk of Hensley in the past tense.

With the change in direction, Olivia was no longer sidetracked by Sinclair and Hensley. She was able to return to the original deal, to have Sinclair carry out a murder, and she pursued it and made it a position she would not abandon again.

*****

With the return of the original deal, Sinclair found out the victim was to be Horace, Hardin's only son. From what Sinclair knew of their father-son relationship, the request was a surprise. He didn't expect Olivia to be a step ahead of Hardin. He thought for sure such a request would have come from Hardin. It caught him off guard.

He knew Olivia saw Horace as the murderer of her son, and Hardin saw him as a homosexual and a business liability; both always seemed to want Horace gone. Sinclair liked the situation; he had gained a new client for his services. He expected Hardin, but Olivia became first; Sinclair knew it was just a matter of time before Horace took his father to the point of no return and the same request would be made. He could get paid twice for one job if he played it right.

Olivia believed Horace killed Blanton and made it look like a suicide. He acted out of jealousy, in that Blanton was more accomplished than Horace in all that he did. Jealousy played into Blanton's death, but not how Olivia thought; it was romantic jealousy. Blanton had taken up another love. When Hardin found out about the two and how they were actually getting along as stepbrothers, he had Blanton killed. Sinclair knew this because he was the one who killed Blanton. He also was the one who killed Hardin's first two wives.

Ever since Gettysburg, when Sinclair learned about chloroform and morphine, then later on about ether, he made it a point always to have them on hand. They helped develop him into a gifted murderer. He was skilled in making murder look like natural or explainable death. He would take his victims to a state of unconsciousness where they could be placed as needed, die in bed of natural causes, or be thrown from a building to appear as suicide if one required a peaceful or violent death to explain what happened. At the time, no one could accurately detect their use; it was a sure thing and easy to use.

Horace wouldn't be hard to kill. Sinclair began to ask himself questions. Who would he get the most from, Olivia or Hardin? Hardin had more cash than Olivia, but Olivia had some money. She could also make the type of payments Hardin could never make. The amount of money he could get from Hardin and the favors and cash he could get from Olivia made him abandon an alternative plan that played in his mind. The alternative scheme was to blackmail Olivia and say he'd tell Hardin of her plans for Horace.

Such was the state of affairs in the Lasbrith household the morning Enoch Mast took over the ballroom. Unaware of all the intrigue, as he waited to get paid.

CHAPTER IV
THE BLOODHOUND LAW

Enoch awoke from an almost perfect nap. The dream Enoch had was vivid and hard to escape. He began to wander his ballroom as he tried to make sense of the dream and what it meant, but it was a puzzle with a few pieces missing. Yet he felt he was one or two recollections away from the clear resolution needed to bring the meaning of the dream into focus.

The crystal water tumbler was three-quarters full of *Old Forester*, and Enoch picked it up and during his journeys, downed it in no time. He consumed the equivalent of about five to six shots, and soon his efforts to recall his dream began to fade and were replaced by another thought.

He began to move from one location to another in search of the perfect site to meet a member or a representative of the Lasbrith family. A location suitable for their formal surrender in yielding him four thousand dollars to end his takeover. A place where he could accomplish what needed to be done to save face with his friends. A place to collect what was owed so it could be reported at the next monthly luncheon and the issue put to bed finally. He couldn't find it.

The whiskey took him to the point where he stared at his reflection in a distant mirror and wondered who the stranger was. He was at the point where it didn't take much to confuse him.

It wasn't the amount of whiskey he consumed, as much as it was the rate. The rate of consumption was rapid and way before noon. It was totally out of character for Enoch and most people in general. However, there were and are those who would consider the time of day, amount, and consumption rate normal.

It would not have been out of character for his father. His father could drink morning, noon, and night; time did not affect his drinking; what did have an effect was the amount. In his father's case it didn't take much to put him in an unconscious state. Uriah Mast had a very low tolerance to alcohol.

The realization brought on a slight twinge of guilt. Knowing the part, he and his brothers, Ezra and Enos, played in the development of his father's alcoholism. The effect the alcohol had on Enoch muddled his thoughts. He had to fight hard to let the notion he was not like his father come to the surface.

He eased up on the drinking and increased his eating to cope with all that ran through his mind. It was a lot for the time of day and something Enoch was not used to. He found a pear that had rolled away from a fruit bowl on a table he came upon and sat and ate it and gazed up at the chandeliers he had installed, trying but unable to recall how he did it.

He became a paradox; he became a body at rest while his mind became a body in motion. Moving from one thought to the next, like one in a gym shifts from one exercise to another. As he sat, random thoughts filled his head, and as they did, he pulled the matches from his pocket and lit a cigar as he got up to stretch his legs and continue his journey.

As he moved, Enoch thought life was made of two halves; the first half was being 'aware.' The other half was being 'oblivious.' The mixture of the two makes life interesting in a harsh way. One always pays more for what they don't know than for what they do. There are timing issues; there are times to be aware and oblivious. Catastrophe occurs when one gets these times mixed up.

Some, the rich, run out of time before money; most, the poor, run out of money before time. Some die with full stomachs, while most don't. Fortune and misfortune come from every direction on the compass.

Arbitrary thoughts like these began to swirl around in Enoch's brain and poured into his mind. He could no longer keep track of his thoughts any better than those who had come into and out of his life. He was wondering who was left and who was gone.

Thoughts rambled through his head until one ended all the others. Enoch was overcome by the realization that he had never seen one book the whole time he had worked inside the Lasbrith mansion.

Their shelves held priceless curios, museum-quality artifacts, and all the other embellishments of great wealth, believed by them to be worth more than the knowledge found in books. The whole time there, not once did he ever come across a tome; the fact amazed him.

*****

"Books and bottles," Enoch whispered to himself. He was thinking back on how one led to the other. How if one wanted to read books, one had to leave bottles. How his mother ensured he and his twin brothers, Ezra and Enos, and later, Brooks, could all read and write by age ten.

Although she never let it happen, Eve Mast knew her husband would feed his animals before his children, if it came to that, and at age ten, would put them on the wagons and work them like fully grown men. Literacy would be needed to deal with him. It would give them the edge over their father, who could neither read nor write. She taught them, then sent them to the different parish schools the churches provided, and always encouraged them.

Eve Mast's sons learned to read and write from the notes they left for her and one another. Most were about their father; some weren't; they were about events or observations. From the practice, over time, what developed in each was the ability to express themselves in the written word and, when read, to be understood by all.

Some things were dangerous to say aloud around Uriah. Reading and writing provided a way to say something without a sound. Eve Mast accomplished the goal she had set from the moment each arrived, and by the age of ten, all her sons were literate.

Uriah Mast was a teamster with some of Cleveland's heaviest wagons and animals. What he could move kept him in demand, but he worked hard, not smart.

His efforts only allowed him to repair and feed what he had; he could never add to it. When his sons went on the wagons, it only took three years to become aware of the mistakes they didn't want to repeat. His shortcomings surfaced early, and they were smart enough to exploit them.

It was always their literacy versus their father's ignorance. When Uriah had to ask for directions, he told those giving them to present what he wanted in terms of distance, in the number of blocks or miles, not in terms of locations defined by street names or signs. Enoch and his brothers read the signs to him when they got on board.

At times directions became roundabout when they wanted to rest. Or they'd talk about something they had read in a discarded newspaper or handbill about a circus coming to or in town. They would talk about what they read about the city, not what they heard on the streets, to annoy their father.

Their father, who never attempted to learn how to read or write, became predictable in his actions.

Anything he didn't understand, he destroyed. Whenever he found a book, paper, and pencils, he destroyed them on the spot in front of whoever was present. What stopped the practice was when he saw a bottle instead. Once he drank it, he either passed out or disappeared, and things became peaceful.

Enoch found a table with a pleasant view and a basket of dinner rolls. He began to tear a pumpernickel apart to eat. As he chewed, he thought of how his mother was never opposed to getting her husband out of the way at home and around their kids. She knew how he was and loved him anyway. She didn't care what method was used. Yet, at the same time, she never wished her husband any harm. There wasn't one time Enoch could recall that she didn't lovingly tend to Uriah's injuries or illness.

By the age of thirteen, Enoch, Ezra, and Enos were pretty much in control of the Mast and Sons Company. In that year, 1852, Brooks Mast showed up, and the operation Uriah Mast had as the town's teamster changed dramatically.

At home and work, the atmosphere was always better when Uriah was out of the picture and at the bottom of a bottle of whiskey. His sons adopted the practice where they would pay in advance and drop him off at a tavern during the day. They gave him a bottle of rye at night if he made it back home. What made this an economic practice was Uriah's low tolerance for alcohol; it didn't take much or cost much to get him out of the way. They felt the alcohol they bought and the bail paid at times to get him out of jail after a few days and nights was money well spent for the tranquility it provided.

They kept up with the old accounts, which led to new accounts. Brooks Mast replaced Uriah Mast in the family business and by the end of 1853 'Mast and Sons became 'Mast Brothers' and the family began to flourish.

*****

Enoch worked his way back to the northwest corner of the ballroom, where the northern window had the view of Lake Erie and the western view of the skyline of Cleveland. No matter how often he got up for this or that or to inspect something, he always returned to what he had set up in the northwest corner.

Enoch subconsciously began to settle in for a protracted occupation as the day approached mid-morning. He began to view his ballroom more tactically as captured territory. As a territory that provided good rations, comfortable quarters, a good view of the terrain, and indoor plumbing. A terrain he could hold on to for a long time.

Since there were no books to be had, Enoch was left recalling the ones he had read. With his dream still in mind, his thoughts began, "I was thirteen, and Brooks was eight." The book that came to mind was *Uncle Tom's Cabin*, and outside of the Bible, it was the most popular book in America, not to mention England, for quite some time. It was translated into many languages and is known on all continents.

Conversations about it being written by a woman, Harriet Beecher Stowe, and the book's plot were never-ending public discourse from the first day it went on sale. The first five years of the characters in Brook's life mirrored some of the characters in *Uncle Tom's Cabin.*

The book and Brook's family experiences introduced Enoch to a world that for the next eleven years of his life would be filled with the issues of abolitionists, underground railroads, fugitive slave laws, state's rights issues, compromises, and conflicts of new territories coming into the Union as a free or slave state. Issues that would not go away no matter how hard Enoch tried to ignore them.

Brooks Mast, at one time, was Brooks Turner. His mother, Evelyn, and father, Momford Turner, brought him with them when they came up from Louisiana on the underground railroad. Brooks was conceived in jail five years earlier when Evelyn's owner and a jailer got together and allowed her to be thrown into the cell of a returned runaway slave in a pseudo-breeding experiment. Evelyn's owner at the time had no way to feed or a place to keep her. The plan was to get her pregnant, sell the baby, and split the money.

Momford Turner was the property of Silas Turner, owner of a sizeable two-hundred slave plantation. Who came for Momford way sooner than expected? When he saw Evelyn, who had been won in a card game, he gave the jailer what he thought she was worth and took her. No different than a large fish swallowing a small fish, leaving the jailer in the awkward position of telling Evelyn's owner they made less than expected on their experiment.

Even more fortunate than going to the same place for Momford and Evelyn was the small amount of time they were given alone to know each other—a time filled with sadness, compassion, and hope. With the misery of being a slave, one would think Mumford wouldn't share his cornbread and molasses with Evelyn. That wasn't the case; he gave all of it to her. As hungry as she was, she left some for him. Most naturally, they shared what they had. They talked about their dreams and who they wanted in them and innately came together.

Against the odds, the Turner family made a break for it when Brooks turned five. He was at an age where he could be sold. Their escape was so harsh, all they could recall was how they crossed the Ohio River into a free state and worked their way to Cleveland. They aimed for Ontario, Canada, but had to stop and find work to move on. Canada offered true freedom; they had no fugitive slave law or Paddy Rollers. There one didn't have to sleep with one eye open.

Momford found work as a ditch digger for the sewers in Cleveland and the Erie Canal, heading towards Canal Fulton and Akron. Evelyn became a dishwasher at a large tavern with a five-year-old holding onto her apron. They mostly ate the scraps from the plates they washed. When they could, they brought some home to Momford when he was in town.

Momford mostly ate any fruit and corn he could find growing along the road walking to work. The only item he bought was bread; the only liquid he drank was water. Once in a while, he would steal a chicken or kill a rabbit; he'd eat the meat and make soup from the bones. When he could, he brought what he stole or killed home.

It was a next-to-nothing existence; money and food were scarce, yet it was enough to keep their hopes of Ontario alive. When they had what it would take to move on at the end of what they thought would be their last day in Cleveland, a race riot at work broke out on the canal. At the end of that day, four Irish and four African ditch diggers were side by side dead. Off the road, waiting to be buried there and then. None of their families were notified; Momford was one of them.

Nothing was accomplished from the riot. Along with the dead, many were crippled by the fighting and could not work again. The riot seemed to be one of many that would occur for no good reason during Momford, Evelyn, and Brooks's early days in Cleveland.

*****

Mast passed Evelyn and Brooks wandering the streets of Cleveland on her way to buy millinery supplies. Eve slowed down when she saw their condition, the compassion in her eyes gave her away, and although she slowed down, she didn't stop. At that point Evelyn went with her instincts and began to follow Eve. As Evelyn walked, a Bible verse she had once heard repeatedly played in her mind: Mark 5:28, "If I just touch His garments, I will get well." A voice tells her to touch Eve's sleeve gently and everything will change. She did, and Eve stopped, and from that moment on, everything changed.

Evelyn told her it had been over a month since she saw her husband. Eve took them home. She told Uriah the two were from her sister in South Carolina, who had freed them. It was news to Uriah and the first he'd heard of such a sister. It made him ask if she had any more sisters or brothers he did not know about. She was an orphan, which in her eyes made everyone like her a brother or sister. Eve answered with a smile as if his question was ridiculous.

She then went on to refresh his memory about her made-up sister. She knew exactly how to deal with Uriah. At first, Uriah objected, but as time passed, he liked the idea of 'negroes' living in his barn after Eve told the neighbors Uriah had hired them to help her.

Evelyn and Brooks made Uriah look important; although he wasn't a slave master, he was a close relative. All he did was try to take advantage of the two every chance he got. However, Evelyn and Brooks could always stay one or two steps ahead of him at every attempt. Both were there when the family business management eventually transitioned from father to son, and Uriah was pushed further into the background. He went from a teamster to a drunk with the help and encouragement of his sons.

The barn was a vast improvement for the two. It took Eve no time to find out Evelyn was also a seamstress. The two worked together to produce dresses and aprons with deep pockets that could be buttoned closed and other features. Features those neighboring women and their friends liked. It seemed out of nowhere; the two created a small but constant market. They could produce one a week and sell it within the next week. They worked at night by the fireplace, when it was cold and, when it was warm, outside by the glow of lanterns. It was pleasant work; each enjoyed the company of the other.

They made enough to make the barn very comfortable and to put a few extra items in the house and on the table. Like Eve's sister in South Carolina, Uriah had no idea they had a partnership. What puzzled him was how he could always be drunk and provide so much. He took credit for any improvement, even if he couldn't explain how the progress came to be.

It went on like this for the next five years, and when Brooks was ten, he joined the Mast brothers on the wagons. He became their real 'little' brother. The fact that he was ten but had a twelve-year-old's body helped but wasn't enough. Brooks would compete with all three of them physically and mentally even though he was pretty sure the outcome wouldn't favor him. The Mast brothers loved this the most about Brooks. They also knew the tables would turn one day, but that day would not be anytime soon. No one teased and protected Brooks like the Mast brothers.

The stars Brooks Mast was born under gifted him with a great aim to hit any target in front of him, endurance, quick hands, and a gifted mind that could pour out a heavy dose of humor. He was not a handsome man. He was a likable person. As time passed, he took on the 'Mast' name, introducing himself as a 'Mast', and no one questioned it, opposed it, or said much about it.

*****

The sunlight streamed through the windows. The way Enoch was positioned in the wing-back chair, he was able to enjoy all of its advantages. As the effect of the *Old Forester* subsided, he felt good enough to pour himself some Riesling wine. He played with the goblet stem, picked it up, and took a long sip. He held the goblet up to the sun, let the light shine through the wine for a few moments, and eventually put the goblet back on the table.

He chose to look out the window that showed the entrance of the Lasbrith estate. With the skyline of Cleveland behind it to continue his version of *Uncle Tom's Cabin*. Only in Enoch's version, the story runs in reverse. In his version, one day, Brooks and his mother, Evelyn, go from being free back to being slaves.

In deep retrospection, Enoch thought about the days Brooks became part of the family as he lit a cigar and stared at the skyline of the city. Those who knew the Masts and those, for the most part, who didn't, looked at Brooks's relationship with the family as being on the same level as a family pet, not as a family member.

The irony in this was Brooks didn't mind what others thought, but the Mast brothers did. Some said the Mast brothers took Brooks along to cause fights because they all liked to fight. Nothing could get one started faster than a "negro" being in what some would say was the wrong place at the wrong time, a place they were not allowed, which some would try to make everywhere and at all times.

At fourteen and fifteen, those older than the Mast brothers found them to be a handful. They figured out that as they got older, it wouldn't be good to have the Mast brothers looking for them down the road. It was better to get along than to take them on.

Most, however, found the Masts to be amiable enough. As a result, after a while, the Mast brothers' friends became Brooks's friends, and he got to go everywhere they went. At an early age,

Brooks could navigate Cleveland on a high level, including all the back streets and alleys in the docks, warehouses, and residences.

At the time, some would argue those free in the North found their circumstance almost the same as being a slave in the South. If it was a better situation, it was only by the smallest of margins. There was hardly any legal protection; often, the authorities were more inclined to turn a runaway slave over to slave catchers or try to collect a thousand-dollar fine from those harboring them and were in violation of the Fugitive Slave Law of 1850. The only absolute freedom at the time was the freedom to keep looking over one's shoulder to see who was coming after them.

Those who made it to the North weren't 'free' slaves. They were 'escaped' slaves. There was a big difference between the two. To be 'free,' one had to make it to Canada, Ontario, and Windsor. Slavery in these parts was abolished in 1833. In 1850 in the U. S. the law sided with the South's position that there were no 'free' slaves in the North, only 'escaped' slaves. Which in turn meant they were property, not people. Property, slave owners wanted back and the reason behind Canada always their destination. The states they passed through were just routes to get there that many escaped slaves got stuck on or adjusted to.

Enoch closed his eyes briefly, not to find sleep but to rest them. He had gotten to the point where he was no longer looking at the skyline but into the city's heart. Not remembering but reliving the time Brooks came on the wagons with them. He relit his cigar and took a sip of wine before exhaling, smiling, and shaking his head side to side, almost in disbelief at how long ago it all took place as he exhaled a cloud of smoke—returning to every nook and cranny of the time.

As Enoch recalled, the slave law was well respected and followed in the South by slavery sympathizers. Mostly, the law was disrespected and hardly followed in the North and rejected by abolitionists. In the North, many counties, cities, townships, and villages wrote their laws to take the teeth out of the Fugitive Slave Law of 1850, which helped the resentment to fester and grow on both sides of the issue.

He chuckled to himself, remembering how they would read the type of company they were in. They could gauge this by the way; whoever they were talking to would refer to the law when looking at Brooks and asking questions about him. Most in the North referred to the Fugitive Slave Law as the 'Bloodhound Law." Those who referred to It by its actual name became the ones to keep an eye on. The chance they were in with the slave catchers became a good bet. They liked to kidnap the victim, take them to a sympathizing county, and judge where they could make good money off of the victim and possibly those who harbored them. The question of "Are they property?" or "Are they people?" escalated from a discussion to a full-blown argument every time the issue came up, and over time, it came up a lot.

*****

Brooks Mast showed up on the wagons at the most critical time in the history of the Mast family business. It was the time Enoch, and his brothers began moving their father to the background of the business through the development of his alcoholism. It was the time when the Mast brothers began to make business decisions. How things began to move after the change, Brooks Mast became the perfect replacement for Uriah Mast. At ten, he had a clearer mind and more strength, plus he was a fast learner. If he had any drawback, he ate as much and sometimes more than Enoch and his brothers.

Regarding specific jobs, Brooks was good at hitching and unhitching the animals, greasing the wagon wheels, holding doors open, putting down and picking up small ramps when they had to use them, or setting up levers and fulcrums. Brooks was familiar with all the block and tackle on the wagons. He could tie ten types of knots, slip knots, and stationery to secure loads. For the Mast Brothers, Brooks was like an extra set of hands and, on occasion, an extra brain. But he became the best at understanding and advancing the technology and use of booms and pulleys that Enoch introduced to the business as Uriah was out of the picture. Brooks was mystified by the principals involved in how something so light could lift something so heavy. Their use of this technology increased their business two-fold.

Enoch stretched his body out and changed his position in the overstuffed chair. Recalling the little over a year Brooks was with them—the time when he was turning sixteen and Ezra and Eli were fifteen. How and when the influence of their father was reduced, and a new and better age fell upon the family. That was sixty years ago, Enoch thought and then chuckled. Like any seventy-five-year-old, he felt he and his brothers grew up much faster than the kids fifteen and fourteen outside the window as he gazed at Cleveland. In a way, he was right. The seven years that followed when he was fifteen called on those his age to do a lot to hold the country together.

During that brief time, all four seemed to work their mind as hard as their body. New customers came by word of mouth from old customers. Every job began by telling the customer their father would be along shortly, then going to work and working smart enough to where the customer eventually forgot about the need for their father to be there.

During the time and their age, the Mast Brothers became very fluid in what they did. They moved two types of freight, industrial and household. Most of the industrial was moving barrels filled with everything from beer to nails to and from manufacturers to warehouses. The household was by floor by item of tables and chairs, cupboards, beds, chests, mirrors, and pianos. Their best effort during the time was winching a stand-up piano into a room on the fourth floor of an apartment building before noon. They began to eat well and dress better. They expanded the business to include land clearing and stump removal. The days at that time had an unstoppable rhythm of working, eating, and sleeping that was in perfect balance, except for Sunday, a day of reading, napping, and eating. Their bodies, minds, and income became stronger. But it all changed within the blink of an eye, and life became different.

*****

It happened downtown, and it happened fast. After it happened, there were several theories about who or what was behind it. There was always a debate about whether it was a setup or an opportunity that popped up begging to be exploited. One early summer evening, Eve, Evelyn, and Brooks went downtown. Eve and Evelyn went for fabric and Brooks for the candy he planned to get them to buy. The three entered Willoughby Dry Goods and soon separated while looking at fabric. Eve looked at the more subdued patterns while Evelyn looked at the brighter ones.

Eve made their enterprise successful by making the dresses' bodies, and Evelyn trimmed them out. Eve used her fabric and Evelyn hers; they never questioned the other's taste; unaware they had found the balance between unsubdued and subdued and created a sought-after fashionable work dress.

Brooks wandered to the cracker barrel and candy counter. It must have happened when Brooks and his mother were the closest to each other and Eve was the farthest from them. Whoever gathered up Brooks and his mother must have told them something to the effect that they would kill Eve, then pointing out the person who would do it and then, if they did not get their complete cooperation. Whatever was said or done made the two vanish quickly.

At first, Eve thought nothing of it when she gave a glance but could not locate Evelynn and Brooks. She thought they would eventually show up, but when that did not happen, she searched the isles and then the street. Within a half hour of entering the store with three, she realized she would be leaving the store alone as one. The realization paralyzed her and left her crippled with sadness for the rest of her life. As much as she resisted the thought, it became clear someone had taken back their property.

She also knew it wasn't a thought but a fact. The only way to explain their disappearance was "slavers" (those from the North and South who hunted down escaped slaves for profit). From that day on, till she died, a day didn't go by where she didn't mention Evelyn and Brooks to whoever was around or to herself. When they found out, Enoch, Ezra, and Eli treated it as a death in the family. A week at work didn't go by where they didn't see or hear something that would bring Brooks back for a few moments.

Some said Uriah got to drinking with some slavers, they worked a deal, and they started to watch the Mast place to pick up Brooks and Evelyn's comings and goings. Others said the slavers were like sharks, and some parts of town were infested with them. The three happened to be in one of the infested areas, and the sharks took advantage of the situation. Some thought there was no point in knowing how it happened; knowing one way or another did not change the outcome.

The Mast Brothers received some insight on the disappearance at the port of Cleveland, hauling barrels of flour off-loaded from ships to the warehouses of some wholesale food companies in town. It was an inquiry by a "leg breaker" who went by 'Scot's Blade Billy.' A Scottish immigrant who didn't give up the kilt, who had a violent nature and little or no conscience, who preferred blade weapons to enforce what he wanted. He was owned by the confederation of the many small wooden offices found on the docks to put down any talk about dock laborers organizing and protecting the bookkeepers in the offices.

Scot's Blade Billy asked, "What ever happened to the black ape that yee let run free all over yee wagons? Yee knows - the nigger?" He asked in a way that would make one think he already knew the answer. The way and the time he chose to ask caught Enoch and his brothers off guard, Scot's Blade Billie decided to start after them at noon when they'd all been in each other's sight all morning. He began to draw a small crowd. He certainly had the full attention of the Mast Brothers, leaving them speechless for a while. It gave him an excellent opportunity to continue making fun of both Brooks and them. His carrying on about Brooks and them caused the crowd to grow and laugh at the Mast Brother's expense.

When Scot's Blade Billy finally ran out of steam, Enoch spoke, "You're a pretty funny man – but then looks aren't everything." It was all he could come up with. Enoch's reply caused a sudden hush in amazement, followed by an outbreak of laughter that drew the bookkeepers out of their offices and onto the street. Two in particular who watched the events unfold never forgot it.

The remark and reaction to it infuriated Billy, and he quickly reached in the purse, hanging from his waist, centered over the kilt, and produced what everyone thought was a bone. He held it up as if he were a wizard, then pressed a button, and a six-inch dagger ground blade suddenly snapped out of the bone. It was a switchblade made in Sheffield, England, around 1850. It was startling new magic to everyone on the dock. He walked calmly over to Enoch and stabbed him in the meaty outside of his right shoulder. The knife went in a half inch with Scot's Blade Billy barking orders to Enoch to get off his dock and never return.

Enoch turned his back on Scot's Blade Billy and walked no more than five paces. He appeared to do as told. He did not grab his shoulder. Instead, he removed his jacket, ripped his belt from his waist, and twirled it several times around his right hand as quickly as he could. He made a fist with about a foot of the buckle end exposed.

He then turned around and ran towards Scot's Blade Billy and, with his left hand, threw his jacket up in the air, and instinctively, Billy went for the jacket, which covered the knife. Next, he began to hit Billy savagely in the face and all over his head with the buckle of his belt. After his opponent folded, Enoch kneed him in the face. When he fell to the ground, a savage kick to both sides of the rib cage ended any ability to resist. The beating left the leg breaker unconscious, permanently blind in one eye and partially blind in the other.

In the end, Enoch took the knife and put it in his pocket. He then positioned the unconscious Scot's Blade Billy's ass up in the air and symbolically kicked it for everyone to see.

Later it was found Scot's Blade Billy didn't know anything about the disappearance, other than he noticed Brooks wasn't on the wagon that day and nothing more. By doing so, he decided to bring it up and became a victim of his own prejudice. He just wanted to get something going, to shake things up, nothing more. It turned out that day Scot's Blade Billy's reputation on the docks died, and Enoch Mast's was born.

Just as Alden Sinclair woke up every morning and put his brass knuckles in his coat pockets like a pocket watch, Enoch Mast never left home without the switchblade in his pants pocket. The knife became a tribute to Brooks Mast, who Enoch, at the time, believed he would never see again.

Enoch relit his cigar, stood up, and leaned against the wall. He no longer looked at the skyline of Cleveland but instead at the Lasbrith Gardens. He gazed in the direction of his home and momentarily wondered if Brooks and Mary Irene were back from the lake. Unaware of what he was doing, Enoch wrapped his hand in his right pants pocket around the knife. When he realized what he was doing, he muttered, "The knife came first and then the accident." The 'accident' was another story. Unable to stop recalling his past, the past of others, and the order of all the significant events of his life, he sat back down and let the day unfold.

*****

Once he was settled into his corner, three strange events occurred. Two he saw, and one he felt. The first was when he reached into his vest pocket and pulled out his watch to see the time. The watch read seven-forty-five; it had stopped when he entered the kitchen. Enoch tried to remember the last time his watch had stopped. It was strange because he couldn't remember. He always wound his watch; it was a nervous habit of his. He went to set it, but it was locked up. He shook the watch hard several times to see if he could get the sweep hand to start up again. Nothing moved; he shook his head and put the watch back in his pocket, still wondering why it stopped.

The second event involved his observations of Sir Carl, and the third was the severe twitch he felt when Brooks and Mary Irene crossed his mind when he gazed out the window at Lake Erie. The three events were independent of each other, and each profoundly affected the future.

He saw Sir Carl come through a doorway on the right side of the far-off stage. The bitch went up the stairs onto the stage and began to perform against the background of the uncleared linen-covered tables. She would appear and disappear among them. The way she moved reminded Enoch of a moving picture he'd once seen at a penny arcade—a movie of a polar bear navigating its way between the icebergs hunting seals.

When Sir Carl was out of sight, the tables would shake violently, tablecloths were ripped from them, and in some cases, chairs were knocked over. In one case, a leg from a chair was torn off. The dog became an imaginary menacing polar bear in Enoch's eyes, a very agitated one that snarled at everything. One to keep an eye on. From Sir Carl's actions, Enoch was glad he was the farthest distance from the stage in the ballroom and that Sir Carl didn't see him.

The whole event was loud, violent and took place in a short period of time. Sir Carl exited the ballroom when she came upon the doorway on the other side of the stage. The door was open, and Sir Carl's behavior dramatically changed as she calmly went through it and wandered slowly through the mansion as always.

No one knew Sir Carl had been in a fight with a rabid raccoon approximately ten days earlier. She killed the raccoon but was bitten several times. The fur on and around her belly had various shades of red bordering on dark brown. It was the dried blood of some poor animal Sir Carl ripped apart. Or so Enoch thought. It never entered his mind that some of the blood was hers. Enoch was surprised he could see it, considering the distance, which told him Whatever took place was brutal in nature.

Enoch believed the dog acted the way she did because she was injured. Rabies never crossed his mind. It didn't matter if the one-act play put on by the dog was real or imagined; all he knew was the impact of what he saw, real or imagined. If it was an illusion, he didn't have to worry about Sir Carl; if it wasn't, he would have plenty to worry about. The thought took up residence in the back of his mind and would come and go the remaining time he spent in the Lasbrith mansion.

*****

Enoch got up from his chair and stood as he gazed out the window at Lake Erie and the northern horizon. He felt a jolt rip through his body for at most a second, like it lasted an eternity. Its intensity brought on an unbelievable pain whereby any duration longer than a second would be a death sentence. The event took a few moments to get over.

The twitch came at the exact moment, across town, Brooks Mast was hitching Emmet the gelding up to a stately split hickory-covered buggy, per the instructions given in the note Enoch left for him. The weather was perfect, and he was to take Mary Irene up by the lake. They would have the beach to themselves during the morning church services. If Enoch could, he'd try to catch up with them later.

Once Brooks completed this, he got Mary Irene, and they headed towards the lake. It was a beautiful morning, and Mary Irene grabbed a doll, smiling and laughing as Brooks took her hand and helped her into the buggy.

Enoch did not attach any importance to the twitch other than it had been a long time since he had had such an episode. For a moment, the last time came to him and was too painful to recall. He backed away from it as soon as it came to him. He went in the direction of more comforting thoughts. To move on and forget what the sensation told him the last time.

This is what he did; for the most part, it worked but did not stop the haunting effect the second twitch had on him.

Enoch reached for a cigar and held it before lighting it. He fell into a period of deep procrastination, lost in his thoughts. Another feeling came over him, one of being in a campaign; he was no stranger to the sensation, he'd been in one before.

*****

Meanwhile, as Enoch stood looking out the window, Brooks Mast and Mary Irene made their way to the shores of Lake Erie. They were enjoying the weather and each other's company. They were very close, and as unfortunate as Mary Irene's situation was, she was blessed with having two fathers who watched over her. Each was equal in their love, which was abundant.

To Brooks, Mary Irene was the only person who told his side of the story about the many things that had happened to him. If one summed up his accounts, there were more positive than negative in his stories. If one ever wanted to know the true confessions of Brooks Mast, Mary Irene would be the one who had heard them all, the only one. They would have to go to her. Everyone close to Brooks knew this. There was more than one who would have loved to have heard these confessions, but to listen to them from Mary Irene would be pointless.

To Mary Irene, Brooks Mast was like having a pet bear that was big and friendly, with a soft and patient voice. One who brought her what she asked for and could pick her up and put her down wherever she wished. One who always ate breakfast and dinner with her and Enoch. One who had always been there. He was one-half of all the love she received. The importance of Brooks and Enoch being in her life she fully grasped.

They crossed a break in the wood line onto the lake's sandy shore. The mid-morning sun glimmered off the water as if the two had come upon the world's largest blue-white diamond. The whole time, Brooks tells Mary Irene something silly about how they owned the entire beach and how the people in the church were missing out on what the two of them had. Right then and there, they were in the heaven the people inside the church were talking about. Mary Irene would nod, smile, and sometimes laugh, not knowing what he was talking about.

When he turned the buggy to go further down the shore, in the distance, he saw a large dark lump that looked out of place. As he moved toward it, he could see it was a body. He put his hand and one finger to his lips to give Mary Irene the sign to be quiet. Then he softly whispered to her, "They're sleeping." He gently pressed down on her right forearm to let her know without having to say a word to stay in the buggy.

He got down to investigate, and before he could react, seven young men were upon them, close to twenty yards from him and Mary Irene. Commanding him, "Don't move, boy!" Best he could tell they came from the wood line. Looking at what was behind them, he could see faint smoke from two small campfires that told him they had spent the night there, that they probably weren't from around town, and this was not a good situation. In fact, at his age, it was the worst of situations. Everything was moving way too fast for his seventy-year-old mind and body.

Brooks Mast's thoughts moved a million miles per second. He'd lived long enough to size up situations fast to know how to react. He had the person on the beach figured out, but the squad coming out of the wood line surprised him.

He thought the dead person on the beach was probably one of them, and they probably killed him over food or money. It was all against one. They ganged up on him; it was an in-house decimation. They probably didn't notice or didn't care that he crawled towards the water for relief after the terrible beating he had taken at their hands. His face was a mess. Brook's last observation told him the victim came close but never swallowed or felt a drop of water, and his companions could not have cared less.

The thought that played over and over in his mind was where he and Mary Irene were about to be robbed, raped, and killed. He first, then Mary Irene, after all of them have had their way with her. It was fast becoming a hopeless situation. It would come to pass that Brooks was right in what he was thinking.

As they got closer, he saw the years of poverty in their malnourished faces. They traveled in a pack because, individually, they were weak, but in a band, they were ruthless. They were a mixed group of every race that had stepped into the country and the half-breeds each race could produce. They were mongrels. Whose looks, along with their torn and filthy clothes, put them on the bottom rungs of society. They acted like they looked undesirable.

They were poor, uneducated, and hungry. They had gotten to the point when they had money; they chose to feed their hunger with alcohol instead of food. They had lived in poverty for a long time and under all the perfect conditions to make them violent people capable of anything. Brooks knew all about them; he was once like them. At an early age, he knew what it was like to hardly have enough to eat to be thrown food scraps from the plates of others.

Under his breath Brooks muttered, "Enoch," as if he was asking what he should do—then nodded without saying another word as if he got an answer. The answer was if it came to robbery and murder, Brooks was the one to be doing it. He raised his hand to Mary Irene to help her off the buggy. The two stood watching themselves become encircled by men who were drunk and carrying clubs, broken bottles, and knives. He then robbed them of what they wanted.

Brooks showed no emotion as he put his hand inside his vest and produced a forty-one caliber two-shot 1866 Mostar Colt Derringer and, in one fluid motion, shot Mary Irene and then himself in the right temple. Both shots produced an immediate clean kill. The two left this dimension in less than a minute and entered another.

They fell to the ground on their left side, and the sand soaked up the blood from the bullet that passed through their heads. Each looked as if they were napping. The band of thugs were shocked, but only for a moment. When the moment ended, they went through pockets and purses, stripped Brooks down to his underwear, and stripped Mary Irene completely, beginning to laugh and joke about what they were doing.

They shoved the victim of their decimation into the lake, and the lake took the body. It drifted towards Toledo, where it came ashore a week later. The group thought it was a good idea to get rid of the person they did kill.

They left Brooks and Mary Irene in the sand. Feeling they didn't need to worry because they didn't kill them. They got about nine dollars, some clothes, and most importantly, Brooks Mast's derringer for their efforts. They had all waited for the day they could get a gun and make real money robbing groups of people instead of individuals.

They looked over the two one last time to see if they had overlooked any valuables and then quickly left the scene. They thought about taking the horse and the buggy but decided against it. They knew they didn't have the appearance not to be asked where they got it. The horse and buggy would do nothing but draw people's attention to them. They slapped the horse, and the rig headed down the beach.

They were in town spending the money when Brooks and Mary Irene's bodies were found. From the time Brooks saw the dark lump on the beach to when he and Mary Irene joined the victim in the hereafter took about twenty minutes.

The derringer proved the robbers undoing. Later that day, they were caught red-handed robbing a small group of people in a cigar store. The Cleveland Police confiscated Brooks Mast's deringer.

At first, the police viewed the crime scene of a nude white woman found with a black man in his underwear as an almost justifiable homicide. Theorizing a citizen came upon them, didn't like what they saw, and took matters into their own hands. They had the bodies taken to the morgue, where later on in the day, they were sold to their anatomy contacts at Western Reserve medical school.

Within a week all the robbers were charged with the murders they didn't commit when the caliber of the gun matched the wounds of the victims. All pleaded not guilty and told the police they didn't do the crime; they witnessed it. They were all found guilty, and all were hanged before the first anniversary of Brooks and Mary Irene's death.

*****

Enoch finally lit his cigar. The first cloud of smoke he produced was delightful; he could feel what he took in and let out to the bottom of his lungs. He loved tobacco. Enoch did not smoke fine cigars as one should; he inhaled any tobacco product he smoked. The second cloud and all the following clouds felt as good as the first. Enoch let his imagination drift with the curling smoke and their upwards movement, with no two patterns of the white turning yellow smoke ever the same.

The smoke took him to the dream he just had. With its twisting and turning, the smoke appeared as stage curtains. They were opening to reveal what had escaped him when he first awoke. When they were pulled back, in front of him was a movie screen.

On it, he saw and heard, in color and sound, Brooks and Mary Irene sitting on a beach below a crystal blue sky by Emmet, the horse, and the stately split hickory buggy. Only Mary Irene is doing all the talking, and it's about a book she has just read. Brooks Mast is the one listening, smiling, and nodding his head. There they were, sitting, talking like ordinary people, both waiting for him on a beautiful beach. It was so vivid and clear.

CHAPTER V
THE OSSTILL MANSION

The dream was too intoxicating to dwell on. Enoch was not oblivious to the mental hangover he would get if he did. All he ever wanted for his daughter was the mind the fever robbed her of, and he began to search for another thought to take its place. He sat, stood, walked, and then randomly repeated the cycle in search of what it might be.

His restlessness ended when he looked outside and saw the red 1912 Ford Model T Runabout. The glimpse turned into a stare as he stood at the window and contemplated what he and Brooks could do with four thousand dollars to that horseless buckboard parked by the kitchen. There were no two ways about it: he needed to get paid!

When he got paid, they would build a pick-up truck the world has never seen. What a garage they would have, stocked with every tool and manual they would ever need. They would take Jessie O'Dell's red truck and make it the father of all pick-up trucks to come. He chuckled at the notion. They would have to start the moment he got paid. He was more than aware time was not on their side.

The realization prompted Enoch to recognize the fact he was old. More than that, it took him back to his mother. He could envision her as she said, "Each year, you get another candle on the cake. The more candles, the bigger the cake, the bigger the cake, the greater the light, the greater the light, the more you see all that surrounds you." That was what she would tell him and his brothers every time they had a birthday. Each year, you get more light to see things clearer and as they are.

Enoch had enough years to say she was right, for the most part. But of all Enoch's birthday cakes, the light from the one that held sixteen candles was the cake he remembered the most. From that point on, the size of the cake and the light from the ones that followed never matched the glow from that one cake, and no birthday since come close to all that happened to Enoch in his sixteenth year. A flash flood of memories overran their banks and flooded his mind to where he put down the knife, leaned back in his chair, and reminisced.

*****

It began at the Osstill mansion. The mansion was gone but would always exist in Enoch's mind. It was the summer he was hired to clear twenty-two stumps from several mature trees. Then, he met Irene Kathleen O'Flynn there, who was in service to the Osstills and a year younger than him.

The stumps were at the back of the residence, perhaps thirty yards from the kitchen door. The Osstill Mansion was one of the first mansions to take root on Euclid Avenue. It was a sprawling three-story stone edifice on five acres with the most prominent doors and windows of any mansion in the area at the time. Its outside appearance gave the impression it protected a lavish inside.

Titus Osstill owned several breweries across the state. In the mansion's foyer was an impressive three-tiered beer fountain, one tier for a lager, one for ale, and another for stout, all choice beers from Osstill's Select Breweries.

It was the day after his sixteenth birthday, July 9, 1855. People talked about the news, which was all about 'Bleeding Kansas' and Border Ruffians and Abolitionists fighting each other. What one didn't hear, they saw in the newspapers. At the time, it meant little to Enoch; he wasn't considering moving to the territory. If he did, he'd side with the abolitionist, but he wasn't, so it didn't matter.

He remembered how he cleared the field with two three-thousand-pound oxen, Ham and Nil. Of all the Mast livestock, his favorite animals were these two beasts. It was a beautiful spring day; Ham and Nil were harnessed up and performed in perfect rhythm what they were taught. The team had no problem overcoming the stump's resistance; they quickly popped them out of the ground without interruption. He didn't anticipate the rate at which he was moving; it seemed each stump they pulled out put him further ahead of schedule. It was a perfect beginning to a beautiful day.

He had his shirt off, enjoying every ray of sun the heavens provided. It was the year after the accident, and for the first time, he felt as physically strong as ever. The memory was an agonizingly beautiful period in his life. It was also why, at times, Enoch resisted returning and fought his memories. He wanted to avoid being captured by what was so perfect that it could never be duplicated again. Experiences that would only live once, die, and become memories that could only be recalled, not relived.

Over the years, just touching this memory was sufficient. To go entirely back, after all the years, was more than enough and maybe dangerous. But what better time than now, Enoch thought? He repositioned himself in the overstuffed wingback, surveyed his ballroom as a king might appraise his realm, and decided to go forward and face any danger.

It was the first time he worked a job alone. It was the first time the Mast Brothers worked two jobs simultaneously. Ezra and Enos worked the wagons, hauling cargo from Lake Erie's docks to various Cleveland warehouses. The pay for both jobs was excellent and the reason behind the attempt.

It was the first time Enoch stayed on a job site overnight. He pitched a pup tent and, with Ham and Nil tied down and fed, would return to it at the end of the day. There, he would dive into the large sack his mother stuffed with a small coffee pot, frying pan, fruit, nuts, a large slab of bacon, and more than one can of red kidney beans and a bag of coffee. Also, two large loaves of bread, a jar of blackberry jam, and a quarter of a birthday cake along with ten fine cigars, contraband he added to the sack.

Best of all, the sack held a book: James Fenimore Cooper's *The Deerslayer*. Enoch would meet up with Natty Bumppo and his Mohican sidekick Chingachgook right after supper. He would be with them until he would be overtaken by sleep, leaving the two to wait for him the following day where they left off.

*****

Enoch Mast met his wife and her patron saints, *Saint Dorwin* and *Saint Bedmir*, who would follow them for the rest of their lives at the Osstill's. It was behind their mansion the first day he was sixteen. They began the first day of many chapters of their life together at sixteen and fifteen then and there.

They first laid eyes on each other under the mid-morning sun by the stumps in the back of the mansion; the second time they met that day was dusk in front of his tent.

The first time began at a distance, with Enoch winding up right next to her at the end of the commotion. It started when Irene threw one of Mr. Osstill's acquaintances, who spent the morning with Mr. Osstill at the beer fountain, out the kitchen door. She kicked him down the set of steps. She shoved him off the cobblestone into the backyard with such authority he lost his footing and, hit the ground hard and bounced up running from the property.

When Enoch noticed what was happening, he rushed to aid Irene; he was halfway to her when he realized she didn't need any help. Upon his arrival, Irene said that the man had wandering hands. She warned him, but he paid her no mind; he did it again, so she showed him the door. Her explanation left Enoch speechless; he was impressed; he'd never seen someone so small handle such a situation so well. All he could do was look at her.

It became the most extended gaze ever given by Enoch as he began to notice, observe, and then stare at Irene's body, unable to stop. She never indicated for him to discontinue the nature of his gaze. She was held in place by his shirtless body. When they saw what was in their eyes, a lifelong connection was instantly made. Neither knew what to think or say at that moment. All they felt was the magnetism from their attraction for each other. A charm that would never fade no matter how far apart they may be from one another

* * * * *

Enoch returned to work after the uproar but couldn't pick up the pace. There was a war in his mind between his thoughts he should have concentrated on the stumps; instead, he thought about her. After he fed and tied down Ham and Nil he sat in front of his tent. He returned to the bag he'd tried to think about all day to take his mind off her. He was thinking about the bag if he wasn't thinking about her. Stumps weren't thought about at all.

As he began to pull it towards him, he caught some movement out of the corner of his right eye. When he zeroed in on the object, eighty to hundred yards off, he could make out the fetching figure of a woman silhouetted against the setting sun. Her figure came through a thin white robe. She ran with a fluttering bath towel in hand, like a butterfly on the horizon.

He became Chingachgook and stayed a safe distance as he trailed her into the woods. He thought he lost her when he came upon a beautiful pond, and she was nowhere to be seen. For a moment, it didn't matter; he was too captivated by the pond's beauty and fell under its spell. The spell was broken when a creature shot through the water's surface at the pond's far end. It surprised Enoch to where he gasped. What, or who, he was looking at had to have heard him.

Irene had her back to him when she surfaced. Enoch took cover; she never saw him; she heard him that day but never saw him at the pond. It was a fact that didn't matter; the sound of him was enough to let her know he was there, which was what she wanted. It allowed her to take her time drying off.

The light from a slow sunset showcased her wet auburn hair as she walked from the pond to her towel and robe on the grassy bank. Each step revealed more and more of her flawless body. When she got to the bank, she moved in the four directions found on a compass. She became a rare gem set in the center of the instrument, which held the needle, exposing all three-hundred-sixty degrees of her nude body to each of the four directions. So, whoever was out there could see every bit of her from all angles. When she slipped on her robe, picked up her towel, and wandered back to the mansion, her auburn hair was dry. That had a beautiful chestnut hew in the glow of the moonlight.

The pond had the most significant impact of all the events in Enoch Mast's life. No event, good or bad, and there were many, had struck with the force of the pond. His life changed direction from that moment on. From that day forward, whenever the subject came up, and Enoch would describe in great detail what he saw at the pond, Irene would tell him he had quite an imagination that she would never swim nude in a pond. She always told him with a coy smile. She told him he was never at the pond even though she knew the truth.

The seed of doubt she always tried to plant never took root. There was never any doubt in Enoch's mind about what he saw. Over the years, the debate over who was and wasn't at the pond and what they saw usually led to a compromise where both could take some enjoyable positions during their discussions.

Soon after Enoch watched Irene walk-out of sight, he returned to his tent. What he saw, playing over and over in his mind, with each episode the same as the previous one, but only better as if somehow, she could become even more naked. It wasn't too long after his return, while sitting with his back against a tree and Irene's nude rampage flooding his mind, Irene appeared, for the second time, as if out of nowhere and as if his thoughts produced her.

This time, she was fully clothed and just as appealing as she was at the pond, in a flattering blue dress with white flowers. They spent the night lying on the ground looking up at the Big Dipper and the stars surrounding it—touching each other with their words. They talked about what they knew of the sky and the stars that filled it.

Eventually, they talked about where they came from and whose children they were. Irene spoke about how Titus and Muriel Osstill lived and why she loved them; they were childless, and she was parentless. Enoch could only talk about his mother, who was surrounded on all sides and at all times by males and their equal or better more times than not—the love he had for her and those who surrounded her.

Irene also talked of her patron saint, the saint of 'doors and windows,' Saint Dorwin, who watched over her. She told of an old, very eccentric, childless couple who lived only in two rooms of a thirty-room mansion, the well-stocked pantry and the well-equipped kitchen. They were hoarders who stuffed the remaining twenty-eight rooms with every artifact they could afford. They loved looking out their windows and wanted the doors to all rooms kept open to receive more of what they didn't need.

When they weren't in the two rooms, they wandered the mansion and conversed with the objects in whatever room they were in, asking, "When did you arrive?" Irene stated she had to do three jobs: cook, clean the windows, and keep the doors open. She spent her time in a different room, dusting pretty and diverse objects daily. She spent her evenings reading in the library to her benefactors. It was perfect, far - far, better than the orphanage. She lived with people she felt would do anything for her, and she, in turn, would do anything for them. They had this type of balance in their lives.

Enoch talked about his mother, who was also an orphan, his brothers, and what he and the two of them did for a living. He mentioned he had lost a brother but never said how. He spoke little of his father, other than he had one, but hadn't seen him in quite a while. He talked about the animals they had and about high school. From that night on, there were times the two could look at each other's eyes and still see the stars of that night.

*****

Enoch poured a glass of wine, lit a cigar, and repositioned himself in the wingback chair. A few moments later, Crandel Poachfield appeared in his mind. He also was in the running for Irene Kathleen O'Flynn's attention and hadn't crossed Enoch's mind in decades.

There he was, twenty years old, the morning of the second day, stopping to talk down to the sixteen-year-old stump remover on his way to the kitchen door like he owned the place. He was about twenty-five yards away when he shouted to Enoch, 'Boy!' Stated her name, "Irene Kathleen O'Flynn," then barked, "Have you seen her!"

Enoch made the fastest character evaluation of his life when he looked up and saw Crandel Poachfield, and it wasn't good. With a menacing smile, he decided to tell Crandel the truth and answered, "Sir, I've seen all of her." Crandell Poachfield took considerable exception to his remark. He stopped, turned towards Enoch, and began to walk deliberately in his direction.

He expected Enoch to know his place and not move. He was somewhat surprised when Enoch walked towards him with no hesitation and just as deliberate.

Irene caught the preliminaries from the second-story window she was cleaning. They began to circle each other like two young but fully grown alley cats, hissing and spitting right before the fur began to fly. When the two got within striking distance of each other, looking for the right moment to unleash, Crandel's back was to the mansion, and Enoch faced it.

Irene caught Enoch's eye and could work the large second-floor window to their advantage, provocatively removing some of her clothing. If Crandel Poachfield turned to see what held Enoch's attention, she wouldn't hide. It would show him who the show was for. The message couldn't be more explicit.

She did this to save Crandel Poachfield's life. She knew him and couldn't stand him. He was an employee of AHP&D introduced to Mr. Osstill by Malcomb Lasbrith at a party. He always came over attempting to sell Mr. Osstill options and securities, which she warned him not to buy. He was always proposing marriage and was worse than the man she threw down the kitchen steps. As much as she despised him, she still wanted to save his life so Enoch wouldn't get hanged for taking it.

While Enoch kept his eyes on the second-floor window most of the time and paid little attention to the lecture he received, Crandel abruptly stopped and began studying Enoch's face. Something about it kept coming back to him in an ominous way. It gave him quite a jolt when he realized who he was trying to intimidate.

The flashback was as vivid as it could be; he was on the docks talking to a young man named J.D. Rockefeller, who was a bookkeeper for a subsidiary of AHP&D. When both of them saw the exact person he was lecturing, he almost beat Scotts Blade Billy to death and literally did kick his ass for all to see and remember.

The realization changed the complexion of everything. In the end, Crandel Poachfield moved on briskly; he turned from Enoch without a word and traveled on, never to be seen or heard from again by Enoch or Irene.

*****

After Crandel Poachfield, Saint Dorwin introduced Saint Bedmir to Enoch and Irene. The saint of open doors and clean windows, who had pleasantly filled Irene's life with the Osstills, departed the summer of her fifteenth year, replaced by the patron saint of beds and mirrors, Saint Bedmir. All his life, Enoch marveled at how Irene held on to her belief in them and got others to believe they were real saints.

Eve Mast would remember it as the summer Enoch left home and moved in with Irene. In the summer of 1855, Irene would explain that Saint Bedmir, the patron saint of beds and mirrors, led Enoch and her to a room in the mansion with thick plush carpet, filled with beautiful expensive mirrors and a charming canopy bed. They set it up to their liking, encouraged by the Osstills.

At first, after work, it was one night, then three, to where it was every night in a short period. At first, he brought Irene to his home, and all accepted her, except his father, who had disappeared. There were always rumors he either fell or was thrown into the Cuyahoga River and drowned, and just as many he'd been seen here and there.

Enoch worked the wagons or oxen daily with his brothers and slept in a mansion with a beautiful woman every night. They both ate well at the Osstills and the Masts. It went so smoothly and effortlessly that by the following summer, they found themselves married with twin boys, Seth and Simon, and living with Eve Mast.

Sixteen years later, in 1872, while reminiscing about the pond at the Osstills, Enoch and Irene conceived a daughter, Mary Irene, who was born normal but, at four, almost died from encephalitis; the fever damaged her brain and left her with the mentality of a six-year-old.

*****

The Osstills, as much as they wanted the young couple to stay, at their age, would be more a hindrance than a help around a newborn. A small child could be lost forever among all the objects their rooms held.

Seth and Simon were almost a year old, and on their first visit, when Titus and Muriel Osstill were found dead at their kitchen table from the poison they took. There was no note or will. The fact both were absent in the end bothered Enoch Far more than Irene. It didn't bother her at all. She would tell Enoch she wouldn't trade one memory she had of them for what they left behind.

*****

Enoch closed his eyes and, for a moment, changed thoughts. When he opened them, he began to gaze over the ballroom, noting what he had created and how satisfied he was with it. As he looked from ceiling to floor, it gradually came to him and gained more momentum as he thought about it. The ballroom was a piece of work that needed to be signed.

With no hesitation, he pulled the switchblade from his pocket, hit the button, and it snapped open with authority. The knife would become his pen. He looked at the walnut sill of the window showing the gardens, stared at it, and decided this would be where he would leave his mark.

The knife was well suited for the job, and the walnut was the best wood to carve. He placed the knife on the sill and stared at the open space provided, putting one hand in his pocket and scratching his chin with the other, trying to visualize a design that would hold his name and the year the room was completed

Suddenly, he was hit with a better idea; Enoch decided to put Brook's name down instead of his own. It would be his and Brooks's inside joke on the Lasbrith family—the room signed by one who would never have been allowed on the property. Let alone inside the mansion.

One couldn't ignore the opportunity the Lasbriths provided by not paying on time. It wouldn't be hard for those in the future to be let in on the joke when they observed the carving at a ballroom event thrown by the Lasbriths.

Enoch was a superior wood carver; some often told him he could make a living on his carvings alone. Enoch knew there was no reality in what they were saying. Carving wasn't work. It was relaxation. He saw himself more as a tradesman than an artist. He felt good he had come up with a pleasant way to spend his remaining time in the ballroom.

He stared at the window sill with a hundred designs running through his head. He gazed at the open knife, with its six-inch blade and six-inch handle, as a pen and ruler. Enoch decided against the center of the sill, muttering, "Everyone goes for the center." Instead, he went to the bottom left corner of the window and would work the mark on both a vertical and horizontal plane of the right angle the corner formed.

On the sash or vertical, he would carve out a ribbon banner with the year 1914 centered on it. On the sill or horizontal, he would carve out the figure of an opened scroll with Brooks Mast's name.

Enoch sat on a chair brought over from the nearest table. He measured the design using the knife and then scratched it in the wood. Next, he lit a cigar and stared at the plan for some time. He made minor changes, and he went to work when the cigar could be smoked no further. The restlessness left him as the past slowly returned, unable to overrun his every thought as he worked the carving.

*****

Enoch wished he could carve his sons, Seth and Simon, into the walnut, but they headed west with their uncle Ezra the year of the Centennial. By 1876, Ezra had read one too many dime novels about the 'Wild West', and Enoch's sons had gone to one circus too many featuring it. Cleveland was no longer in their future.

The same year General Custer was killed at Little Bighorn and Wild Bill Hickok left 'Aces and Eights,' the dead man's hand, on the table in Deadwood, South Dakota, the three started to make their move. The move picked up steam when the three found out about the gold rush in Deadwood. By the end of 1876, they were in town.

149

The Masts soon established a reputation for knowing how to handle themselves in a saloon and how to behave on the streets. The sheriff of Deadwood, Seth Bullock, who had a reputation for maintaining order, liked them. He was also a businessman. In a short time, the Masts went in with Bullock, selling supplies to the miners. They invested in Deadwood, bought vacant city lots, and were also for hire to provide private investigations for lawyers and personal property security for the merchants. After a while, they became known as the 'Ohio Trio.'

*****

For the most part, The Ohio Trio wandered the west unafraid to test its boundaries, and when they had to, took on high-paying private jobs that were as dangerous as they were profitable. They developed the type of reputation where John Wesley Hardin stayed on the other side of the street when they were in Abilene. Tom Horn kept his distance whenever they shared the same territory.

By the mid-eighties, Seth Bullock introduced the Ohio Trio to a man who came west to escape the pain of losing his mother to typhoid and his wife to Bright's disease. Both on the same day, Valentine's Day, 1884. His name was Theodore Roosevelt. For a time, Ezra, Simon, and Seth worked both his ranches, the *Maltese Cross* and *Elkhorn*, as foremen. It worked out well, and Roosevelt never looked at them as employees.

Ezra was eighteen years older than 'T R,' as they called him, Seth and Simon, two. T R became the twenty-sixth president, and the Ohio Trio's influence on him overlooked in all the records of the man's life and times.

*****

Eventually, all their pursuits in the West paid off. They had enough cash to change occupations, and they became ranchers. Ezra started the *Bar Z* outside Deadwood, South Dakota, on the outskirts of Laramie, Wyoming. Seth formed *Saddle Ridge*, and a stone's throw from Abilene, Kansas, Simon built Shadow Run. Every four months, they rotated from one ranch to the other.

Their management method made the ranches successful, each well-known throughout the territory in three large towns. It also kept them single. They made romance a four-month habit with another woman in a different town.

*****

The brother who stayed back with Enoch was Brooks Mast. After 1876, with sixty percent of the workforce gone, The Mast Brothers became a two-man operation. They went from teamster to carpenter, from the logistics involved in moving items from one place to another to developing what needs to be built to hold these items. The change was Brook's idea and couldn't have been made at a better time in Cleveland, Ohio. It worked, and they did well from that year on.

*****

Enoch Mast shook his head when he realized thirty-eight years had passed since they went out West. The last time he saw them was in the winter of 1910. They returned home at random intervals, ten years the longest and the shortest two. Their visits, for the most part, were quick and vague. No mention of wives and children. When asked what they did? The answer was "Ranch," which would soon evolve into a discussion on the scenery of the West. They let it be known they came back to talk about the past, not the present. Ezra liked to return to the days of the parish schools, Seth and Simon being on the wagons, the war, and the days of their mother and father.

When they were in town, a small group of close friends, made over the years from school, work, and the war, would show up at the house. Those nights came with eating, drinking, stories, and laughter. It would go on for a few days and end when the three would leave without a word.

The last time Enoch saw them, they looked sturdy and weathered. When home, they never asked for money or anything for that matter. They all seemed pretty self-reliant, well-fed, and clothed. News from the West hit Cleveland all the time from various sources. He'd heard of the Ohio Trio. When he asked if they had ever heard of or run into them, they would shake their head' no' and smile 'yes.' It became a known secret they didn't talk about.

*****

As the morning sun moved towards noon, Enoch was comfortable with his new project and the reflections of his past, which moved like an old river through his mind, at times calm and crystal clear and at times dark and foreboding.

*****

Enoch stopped carving. He brushed the wood chips that were starting to build onto a napkin with his hand, closed the switchblade, and placed it next to the ashtray, which held his unlit cigar. He decided to go on break and grabbed a peach and some napkins.

The peach was tasty. Enoch lit the cigar in appreciation. His mind began to wander like the smoke he exhaled, and he recalled the preamble leading to any intimacy required going back to the pond and who knew what about what took place there. And his conditional recognition of her two saints as legitimate. On many occasions, these two notions always helped him get what he was after.

He smiled from ear to ear and gazed toward the Osstill mansion as if it were still there and what he had just recalled had taken place minutes instead of years ago. She had a great sense of timing in all she did. Her behavior, Enoch's reactions, and the times of Saint Dorwin and Saint Bedmir warmed his heart enough to overcome the pain of missing her.

*****

His mood suddenly changed when he repositioned himself in the chair, and beyond his control, his eyes began to glaze over. It was Irene's first and last trip out of town without Enoch. He had to wrap up putting in a grand staircase, a very lucrative project, at the Brecht mansion. She had a friend from the orphanage, Ester, who she said was her sister; there were no records and no way of knowing if she was or wasn't.

Ester lived in Johnstown, Pennsylvania. Irene was a year younger than Ester. She went to Johnstown to celebrate her sister's fiftieth birthday in her forty-ninth year and never came home.

Ester's birthday was May 31, 1889, the day heavy rains caused the dam at the South Fork Hunting and Fishing Club to fail and sent a thirty-foot high wall of water, close to twenty tons, moving forty miles per hour, through a valley, a distance a little over eleven miles that slammed right into Johnstown, Pennsylvania. It killed over twenty-two hundred people and caused over seventeen million dollars in damages. It took the town five years to rebuild.

The Johnstown Flood resulted from the negligence of some of America's wealthiest families. The sixty or so members of the club included Andrew Carnegie, Henry Clay Frick, Andrew W Mellon, Philander Chase Knox, and people with the wealth to build a world-class dam if they wanted. Instead, they chose to keep their money in their pockets; the dam didn't threaten them if it failed.

At the time, Johnstown Flood was the worst disaster in U.S. history and the first large-scale relief effort by the Red Cross. The first request from the town in the aftermath was to send morticians and coffins. Henry Frick donated money, Andrew Carnegie built the town a library, and others in the club sent blankets. None of their donations came close to covering the damage done. There were claims and litigation, but the club and its members were never found to be liable for monetary damages. Their wealth overpowered the truth and got the courts to view the flood as an Act of God.

In the end, *The American Law Review* weighed in and stated, "A jury of Pennsylvania Lutherans, Reformed Dutch, Presbyterians, Methodists, Baptists or Catholics will not take readily to the attempt to cast the responsibility of such a catastrophe from the shoulders of the fine rich gentlemen who owned the fish pond and the rotten dam to the shoulders of God,"

Enoch gritted his teeth as he thought about who had taken Irene from him and again swore to himself if he ever came across a member of the South Fork Hunting and Fishing Club, he would kill them with his bare hands.

*****

Enoch extracted himself from the memory when he exhaled a cloud of smoke and watched it bounce off the glass window pane. The incident made him chastise himself, muttering, "Look at this day! What's wrong with you? Open the damn window!" He followed his orders immediately, and the warm air flowed from the room and the smoke to the cooler air outside. He stuck his head out the window, breathed deeply, and exhaled with a pleasant sigh.

Next, he pushed a small pile of wood chips from the sill out the window and smiled as they floated to the ground. He turned away from the window, grabbed the napkin with the wood chips, held it outside, and shook it out, pleased with the new method he found to handle the scrap.

He went for his pocket watch and was halfway to retrieving it when he remembered it had stopped. He gazed out at the horizon and found the sun had moved further west. It was mid-day, noon, or close to it. That was his guess; he had been in the ballroom for maybe five hours or more. He couldn't decide if he felt this was short or long. What he did know was so far, for the most part, it had been pleasant. He wondered if there would be another agreeable five hours and if they would bring him his payment and freedom.

Enoch's mind wandered, returning to the dream of Mary Irene and Brooks. He began thinking about what else he saw and came up with creamed chicken, biscuits, and some green peas. He saw it all in his dream—a long with a small pitcher of cold milk and a piece of coconut cream pie.

His next thought was it sure, at that moment, would make it a damn near perfect lunch. What would make it beyond perfect would be if Jenny delivered it. He relit a cigar and knew the odds of lunch unfolding this way were almost nonexistent. The better odds, which weren't great, were on the possibility of Jenny showing up with something.

He leaned back in his chair and smoked away. The smell of the tobacco masked the growing smell of the unfinished food that had been out for almost twenty-four hours, starting to linger in the ballroom. He began to wait and see if Jenny would come.

*****

Downstairs in the dining hall, Jenny was not thinking of lunch as much as she was about escaping to see Enoch. At that moment, she and all the staff, except for Sinclair, who was in Olivia

Lasbrith's bedroom, were busy carrying out the orders Hardin Lasbriths issued after he saw the cobweb and smudge.

The Dining hall was in chaos, with two factions fighting for control. Some lived in fear and would clean and clean until told to stop, and those at the point of rebellion would clean it once and state they cleaned it many times when they hadn't. Some were working, others chose to sit, and the resentment one group had for the other could be cut with a knife.

Jenny did both. She sat, and she worked, scrubbing the back of a painting per the earlier instructions, traveling on her reputation. It was easy to think she had done the backs of several paintings, but she was on her first. She concluded that with the state of affairs with the staff, she couldn't get away without being noticed. It seemed everyone had their eye on someone. She decided to stay put and use the time to plan a safe getaway.

It was very odd; the first thought to come to her after she made her escape was to make creamed chicken. The whole time she sat washing the back of the painting she kept thinking about what she would do once she made it to the kitchen.

She recalled the day Enoch finished the scaffolding in the ballroom and how he came down to dinner unaware of what they were to have. They had creamed chicken and biscuits with the trimmings. Jenny remembered it was one of those chance glances one hardly catches, yet at the same time, a glance, if seen, that could not be forgotten.

How Enoch sat down with them and ate, how his eyes let everyone know how much he enjoyed the meal and the company. Jenny recalled he did not back off on the helpings. The whole time, all at the table teased and joked about his appetite. Enoch took it all in stride, in the best of spirits, and even joined in on making fun of himself before targeting others to test his wit with theirs. It was a meal well worth remembering.

She began to visualize making the meal. Her thoughts turned to her current situation and how Hardin and Sinclair had victimized the staff with their actions. She knew, for a fact, they should all be working in the dining hall until Hardin's return. She knew whenever he wanted, Sinclair could put a stop to the nonsense, but he wouldn't.

She knew Sinclair's reward was found in knowing Hardin would like nothing better than to put the staff in an uncomfortable situation. After the leftover food began to turn rancid, the ballroom would fit the bill. That was how Hardin and Sinclair governed over those who worked for them. Jenny next began to wonder how long Hardin would be gone and how long Enoch would wait. She didn't know the answer to her first thought, but she did for her second.

*****

Enoch returned to work, he started carving the year 1914 into the banner. He then decided to carve the month, June, and the date, twenty-eight, above the year. Initially, he had decided not to, but the "1914" was coming out better than expected. He had just enough room inside the banner to present the date of when the room was completed in his eyes. He would leave a mark for the observant to show others.

It would turn out to be June 28, 1914, the day after Hardin Lasbrith's granddaughter's wedding reception. The day Hardin had been looking for, when demand for wire worldwide would go through the ceiling, telegraph, barbed, and razor (concertina) wire. The day Hardin Lasbrith left for Cleveland to take all the necessary steps to take advantage of the oncoming misfortune behind the demand.

The world crisis he'd hoped for erupted the day Enoch Mast left his mark. The news from that day would make him unbelievably wealthy. Unaware of what the day brought him. The tipping point to the First World War. All that ran through his mind as he constantly snapped the buggy whip, at first above the horse's back and then on it, as he made his way to town, was all the good fortune a war would bring him.

After dropping his satchel off in his office at AHP&D, he decided to spend the night at the Turrets, a very exclusive men's club for the very wealthy on the west side of Cleveland. It was a good decision but one he could not see through.

The family history at the Turrets was not good. Members disliked Hardin's grandfather, father, and they blackballed Hardin no less than six times. Eventually, Hardin bought his way in. Members treated him as one who had converted to their religion instead of one born into it. They were neither warm nor accepting, just tolerant, and that was marginal at times. However, he was no victim of prejudice; over time, as with most people, Hardin brought on the members' sentiments towards him by his own hand.

He went to sign in for a room. Everyone there knew it was him by the demands he put on the clerk for the type of room he wanted. At the Turrets he was often heard before seen. He made sure all heard him when he stated the price didn't matter. Hardin looked around at the members after he said it as if they were his audience and was unaware, they were unimpressed.

In the first place, the members didn't feel like being his audience, and the feedback he got was blank stares and exasperated sighs.

Secondly, he didn't have a friend among them. The clerk said pleasantly, "Here you are," and handed him the keys. Then, he added in a firm voice heard by all, "We are expecting a prompter payment this time around," and by doing so, with his request, found the audience Hardin looked for when making his demands.

It infuriated Hardin, throwing down the keys as hard as he could and storming out. He could still hear the laughter from inside as he approached his rig. The only thought going through his head was total revenge and that he had to make enough money to destroy the Turrets and all the members one day.

It was fortunate for the horse that Miss Chiffon's was less than ten blocks from the Turrets; otherwise, a veterinarian would need to be called to salve the horse's back. The way he treated the animal did not go unnoticed by those on the streets and sidewalks. Midway there, Hardin pulled back on the reins to where the horse slid to a stop and had to fight to keep from going down. Hardin was no different with animals than with people; he abused both.

The incident with the horse happened when he spotted Cyrus Winford, a pimp Hardin had known for years. Cyrus told Hardin, "This is your lucky day!" They talked about a new pony Cyrus had just added to his stable. When they were done, for a hundred dollars, Cyrus would bring the thirteen-year-old girl to where Hardin was staying.

Miss Chiffon did not tolerate foreign 'split-tails' in her whorehouse. To bring in outside talent had been tried once, maybe twice and no more, the attempts never ended well. Everyone who patronized the house knew how they ended and how vindictive she could get. She had an army of thugs capable of anything. It was a terrible idea in Cleveland to cross her.

It didn't matter, Hardin was too excited about the adolescent girl to pay attention to Miss Chiffon's rules. He would book a room, and he and Cyrus would carefully sneak her into the room.

When Hardin arrived at Miss Chiffon's, he entered the large parlor, and there wasn't a predator or pervert he didn't know. He had no problems the second time around getting accepted. He went out on the veranda and hand signaled Cyrus, showing four fingers on his right hand and two on his left. Cyrus nodded and took the girl to the fourth room on the second floor.

Hardin had his bags sent to the room. Socialized and bought a bottle of top-shelf whiskey from the bar. He made sure Miss Chiffon saw the purchase as they exchanged smiles. He went to the room and waited for Cyrus and the girl. There was a knock, and Cyrus and the girl were let in.

The girl was like a brand-new buggy who had yet to experience the ruts, mud, uneven terrain, dead animals, and other hazards of the road she was on. When Hardin saw her, he wanted to ride her until she couldn't move. She took her clothes off with little hesitation and very little modesty. There was no emotion, teasing, or foreplay, and Hardin liked that; it was as if she understood that, at his age, he had no time for it. Cyrus Winford found a chair when it became apparent Hardin no longer noticed or paid attention to the fact he was still in the room.

Hardin began to work his way down to his underwear. He wore the button-up type where shorts and shirt were one piece. The shirt part was a grayish white, but the bottom shorts were stained front and back. Hard evidence of the severe control problems Hardin had. With Cyrus still in the room, the girl looked at it as training, and she had to act as if she wasn't repulsed, which was difficult.

Hardin walked around the young girl, wrestling with his underwear. The first signs of what was about to take place were misread by both the young girl and Cyrus. Hardin's eyes glazed over, and he began to drool from suddenly not being able to swallow. Both thought these were the typical signs of an old man about to pounce on a naked girl.

Then, every muscle in Hardin's body tightened so he couldn't move. Every single muscle was severely cramping to the point where he froze. The tips of his fingers, the first joint of each finger, painfully bent down, and so did the first digits of his toes. Every joint under the badly cramped muscles felt like they would eventually explode. Neither the pain from his muscles nor his joints dominated; they were both equally excruciating. All these events were followed by the complete loss of speech along with the ability to make any sound.

The thought of a massive stroke never crossed Cyrus or the young girl's mind. They thought he was dead as soon as he hit the floor after the girl touched him. Hardin went down hard and did not attempt to break his fall. On the way down, he caught the corner of a table that left a severe gash on his scalp, and blood poured from it. His eyes froze in place, but he could see; he just couldn't move them. The only sense left in tack was his hearing, he could hear everything around him.

The two caught Miss Chiffon's eye as they ran from her veranda to the stairs and into the alley. She knew who he was, but the girl wasn't one of her whores. It wasn't too long after this she found Hardin and put two and two together, believing it to be a robbery. She also thought he was dead. He was motionless. His head was in a large pool of blood.

Instructions were given to get the body out as soon as possible after dark. The only people who got close to the body were the bouncers who rolled Hardin up in a filthy old rug and didn't notice his shallow breaths. Had they, it wouldn't have mattered. They were told to get the body out, period. Nothing was said about dead or alive. He was to be taken to the garbage dump, where he died of fright later in the night after being discovered by the rats. Norwegian wood rats, the size of well-fed house cats, began to rip into his scalp and feast on his bloody head.

After the two dropped him off deep in the garbage dump, they were instructed to find Cyrus and the young girl, shoot them, and throw their bodies into Lake Erie, which they did. To send a message to whoever else Miss Chiffon thought might be in on what she assumed was the robbery/murder of Hardin Lasbrith. Which she believed over the years was one of Cleveland's best-kept secrets, and she was the one who kept it.

No one ever saw Hardin Lasbrith after June 28, 1914. Like his wives and stepson, there was plenty of talk and rumors. Perhaps the greatest irony to be found in all the events of that Sunday was that Archduke Franz Ferdinand was assassinated by Gavrilo Princip, a Serbian nationalist dedicated to freeing all Slavs from Austria-Hungary's control. It occurred in Sarajevo on the same day Hardin Lasbrith wound up in the dump. Within a month Europe began to cover itself in both barb and razor wire, they couldn't get enough of it. The First World War broke out, and AHP&D made a fortune and Hardin Lasbrith never saw a penny.

*****

Enoch stood for a while admiring his rendering of the 1914, he had just carved. He was at that point where he wanted to do more but knew any additional work on the year could ruin what he had completed. He felt lucky he had scratched in the month and date on the banner and had somewhere to go. He skillfully began to bring the date out of the walnut with the point of the knife and began to work through lunch and into the early afternoon.

He thought about Jenny and the lunch she was to bring for a moment, but the thought came and went. He ate a large pumpernickel roll with a nice amount of provolone cheese on it and gulped down two glasses of wine in five minutes. He learned how to eat fast in the Army and was good at it. The most common demand made by Irene over their thirty-four years together was, "Jesus, Joseph, and Mary – will you slow down!"

When he was done, he freed a fresh cigar from the fine wooden cigar box and lit it. He drew on it a few times, with the last one being the longest, and exhaled the smoke slowly. He placed the cigar in the ashtray and returned to work, totally absorbed in what he was doing. He was unaware of all that surrounded him other than the window he was working on and the view it provided.

As he carved, for the first time since he entered the Lasbrith mansion, he began to feel he was running out of time for the unfinished work he had discovered, the need to see Hardin Lasbrith, his attorney, accountant, or family representative no longer had an urgent feeling. What had an urgent feel was he might need the afternoon, night, and at least the following morning to leave the Mast brand on the window in the ballroom. He knew there was as much chance he would get kicked out as for getting paid, but he didn't want it to happen before his carving was finished.

Of all the work done, Enoch felt the carving on the window would become the most significant piece of work he did in the Lasbrith ballroom. He began to think leaving the mark was the real reason he found himself in their home. That he wasn't there for money but to leave his mark.

*****

Horace Lasbrith was in the room above the window Enoch worked on. He had just returned from a two-day bender. As soon as he woke up, self-loathing came over him. He was in a urine-soaked bed. He had no idea where he had been and what he did the previous night. He had no idea what time it was, or did he care. The sunlight had to fight its way through the cracks in the drawn curtains. Its intensity showed it was midday.

The ritual began; he stripped his bed of the soaked sheets and started another ever-growing, slow-drying pile of soiled sheets in the farthest corner of the room from his bed. Every day the smell would grow to the point where he would eventually have to leave his room for at least two days and wreak havoc on the outside world with the things he would say and do. It was the amount of time given to the staff to make the room inhabitable.

When his mess was taken care of, he would return to recover.

The morning Enoch worked below his room, Horace wanted to find his bottle of heroin. The bottle that the scientist at the giant German pharmaceutical Bayer developed trademarked, and marketed as a non-addictive substitute for morphine.

The bottle was nowhere to be found. Knowing it would hurt his eyes, but beyond the point of caring, he finally threw open the drapes to help in the search for the drug. He became frantic as his eyes watered, and tried to adjust to the light. He found his syringe but no drugs. It was the final straw. He could take no more.

With little hesitation, he skillfully tied three leather belts together, fashioned a noose at one end, then secured the other end to a finely carved walnut support beam that ran across the room. His room was opulent, with heavy dressers, a writing desk, tables, all made of the best woods, two fine leather oversized wingback chairs in front of a fireplace, deep closets, big mirrors, fine drapery, thick Persian rugs, large oil paintings of Cleveland landscapes and landmarks.

He took the chair from the writing desk, stood on it, placed the noose around his neck, and realized he had not left a note. He wanted to leave a note, tried to undo the noose, lost his footing, the chair fell away, and accidentally accomplished what he had set out to do before he thought of the note and hanged himself.

A few days later, the staff noticed an unfamiliar but equally noxious smell from his room began to linger in the hallway. The scent came from the feces of his final evacuation. The obnoxious odor gave way to what Horace Lasbrith had committed.

Almost nothing was known about Hardin Lasbrith's disappearance, and Horace Lasbrith's suicide. Hardin's body was never found, and Horace left no note. Hardin's disappearance was talked about for the rest of the summer and part of the fall. All the predictions and speculations had all been made in this time interval. By winter, word of his disappearance faded and then vanished.

Horace's death was met with little surprise. Most said when they heard, the news didn't come as unexpected. No memorials were held for either; there was no public show of grief for the father or the son. The only interesting fact that never came to light was Hardin's stroke, and Horace's suicide took place on the same day. There were no days between the two events, as everyone familiar with the situation had thought.

*****

Enoch worked in the perfect light of mid-day, each chip that fell revealing more of the date and year, capturing when one era ended and another was to begin. A sudden gust of wind changed the serenity of the situation; it lifted and scattered the wood chips to where they landed in random locations, one being Enoch's left eye. He felt it go in and by instinct, began to rub his eye, even though he knew not to. It began to sting, and the eye became highly irritated.

It turned red and watered, burning tears profusely. When the chip was finally washed away, by pulling the eyelid away from the eyeball, Enoch took a cloth napkin, dipped it in the water pitcher, went to the over-stuffed chair, slouched in it to the point of almost lying down, put the damp napkin on his eye and waited for the irritation to subside. The whole episode returned him to John Brown and the accident.

With his one good eye, he spotted an unfinished cigar in the ashtray, lit it, and with the first cloud of smoke, went back to a time when fate stepped in to save him from himself.

It was shortly after Brooks and Evelyn were taken early October of 1854. The sting of that event was still fresh with Enoch and his brothers. Nonstop work helped alleviate the feeling. A client of the Mast brothers contracted them after they had purchased a rather large spinet, a type of upright piano, from Colonel Simon Perkins in Akron, Ohio, about forty miles south of Cleveland. They wanted the Mast brothers to pick it up and bring it home.

The round trip would be eighty miles and take two days, the pay would be excellent, and the Autumn weather and scenery in Ohio would be the best of the year. The client informed Enoch that Colonel Perkins would send one of his business partners, John Brown, to meet the Mast brothers in Hudson. He would then guide them to Akron and Colonel Perkins's mansion. It was to take place on the first Monday of the month.

On that day in the center of Hudson, a tall, angular, thin, fifty-four-year-old, thick-haired man with piercing eyes waited on the village lawn for the Mast brothers to arrive. He didn't mind the wait. He had a lot on his mind. One was that it was becoming apparent this would be the last year of the Perkin's / Brown partnership in the wool business. In the back of his mind, he wondered if Colonel Perkins was selling the Spinet because of him. He had, of late, made some costly business decisions. In the end, he concluded that it didn't matter and that he had other and more essential causes he wanted to take up that were far more important than money.

As it turned out, John Brown was expecting teamsters, not kids, and the Mast brothers were expecting a guide, not a grandpa. Without saying a word, John Brown tied his horse to the back of the wagon, jumped up and took the reins from Enoch, and told him, "I'll take it from here."

John Brown was impressed with Enoch's grip on the reins. Enoch didn't give them up readily. They stared at each other momentarily and realized they had the same type of eyes, not in color, but in determination. A few moments passed, and Enoch gave him the reins, realizing he had no idea how to get to Colonel Perkin's mansion.

The Mast brothers saw right away there was some hard bark on this old man. He was captivating when speaking; his physical features only added to his charisma. It didn't take long to find out he was a fervent abolitionist. Before they went any further, he wanted to know Enoch's, Ezra's, and Enos's position on slavery. He couldn't have caught the Mast brothers at a better time. They all told John Brown about Brooks and how it was like losing a brother.

From that point on, John Brown kept the conversation on the abolition of slavery. From Hudson, through Kent and Cuyahoga Falls, on into Akron and Colonel Perkins mansion, the evening spent there, the crating, loading of the Spinet, and their departure the following morning, the topic of slavery continued to grow to where it took on a life of its own and became a subject that refused to die.

Enoch and his brothers embraced what was being said and were captivated by this old man. However, during their time together, the brothers learned nothing new from John Brown; they knew the country had thirty-one states and more would come. The overbearing issue - would the new states be free or slave - would the country be free or slave? With John Brown, it wasn't 'what' he said about the issues but 'how' he said it.

At the time, it seemed there were plenty of answers but no solutions. John Brown told them about the *Free Soilers* who arose from one issue. That issue was slavery.

They were vehemently opposed to it and determined to halt its expansion in the western territories. In Ripon, Wisconsin, the Soilers had recently evolved into a new political body called the Republican Party. The party was formed in response to the Kansas-Nebraska Act and their opposition to the act. Their goal was to run a candidate in the next presidential election.

The Kansas-Nebraska Act was told to Enoch and his brothers by lecture and sermon; it started out as a mind-stimulating lecture and wound up a spell-binding sermon. One would not forget its content or the protagonist who delivered it.

The knowledge of the act was imparted to them after supper with the Brown family. They weren't the only audience; John Brown was prolific when it came to fathering children, and they listened as diligently as the Mast brothers. Even though they had heard what was said many times before. They were true disciples, there to aid their father's conversion of the Mast brothers.

The basic idea behind the act was to open the Kansas and Nebraska territories up to farming. To develop a rail system to get the crops to market and to help further western expansion beyond the territories. No one had a problem with this. The problem came when the question was asked: Would these present territories and future states be free or slave?

The question became a double-edged sword, one edge pro-slavery and the other edge anti-slavery. The slavery issue, at the time, seemed to have as much support as opposition. Still to be determined which edge of the sword would be best for the country. Slavery was an institution for centuries in the United States.

As John Brown explained, Congress could mandate the new states from these two territories to be free states and have it stated in their constitutions as a requirement for statehood. Or Congress could let the inhabitants of the territories decide to be free or slave by vote.

Either way, as a result, pro and anti-slave settlers poured into the territories to gain control. The consequence of the act was that one issue created two groups who were continually at each other's throats. It became apparent compromise could not solve the situation. What was left to solve the situation and settle the issue was conflict. The institution of slavery in the late 1850's went beyond being a political issue. It evolved into a moral issue, making all the difference as the country moved towards its eighty-fifth year of existence.

*****

It went on like this from when they met John Brown to when they loaded the Spinet and headed for Cleveland. Not only did the Mast brothers learn of the Republican Party, but they also heard about the *Know Nothing Party*, but their issue was immigration. John Brown told them that in early August, on the seventh through eighth, the Know-Nothings started a riot against immigrants in Saint Louis, Missouri, that led to ten deaths.

The story he told them left the brothers with an uncomfortable subconscious conclusion that the country had more than one issue to solve and probably always would. That if it weren't slavery, it would be immigration. It wasn't what they knew; it was what they felt. The problem with democracy is the issues it creates through the functions of free speech and press. Countries that put the brakes on these two have fewer issues but more significant problems.

*****

Their topics changed like the weather that goes from bad to worse as they sat hunched together on the wagon bench, the chill of an Autumn morning upon them. The case of Anthony Burns, a runaway slave captured May 24 in Boston, Maine, who on June 2 was shipped back to a life of slavery in Virginia, came up and was commented on in the harshest manner. They forgot it was told to them by John Brown right after they told him about Brooks Mast. John Brown told it to point out how the slave-holding South could impose their will on the North. That they were winning, and that had to change.

The case of Anthony Burns infuriated John Brown and the abolitionists. Just as the taking of Brooks Mast riled Enoch, Ezra, and Enos, all John Brown did with Anthony Burns was cement the Mast brothers' complete support of the abolitionist cause from there on out.

The temperature started to drop, and it began to rain. They stopped to check the crate they built that morning to hold the Spinet for leaks. They took a sizeable oil-cloth tarp from the wagon's tackle when the crate passed inspection; they got under it, smiling as they ran the tarp over their heads and shoulders, staying warm and dry.

Enoch was in the middle and told his brothers that John Brown was different from any abolitionists they had ever encountered. He told them Brown was right, that when one thought about it, all the abolitionists ever do is talk. John Brown, on the other hand, believed in action through armed insurrection as the only way to overthrow the institution of slavery. Arm the slaves, and they'd do the fighting.

"It's that simple." Enoch liked this position, and what he said about John Brown surprised Ezra and Enos. They saw the issue as a problem, not a fight, and the John Browns, on both sides, were a big part of the problem.

*****

Enoch moved the ashtray closer, drew on his cigar, and then chuckled at how he thought at fifteen. As he exhaled, he remembered what he told his brothers, that he and John Brown stayed up and talked after they had turned in. "Talked about going out to Kansas together, all of us, soon. That we should consider the idea." He remembered how his brothers shook their heads in disbelief.

Enoch told them, "It was the conversation we had right after I told him about how we all hauled a wagon full of blankets to Harpers Ferry, Virginia, a few months back. I told him about the armory there."

He recalled how it surprised Ezra and Enos, and they immediately started on why going to Kansas and telling John Brown about the armory were two colossal mistakes. They were right. In the years that followed, whenever Harper's Ferry came up, he and his brothers would have to deal with the possibility John Brown could have found out about the armory from Enoch that he may have planted the seed five years before he raided the armory. What he told John Brown and what John Brown told him, Enoch said to his brothers.

On the return trip, the decision was made to go home first and deliver the Spinet to the customer the next day if it was raining. The following morning, after a good night's sleep. On his way downstairs, Enoch heard his two brothers talking about how crazy they thought he was, in concerned voices, to buy into John Brown.

Rather than put their minds to rest, Enoch chose to increase their anxiety. He picked up right where he left off, talking about going to Kansas and straightening out some people. On the way to the customer, they argued back and forth, and just as they were about to come to blows, about whether or not to take up with John Brown. They arrived at the address and entered the gates of a stately mansion. They were met by some of the household staff and shown the drop-off point. They let down the tailgate, retrieved the heavy-duty ten-foot ramp from the wagon's undercarriage, and set it up.

There were two coiled ropes side by side in the tackle, it was decided to use the newer of the two. The one had only been used once and had a severe unseen flaw hidden in its coils. On its first job, it got caught up in the thin-edged, sharp metal flashing surrounding the chimney's base on a roof. The tug to free it created a half-inch-deep slice in the rope. At the time, the decision to use the 'new' rope proved one of the worst decisions the Mast Brothers ever made.

They lifted the crate onto a dolly and moved it towards the ramp. The rope was put around the front end of the crate going down the ramp, with the ends of the rope brought back and held by Ezra and Enos standing on the wagon bed. Enoch would guide the crate and offer token resistance once the crate started down the incline. Ezra and Enos let the crate's weight take out some of the rope to slow down the momentum of the crate as it traveled down the incline.

For the first five feet, the crate moved just as planned. The last five feet turned into a total catastrophe when the rope broke, and the wheels on the dolly were set free. The crate picked up speed as it moved down the ramp, its momentum more than Enoch could handle. His brothers and the household staff looked on helplessly as the heavy, out-of-control load drove him into a wall with no mercy. There was no scream, just a horrifying loud snap.

When it ended, all rushed to Enoch and quickly turned their heads away from what they saw. The bone of his lower left arm, not only broke through his skin but his shirt as well. Along with the compound fracture of his lower left arm, he also broke three ribs on the same side. Through it all Enoch never lost consciousness which only added to his suffering. Thankfully there was no damage to the Spinet, only to Enoch who would be off the wagons for quite some time.

*****

Enoch thought, what a strange day, as the irritation of his eye subsided. One episode of his life after another. Events he hadn't thought of in years. The recalling of his life seemed unstoppable, but why here and why now? The answers and speculations of 'here and now' were quickly run over by recalling what happened after the accident. He repositioned himself in the chair and returned to the time without hesitation.

His brothers got him enough whiskey to drink himself unconscious. The bone was set the day of the accident. Enoch did nothing but smoke cigars and shoot shots of whiskey the next two days. On the third, he began to eat and stumble around with his broken ribs protected by an arm in a sling. The only job he was good at was getting in the way of whatever job was at hand for Ezra and Enos when they were at home.

Winter was coming on, and they would go out on fewer jobs and have more time for maintenance. This was the rhythm of their work, the pulse they had to keep to be a healthy business spring, summer, and fall. Winter was a time to maintain the wood and leather of their rigs and tend and rest up the animals. Winters were a time of big meals and big fires in the stoves and fireplaces. A time of pleasant conversation and naps

Every winter was played out that way except the winter after the accident. Enoch took that winter to the point where each day Ezra and Enos would threaten him with breaking his other arm and smashing in the ribs on his right side if he didn't stop trying to help. They told him that getting in the way was not helpful. More often than not, a day would end on the threatening note of Enoch snarling at Ezra and Enos, "You Two will get fixed when I'm healed up. One at a time or together it doesn't matter."

The friction subsided before October ended when Ezra and Enos overheard a customer talking to a house guest while delivering a very expensive dining room set. It was a lively conversation about Ohio's first publicly funded high school. It was located in the Universalist Church on Prospect Avenue in Cleveland. It was called Central High School, the only public high school west of the Alleghenies. It was 1855 and the last year at the church. The following year, 1856, it would be in a new building on Euclid Avenue, west of East 9th. The conversation was more of a debate on the virtues of private education over public.

The guest believed educating the public was dangerous, whereas his host held the opposite view. Stating the country's strength is found in public libraries, and if they were public, why not the schools? The guest replied along with schools, and libraries should also be private.

What came of Ezra and Enos's eavesdropping was the idea to get Enoch to enroll in Central High School. An idea that occurred independently of each other but hit both at the same time as their solution to a big problem.

The two having the conversation, the host and guest, were at the point of blows when Ezra and Enos left them. After they got paid, the two brothers smiled like idiots and egged the two on. They were gone from view when the host and guest lunged at each other, but they heard the racket. Nothing could take away their newfound hope Central High School would be the answer. Which it turned out to be. What followed saved the remainder of winter that year.

It was one of the best decisions ever made by the Mast brothers. The curriculum was way beyond those of the parish schools their mother made sure they finished. Central High had history, Latin, geometry, algebra, music, and art. Enoch enrolled and took to every aspect of it.

Without a doubt, the best thing about the situation was the friends Enoch made; one in particular was exactly as old as Enoch. His name was John David Rockefeller, and he and Enoch shared the same birthday, July 8, 1839. Both shared that they had fathers who were more of a hindrance than a help to the family, one an alcoholic, the other a grifter. They had a lot of common ground between them. Each displayed a delightful sense of humor in the other's company. They were direct and honest with each other and had dueling wits that made any topic discussed interesting. They were equals in so many ways and aware of the fact.

They bonded in the way they tried to speak Latin to each other. They knew to string a few sentences together for use in public to let their audience know they were in the presence of scholarly men. That they were similar to Romans. They committed many Latin sayings such as: "Sic semper tyrannis" (Thus always to tyrants) and "Aut cum scuto aut in scuto" (Either with shield or on shield) to memory. For the short period, they took the language, they developed quite a vocabulary of nouns and verbs. The language became a humorous code to use with each other, which sometimes led to laughter when corrected by those who knew the language.

Also, along with Crandel Poachfield, John D Rockefeller was the second person on the dock the day Enoch kicked Scot's Blade Billy's ass. Both knew about the dock, but neither talked about it. "J.D." is what Enoch called Rockefeller, "E.M." is what J.D. called Enoch. The way he would say it, though, made it sound like one letter "M." Enoch would ask, in Latin, "Quare una littera?" (Why one letter?), When he gave J.D. two. J.D. would answer, in Latin, "Est multum," (it is a deal). And add for one sound, you get two letters."

John D. Rockefeller eventually became the world's richest man. It happened by accident. No one knows if it would have ever come to pass had it not been for a rope that broke. Had it not been for Enoch Mast and the half a year he and J D Rockefeller spent together in high school.

All recalled by Enoch the day Mary Irene and Brooks Masts were shot, Hardin Lasbrith disappeared, and Horace Lasbrith committed suicide. Enoch too lost in the past to care anything about the present.

CHAPTER VI
WINSLOW HOMER'S GULF STREAM

In the late afternoon, after Alden Sinclair visited the dining hall, Jenny moved to the kitchen. The first phase was completed and, per Hardin Lasbrith's instructions, to be repeated nine more times or until his return, whichever happened first.

Alden Sinclair showed up to remind the staff. He was there and gone in a matter of minutes. He arrived at the hall's entrance and, for a moment, gazed at the staff. He didn't speak until everyone noticed him. When everyone's eyes were on him, in an icy and demanding manner, he told them, "Carry on!" and nothing more. He kept his distance from everyone and waved off those who approached him. He did it to hide his breath and minimize his movements to appear sober.

He was on his way to the wine cellar. His appearance at the entrance to the dining hall at the end of the first phase may have seemed planned, but it wasn't. It happened by luck. Sinclair's appearance was secondary to the actual mission he was on. The primary mission he was on was to get four or five more bottles to replace the ones Olivia Lasbrith, and he had consumed during their late morning and early afternoon activities in her bedroom.

Jenny's move to the kitchen wasn't made without thoroughly observing all in the dining hall and what occupied them. The physical appearance of the dining hall was in a far better state than it was before the decimation. It was pristine. The smudge and cobweb that created Hardin's 'ten phases' was gone. The smudged mirror and all mirrors were cleaned, the giant cobweb removed, and all the paintings wiped down and returned to their original locations.

The issue was the work completed and the work at hand. Hardin's duplicate phases led to chaos. She took advantage of the situation, knowing the remaining phases would be a complete waste of time and effort, an exercise in futility. She doubted the staff had the stamina to surpass five phases, let alone ten. She believed each phase would have its desertions.

Jenny's desertion was difficult. She was captivated by all that was going on. She saw the dining hall become an imaginary country that had lost its way over what to do. A country whose population was caught between, what they were told to do and what they wanted to do. Most wanted to ignore the remaining phases and viewed them as punishment work, not productive work, like the ballroom. However, a considerable portion believed it was in the best interest of all to do as instructed and not question what they were told.

There were those in favor of Hardin's ten phases and those opposed. The dining hall evolved into a place where some sat while others worked. Those who worked called those who sat, "lazy." Those who sat called those who worked "stupid." Neither side could find common ground and the trade-offs needed where all could agree to stay in the dining hall or move on to the ballroom.

No, the nature of all was to quarrel. A compromise was not on the table. Both sides bickered back and forth over the issue and paid more attention to what was said than the chaos it was creating. The bickering was what occupied everyone's thoughts and movements. They were in constant agitation, no different than bees in a hive, when disturbed. Their frustration with one another provided the perfect opportunity to disappear.

*****

If one was to ask all there at the time, "Did Jenny ever leave?" They would all say, "No." Believing, rather than knowing, it would be something she wouldn't do. She played the role of the one everybody least expected to perfection.

She was gifted in the way that all who knew her always saw her in a positive light, yet she did sneak off and do what she wanted on more than one occasion. Her gift was the ability to pull off the unexpected. Her insurance was her personality; the one or two times she got caught, most didn't care or wouldn't believe what was said. Jenny did many things that went unnoticed. Going to the kitchen to cook up some creamed chicken for Enoch Mast would be just one of many.

Her timing couldn't have been better, no one was in the kitchen when she arrived, and no one came in it while she worked. She got a box of matches to light the stove and went to the ice box. The cook always had four chickens in reserve, two dressed and two cooked. On a large counter she took the cooked ones, placed them on a large platter, gathered up a carving knife and fork, and placed them next to the chicken.

A batch of biscuits was quickly mixed up, the oven lit, and they were placed in it for time it took her to cut up three cups of chicken. A match was struck to light the pilot for a front burner on the top part of the stove. A saucepan was placed on it. Over medium heat, some butter was melted in the pan. Flour, broth, and cream were poured in. Garlic powder, salt and pepper added. As Jenny stirred the ingredients, she added the three cups of chicken last.

She stirred till it felt right and became a thick sauce. Some thinly sliced mushrooms and crushed cashews were folded in. All was stirred to where, the meat was hot, the mushrooms cooked, and the crushed cashews hidden in the thick sauce.

The burner was turned off and all the ingredients in the pan waited for a dozen hot biscuits to find their way to a plate and a basket. She rounded up the best China and silverware, linen napkins, serving tray and cover available in the overwhelmed kitchen from the previous day's wedding reception.

Six biscuits were placed in a white cloth napkin and put in a small basket and covered with another white napkin. A small trivet was filled with blackberry jam on one side and a large dab of butter on the other. The remaining six biscuits were put on a large plate and smothered in the sauce from the pan. A napkin was folded and the plate was placed under a silver dome and put on the tray along with the basket of biscuits and trivet of condiments.

The silverware was placed on top of the napkin and the salt and pepper shakers next to the plate. Jenny looked several places for either some ale or wine but the only drink she could find was a small pitcher of cold milk in the icebox. That, and half of a coconut cream pie which could not be overlooked. She put both on the tray along with a large water glass.

All that was placed on the tray was organized more than once to get the absolute perfect appearance for the presentation of the meal. She created a meal for Enoch on the level of what one about to be executed would want as their last supper. On the same level as those condemned get for their journey to heaven or hell.

*****

Before Jenny picked up the tray to make her way to Enoch, she went to the mirror provided for the staff to check their appearance before going out on the floor. She unpinned her hair and let it fall to her shoulders. She bit down on her lips to fill them out and give them color, then unbuttoned the top two buttons of her blouse. She thought of her age and laughed in embarrassment at her arousal. Yet at the same time welcoming the feeling, that had been absent for such a long time, with open arms. She stood for a while in front of the mirror, not looking at herself as much as picturing in her mind the perfect evening with Enoch.

*****

Enoch at the same moment, pushed the wood chips from the sill and watched them float to the ground. He decided to fold his knife, put it in his pocket and, for a while, rest his eyes.

He didn't want to close them, he wanted to turn down the intense focus they had been in for most of the afternoon. After the knife was put away to assure a period of rest, he lit a cigar, found his way to the overstuffed chair sat down and could not take his eyes off the sky. A sky that was transitioning from late afternoon to early evening.

A sky filled with the softest clouds whose shapes led to pleasant, imagined images. Which would tail off into a pallet of blue, red, orange, and pink. Shades are eventually overtaken by a dark blue background that patiently waits to show off the silver stars of its constellations.

Enoch and Jenny's second meeting in the ballroom wasn't anything like the first. There was a significant difference between cake and coffee, chicken, and biscuits. The difference was measured in the hours consumed between the two events. With a desire to meet again that increased with every hour that passed. The intensity of the second meeting was greater than the first. The anticipation for Jenny and Enoch was almost unbearable.

In their second meeting, Jenny anticipated Enoch would be where she left him. When she entered the ballroom that was not the case. She walked unnoticed to where they first met. Stopped, held the tray steady and began her search of the cleared and uncleared tables with the same intensity a sailor in the crow's nest has for one who went overboard.

In the fading light of the day, it took over a minute to find Enoch. A short amount of time, in most cases, that magically turns into an eternity when one isn't where expected and a search is required to find them.

It was the overstuffed chair between two tables that broke the pattern of tables surrounded by chairs. The break gave Enoch's position away by the window. It was the only furniture out of sequence and was hardly noticeable by the wall.

When she found Enoch, she saw how locked in on the clouds he was and was able to come upon him and place the tray on a table next to him completely unnoticed. It pleased her to pleasantly startle Enoch as if she appeared out of thin air. Her actual arrival better than what she had pictured.

Jenny quickly took the lid from the plate and let the heat escape along with the aroma. Put the plate, silverware, and napkins in front of Enoch and began to organize the condiments on the table for his convenience. Her actions left him speechless for some time. All he could do was keep his eyes on her in amazement wondering if she would disappear as fast as she had appeared.

When he finally concluded she wasn't a vision and looked down on what she had put before him, it took quite a few moments, for him to look up again. When he did, she was still there and all he could do was ask himself, "How'd she know?" He moved from pleasantly startled, to pleasantly puzzled. It was turning out to be remarkably similar to a summer night at the Osstill's. The long-lost wonderful feelings of those distant nights familiar again.

*****

As Enoch gathered his composure, he spotted on a far-off table near the stage a candle-labra that held five candles. He smiled at Jenny and without a word, got up, and headed for the candle labra.

He needed some time to think. As he walked, he thought about all the short conversations he and Jenny had when he worked on the ballroom. They were always about how the day was spent and the characters that filled it, like Sir Karl, Sinclair, Horace and other family members and household staff.

Finally, the time had come where the conversation would go beyond the activities and characters of the day into the activities and characters that filled their lives. What would he say? Jenny watched him as he walked down and back and had the same thoughts.

He put the candle labra on the table and the matches by it so he wouldn't have to search for them later. he thought it was a nice romantic touch, for when they ran out of day light. If the conversation ended before dark, he would use it for when he'd go back to work on the carving. He grabbed a chair, placed it behind Jenny and helped her to take a seat at the table.

At first all they could do was speak to each other with their smiles. Enoch began to eat, and Jenny found a saucer, placed a biscuit on it, tore it in two, spooned the blackberry jam on the parts and began to eat. They would eat, then gaze at one another and return to their plates, after a time they began to eat more and gaze less.

They didn't speak till Enoch was past his fourth biscuit and on his second glass of milk. Jenny drank from Enoch's glass as well and was past her second biscuit and thinking of another before any words were said. Enoch caught her gaze at the biscuits and spoke first. In a worried voice he asked her, "You're not thinking of another biscuit – are you?"

It caught Jenny off guard, it surprised her. She anticipated an inquiry of a far more romantic nature not one about a biscuit. As she thought about it, she began to laugh. It was the nature of the question that made her laugh, it was just unforeseen, that was what amused her. She wanted to answer with a sarcastic laugh, but the laugh she gave turned out to be more genuine than she intended.

They tested each other's wit. They delved into the math of the meal, Jenny's two biscuits with blackberry jelly as a ratio to Enoch's four biscuits with creamed chicken. She was quick to point out to him he'd consumed twice her amount in half the time.

Enoch didn't know if she was right, for a moment he questioned it in his mind, but didn't want to do the math. From experience, having lived with a woman over three decades, he was aware they were the ones who were right more times than they were wrong when it came to this type of reckoning. His reply to her finding was "It comes as no surprise to me that in a short period of time I accomplish more, I've always strived to be efficient in all that I do."

Enoch moved on and stated his brother and sons were out west to start a conversation. Jenny ignored the information and stayed with his last comment on efficiency and answered "I would hope not in all undertakings. There are some efforts whose good outcomes depend on one's endurance, not their efficiency, in fact there are undertakings where efficiency is not what the situation calls for."

Her reply stunned Enoch and left him speechless for a few moments and then brought on the first aloud laughs of the evening, which would be followed by many more. It came from Enoch who was more than willing to pounce on the topic of 'endurance and efficiency.' He knew what she was really saying. He was prepared to go all the way and tell her he had the most "efficient endurance" on the planet.

However, before he could get the concept out, Jenny switched gears on him and in all the beauty sincerity can bring out of a person, looked deep into Enoch's eyes, and made a plea. "Tell me everything about you Enoch Mast - everything!"

Of all the people in his life who'd made the same request, Jenny would be the one to know the most. Others only have part of the story. Enoch was quick to make terms with her, he'd acknowledge her request if she would do the same. Terms were quickly agreed to and Enoch went first.

*****

He began after all the biscuits, on his plate and in the basket, along with all that covered them, were gone, along with the pitcher of milk and the coconut cream pie. After he took the empty plates, basket, napkins, and silverware from the table and placed them on the tray. The tray taken to a far-off uncleared table to become part of the future clean up.

The odor of the leftover food had increased to where the windows by the overstuffed chair needed to be opened. To help hold off the growing smell which would eventually overtake the room regardless of the open windows.

Next came the necessary preparations to take his place in the overstuffed chair by the window. He placed the candle labra on the window sill for when he would return to his carving. He lit a cigar, sat down, and let the fine meal settle in. Just as the feeling he was after came upon him the momentary rest ended as fast as it began. It came to him almost immediately after he sat down. That he wasn't the only one in the room and he couldn't leave Jenny at the table while he lounged in such a chair.

He got up as fast as he sat down and went in search of and found another overstuffed chair and wrestled it next to his. This act of equality did not go unnoticed by Jenny, and she smiled as she settled in as close to Enoch as she could, with her right arm touching his left arm and her hand searching for him on the arm rests of the two chairs. As they held hands Enoch exhaled a cloud of smoke and behind the cloud came the words Jenny wanted to hear.

His story had an unusual prologue as the thought of the morning and Sinclair's warning, "Ego te interficiam," for some reason came back to him in the form of a premonition. He immediately told Jenny, "Before I forget," and invited her to a window to show her what he was talking about, "See that 1912 Ford Runabout, it's mine, anything ever happens to me, it goes to Jessie O'Dell's widow and children, you're the only one to know, so don't forget." Jenny responded with a confused look as she nodded in agreement.

With the prologue out of the way Enoch began, "My mother's name was Eve, my father's Uriah.", He admitted he never knew his mother's heritage, but his fathers were Russian, and the family last name was actually Mastinoff. His father began to use 'Mast' for two reasons, it was one syllable and sounded German. He felt it to be a more acceptable name in that there were far more Germans than Russians in Cleveland.

Enoch told Jenny he was the oldest of three. He had twin brothers, Ezra and Enos, who were a year behind him. That at first, they grew up poor, his father was a teamster and cared for his wagons and animals more than his children. He pointed out if given the choice, when there was little or no money, his father would have fed the animals before Enoch and his brothers, had it not been for their mother.

Not only did his mother make sure all were fed, she also made sure all were educated in the parish schools and that they could read and write before their father put them on the wagons at age ten. At night when Uriah was either asleep or gone, she read Bible verses to Enoch and his brothers and through her efforts her sons learned both compassion and endurance.

Enoch told Jenny he and his brothers were diligent students and that he had also gone to high school for half a year. His brothers and he could all read and write by ten, the only one who couldn't read and write in their family was their father.

He pointed out to her, nothing irritated their father more than to see them read or write. He was always at a lower level than his wife and kids and because of this took to drink instead of bettering himself. It turned out they didn't hide alcohol from him they hid books, the ones they owned and the ones they had borrowed. The few times one was caught by him with a book or paper and pencil, they were beat and the book destroyed, the pencil broke and the paper torn up. They never hid the whiskey, always hoped he'd drink till he'd pass out for hours or disappear for days.

Enoch put his cigar out, reached for another one to hold in reserve knowing he would need plenty of them if he was to continue. "We started to make enough money to have a decent life when we got our father out of the business." He went into the unconventional way his brothers and he did this by encouraging their father's alcoholism. He talked of the Osstill's and how he met Irene at the back steps of the Osstill mansion. How she became his wife of thirty-four years.

How they were married when he was seventeen and she sixteen. How they moved in with Enoch's family eight months prior to the birth of their twin sons Seth and Simon. He also told Jenny of his daughter, Mary Irene, who was born in 1875 a year before his sons left home. She was robbed of a normal life by an infection that brought on an extremely high fever when she was an infant.

Enoch didn't leave Evelyn and Momford Turner and their son Brooks out. At that point Jenny asked how it was Brooks had the family's last name? Enoch went into a detailed history of how that came about. Every word told her about the life and times of Enoch Mast after the introduction of Brooks Mast captivated her. To where she became pleasantly paralyzed and could neither speak nor move, only listen.

*****

Enoch continued, "The first year I was out on the wagons, I heard talk and even read some of the *Compromise of 1850*. They made it sound like it was one grand compromise that would handle everything, when it turned out to be several compromises that handled nothing. At the age of eleven I was even able to figure this out. It never resolved the issue of free and slave states coming into the Union, it just kicked the problem down the road. To where, ten years later, at twenty-one, it's clear we're out of compromises and are left with conflict. April, twelfth, 1861, Fort Sumpter, in Charleston harbor, South Carolina, fired on to signal everyone was done talking."

April of that year brought on the terrifying tumult. It swept uncontrollably over the nation with an underestimated fury. Enoch's expression turned sober when he told Jenny, "You were one year old when it took place."

This was Enoch's subtle way to remind Jenny of their age difference. His way to drive home the irony he found in the fact they shared the same war in separate ways. How she was fortunate to have lived through the war and have no real recollection of it, other than what she was told. Enoch could only wish for such a case; all his recollections were very real and unforgettable. When it came to the war, memories were all he had. It was different for her, all she had was the history. The Civil War was not a shared experience for them. Enoch had deep feelings for Jenny but felt to be fair she always had to be made aware of the one big gap between them and the war was the perfect example.

The age difference was completely ignored by Jenny. It didn't matter to her. Normally she would have debated its importance but she was more interested in the impact the Civil War had on him. She wanted to hear how he got caught up in it. Jenny wanted to gain further insight on the troubles he had seen and how they shaped his character.

Each told Jenny "To me and many others, it came down to two issues: the first, was whether one man could own another, and I believe now as I did then, if he could – he shouldn't. Second, citizenship only belongs to those born here. At the time our democracy wanted to change from being 'for all' to being 'for some.' I didn't like the idea."

Enoch explained, "Around twenty I began to question the direction some wanted to take as to who was, and who wasn't, entitled to the rights of human dignity. There were many who thought only 'some,' to be the answer and just as many, if not more, who thought the answer was 'all.' To me, one was right and one was wrong, it wasn't hard for me to pick a side."

He continued with what he believed to be good examples of what he was talking about, "There was Harriett Beecher Stowe's portrayal of the evils of slavery in *Uncle Tom's Cabin* to read about and each year as the literacy rate increased its impact was felt by more and more people."

Enoch gently ran his hand through his white hair and went on "There were those who followed the likes of former president Millard Fillmore and his *Know Nothing Party.* It was made up of people who demanded no more German and Irish Catholics be let in. Party members were no stranger to violence when they came across these immigrants in places, they thought they didn't belong. What was read about and talked about at the time whipped everyone into a frenzy."

*****

He paused for a moment, gazed out the window and then lit the cigar he had held in reserve. Poured some wine for himself after Jenny smiled as she declined by placing a hand over the brim of the goblet, he had brought her. Both sat in silence for a few moments and enjoyed the soft warm breeze that came from the open windows.

What Enoch said next was out of context or took the subject at hand in a different direction. At first it seemed so totally unrelated, but in the end fit perfectly with what he wanted to express about the war Jenny was born into and he survived.

To see and understand the impact it had on him required a painting he once viewed. Its composition of the images it used from that point on never left him. He softly whispered to Jenny as one does when telling a secret "I'm going to tell you about three things: 1899, desolation, and a place everyone has been."

He began to tell Jenny about an artist who exhibited a painting in 1899. The artist's name was Winslow Homer, the painting was called *The Gulf Stream*. It was never privately owned. It always belonged to the public.

Enoch explained how this came to be. How fifteen years ago he was in Pittsburgh, had some free time and went to the Carnegie Institute, where it was first shown. Its price was four-thousand dollars. Enoch told Jenny for most it would take a full year's salary for at least the next four years to own the painting. He then told Jenny, "Know what? It should be four thousand times a year's salary. Even that wouldn't be enough, it's priceless."

Enoch continued "It did sell but it didn't sell right away. It was sold in 1906, after it left the Carnegie Institute and was on exhibit at the National Academy of Design, where it was introduced to the Metropolitan Museum of Art. The work made enough of an impression on the museum that they purchased it.

They had to have seen it as too important a work to be in a private collection where some had the privilege to view it. To avoid this, they made the purchase. The painting went from institute, to academy, to museum for a reason and that reason was the work was on a level that had to be open to all not some."

Enoch then footnoted all he said with an afterthought of appreciation. "When you think about it, it's the public schools, public libraries, public museums that make us what we are which makes us great. The painting never belonged to a private soul; it always belongs to us."

Enoch took a moment to gather his breath and then continued. "Reviews appeared in the major newspapers and they were mixed. Some believed it belonged in the Metropolitan, others that it belonged in the trash. Most referred to it as Winslow Homer's *The Gulf Stream*, but there were some who referred to it as Winslow Homer's *Smiling Sharks*. To me the work is a masterpiece, it comes back to my mind often, I see it all the time."

Jenny was overwhelmed with the impression the painting had on Enoch. She could no longer hold back and blurted out in a voice heard more as a command than a request. "Describe it to me!" It stopped Enoch in his tracks and got his attention. She did this on the chance she might know the painting, the thought excited her. Enoch relit his cigar, smiled, to ensure that her request was not taken the wrong way, nodded, and pleasantly whispered "Sure."

He told her it was a large painting; he knew it to be thirty-eight by forty-two inches. Its dimensions burned into his memory like an address he didn't want to forget. He told her that Homer used a full pallet with shades of blue, brown, yellow, grey, white, and black to create a scene of desolation. The subject is a Negro centered in a triangle of grief sorrow and woe.

The man is on a rudderless fishing boat with a broken mast in rough seas. The first point of the triangle is to his left on the far-off horizon. There is the image of the ship that could save him sailing away from him. The second point is on his right, where off in the distance a huge waterspout has formed, it moves towards him. The third point is made up of the crippled boat and menacing sharks gathered around the boat adrift in rough seas. The sharks are aware it's not 'if' but 'when' something drastic will happen, the boat will sink, or the storm will hit. Either way they intend to be the beneficiaries.

Enoch gave a synopsis "There the Negro sits between all three: the ship that isn't coming, the impending violent storm and the waiting sharks." Enoch ended "The painting is the perfect illustration of the hopeless situation and the desolation that will follow. At one time or another we have all been on Winslow Homer's boat."

He stared at the curling smoke that came from the cigar at rest in the ashtray. Like a lawyer addressing a jury in a court room, told Jenny, "The boat sailing away – that's the government - it provides the grief. The storm is the war governments are known to start - it provides the sorrow. And the sharks are those who take advantage of what grief and sorrow gives them – they provide the woe."

He then let Jenny know, "Thirty-five years after the fact I find the Civil War in this picture and understand I was once like the man on the boat. Only I survived and always wonder if he will. The canvas I found myself on always changed – the canvas he finds himself on never changes – he's always in danger. It's hard to explain, seems I can only talk about it, not to where you understand it, but, to where I understand it."

＊＊＊＊＊

What Enoch told Jenny filled her mind to capacity. His personal history was told effortlessly, and it all fell into place. It was unembellished and easy to follow. She was spellbound by the sequence of events that made up his life and formed his character.

Enoch got up from the overstuffed chair and stretched. He took a chair and moved it, so its back was as close to Jenny as possible. He sat backwards in the chair, using it more as a stool, resting his arms on top of the chair's back. He gazed out into his ballroom as it began to fill with the shadows of the day's end.

He gazed at Jenny, smiled, and then returned to the openness of his ballroom with its sea of cleared and unclear tables. The gaze was replaced by a focused look. He began to search for the features of the room that borrowed the best of his past works. The ballroom was a direct reflection of everything good he had done over his forty-year career, and it pleased him.

Enoch began in a soft but firm voice, "It was every bit of two years after Brooks was taken that I had a wife and two kids. It happened that fast. My mother took to Irene the same way she took to Evelynn." Jenny asked "Evelyn?" and Enoch explained. He then continued about the changes, "My father didn't come home one night, or any day or night thereafter."

Enoch' cigar had gone out and he relit it, then continued, "It was as if a great weight had been lifted off the family. Fate brought on his departure to make room for grandchildren. One night when I was twenty, my mother read to Seth and Simon, had them giggling before sleep overtook them, and then kissed them goodnight. She turned and gazed at the fireplace and used its glow to give Irene as pleasant a smile as one can give and then fell dead in front of us all. It couldn't have been more unexpected, and it happened in the blink of an eye. Told it to Ezra and Enos same as I'm telling you – it took a toll on them, part of them died with her."

"The boys were five when they fired on Fort Sumpter, just as we were getting over our loss and settled into accepting a life without her – it changed everything. Two years later I wasn't home when they turned seven. I was at Gettysburg. Back then one could make all the plans they wanted, and none would work out. The times wouldn't allow it. One could only react to what was in front of them and hope for the best."

Enoch put the cigar in the ashtray and told Jenny "Ezra and Eli went in 1861, they weren't about to miss any of it, no wife and kids to hold them down. They had no problem deserting me." Enoch explained, as soon as he heard the news about Fort Sumpter, he knew what would happen next and his brothers didn't disappoint him.

He felt they deserted him but that was not the real issue, the real issue was his jealousy of both getting to go where he couldn't. Eventually that would change. But it took a while. The 'change,' was the direct result of bad luck and desperate times which would eventually evolve into good luck and better times.

Their departure translated into fewer jobs and lighter loads. Unless he hired replacements, which he did soon after his brothers left for the Ohio 29th Volunteer Infantry. It was the first time the business had employees and they seemed to work out for a while until he sent them to Cincinnati, with four Belgian draft horses and a solid heavy-duty prairie schooner to pick up over a ton of wool blankets. Enoch never knew if they fell victim to highway men or made off with his property and into business for themselves. All he knew was he never saw the horses, wagon, or them again.

During the two years that followed, Ezra and Eli's departure, the family went from a comfortable living to one of a hand to mouth existence. Made worse by a lightning strike that hit the barn, they didn't lose any animals or equipment, but they did lose a fair portion of the barn. Enoch rationalized the unfortunate events of the wagon and then the barn to Irene. He told her it was just as well, they no longer had room in the barn for what they lost in Cincinnati. That in the end everything has a way of balancing out for some strange reason to an unexpected and undesired outcome.

The autumn of 1862 and winter of 1863 the war was hard on the Mast family. What had been rumored all winter came to be fact in March of 1863. The war was at the stage where there would be a draft. Whereas the South had to draft each year of the war, this would be the first in the North and it was very unpopular.

Even having a wife and kids wasn't enough. Those Enoch's age became prime candidates. As the Enrollment Act date neared his status was always in the back of his mind. He wasn't alone in his concerns, his old high school friend JD was in the same boat and shared the same status, but felt his situation was far more severe than Enoch's.

*****

"As fate would have it," Enoch began to explain how he was once lost, in more ways than one, on a street corner in downtown Cleveland and how destiny arrived to guide him out.

A corner, whose intersecting street names, he, and an old friend, who met there, could never remember. The only way they knew the location was by the landmarks that surrounded it and as they disappeared over time the location became more remote. They gave the place the fictitious name of 'Mast and Rockefeller,' whenever they talked about the deal, they made on the corner there.

At the time all they knew; it took place on one of those psychotic late March days in Ohio where one day is sunny and mild and the next day Antarctic in its severity. The March day they met in 1863 the weather, unlike the previous day, was as raw, gray, wet and unforgiving as Ohio, can at times, conjure up. A day not fit for man or beast, yet there they were in these harsh elements, one coming from the docks, the other going to them.

Slush on the road made it hard to handle the team, the wagon, and the cargo of household goods. Enoch was headed for the docks where a ship, named the Acropolis, was being loaded with cargo going to Buffalo, New York. The loading and unloading of the cargo he took to the ship was a back breaking one-man job as miserable as the weather, that paid next to nothing.

Enoch thought of his father and for a moment experienced a rare sympathetic feeling for him. Here he was in the same vicious cycle his father had known extremely well. For the first time ever Enoch wrestled with the age old problem of how to decide who got fed with what little he made, the family or the animals? He began to wonder how long he could continue like this.

He had stopped at the corner to get his bearings. Upon leaving the address where he picked up the household goods, he believed he knew a short cut to the lake, which only proved that he didn't. He sat silent on the wagon and had to accept the fact he was, in fact, lost and his anger grew. He couldn't recall the last time he had been lost as he began to vehemently swear under his breath.

Upset with himself and everyone around him on the busy corner, Enoch barked at the first pedestrian he saw for directions, which turned out to be J D Rockefeller. Who had come out of a nearby bank, where he had just closed on a dockside warehouse.

J.D. the one he shared a birthday with, the one who had the same type of father, the one he went to public high school with and the one who became a good friend. The years that had passed since they last saw each other played no part in their recognition of each other, which was the moment their eyes met.

The event of their meeting stunned both in the most pleasant way. In no time at all J.D. climbed onto the wagon, took a seat on the bench, nudged Enoch. Enoch asked with a smile, "Quare una littera," J.D. laughed out loud and replied "Est multum." Enoch grinned as he told J.D. his situation, how he was headed for the docks but was "Perdita." It was beyond J.D.'s Latin but he guessed 'lost' and was right. He told Enoch he knew the way.

As he guided Enoch towards the lake the two caught up on old times and then went into what the future might hold. They stopped at a tavern and ate lunch and by the time they got back on the wagon had made a deal with each other to secure their futures.

A deal Irene, when she heard it, upset her as never before to where she refused to believe Enoch would make such a deal. Why? She would ask repeatedly. Each time he would painfully try to explain that led to a fight and then silence. It went on this way for some time and tested both severely. He told Irene he made the deal and there was no changing it.

During lunch JD told Enoch, due to his father's behavior, he was the head of his family. He was the soul support for his mother and siblings. Enoch had no trouble relating to this. JD went on to say that he had started a business down in "The Flats" that was at the dawn of becoming a remarkably successful enterprise. He explained how the war had shut down the Mississippi and the volume of goods that was once on the river went to the ports on the Great Lakes, like Cleveland.

JD cut through the chase and told Enoch he feared the draft and couldn't take three hundred dollars out of the business, that like a newborn it was fragile and still had to be nursed. At that time making such a move would cause him to lose the business and put his family in poverty. On top of this JD was moving from dealing in foodstuffs into oil refining and was on the verge of finding a way to replace expensive whale oil with kerosene, a cheaper general-purpose lighting fuel for the masses.

Since he couldn't risk the cash, the only other alternative to avoiding the draft was to find a substitute. Enoch agreed, the whole time as he ate, he nodded his head and added a footnote to their conversation about the draft. He mentioned having a wife and kids and that he too shared JD's concerns about the draft. He had no idea he was the target of a request about to be made of him.

Had it been any other day of that year the odds of Enoch making such a deal wouldn't even have been possible. JD was fortunate to run into Enoch when he did. He caught Enoch at just the right time in his life where he could no longer endure it if it didn't change. He was willing to gamble on anything that would change it. Why not take any deal offered? He was soon to be drafted anyway, why not make the situation work for one? In return for Enoch taking JD's place in the Union Army, JD would watch over Enoch's family and secure a clear deed in the family name to a property as Large or larger than Enoch's current property.

It was a groceries and property deal that went to Enoch's family whether, or not, he returned from the war. It was the best insurance Enoch could provide before life insurance was even invented at the end of the Civil War. The deal was closed with nothing more than a handshake.

Despite Irene's rage when she heard it, no one could have known how good a deal it would turn out to be. She had no idea, nor did anyone else, that Enoch had made a deal with the future world's richest man. By the end of 1865 JD Rockefeller was at the helm of what would become an oil-fueled economy and every term of their agreement was met.

In the end the risk Enoch took paid off as well. The family was deeded a grander house with indoor water and a large kitchen and separate bedrooms. Outside a stable flanked one side of the house with a combination forge and workshop flanking the other side, between these two outbuildings was a courtyard. The property was just on the outskirts of Cleveland and had an unobstructed view of the lake. Both Enoch and Irene appreciated the property, but never discussed how it came about. One saw it as the shrewdest decision they ever made, the other saw it as a reckless move that could've cost them everything and neither ever budged from their position.

Enoch, JD, and Irene were the only souls on earth who knew of the deal. Enoch took JD's place and records show JD made a legitimate substitution. What isn't known is who that substitute was, the records that showed who it was, were either lost, or incorrect at their inception. The date of birth each shared played a part, in that it was treated as a clerical mistake. The deeper one got into the records to find and correct the mistake, the more the trail grew cold and unable to follow, even to this day.

It wasn't too long after the war that JD became the world's richest man. Eventually people became curious as to who took his place in the war and asked a lot of questions when the records couldn't satisfy their thirst. Interest in the topic would sink and then surface over time in the public conscience.

Enoch kept his silence on the matter and never came forward, neither did JD and the two kept it a mystery their whole lives, not that they had anything to hide but for the sheer reason they could keep it this way, that they had the answer everyone wanted, and they weren't sharing it. That it was Enoch Mast who took John D. Rockefeller's place in the Civil War. It made the bond between the two unbreakable that they were the only two on the planet that knew.

The few times they discussed their reunion on that March day, JD would say it happened for a reason, whereas Enoch would tell him it was a random event that worked out well, nothing more, nothing less. The two enjoyed debating the issue, neither accepted the other's view and each could present a compelling case for their position.

From 1889 to 1914, the twenty-five years between them, only two knew who took J D Rockefeller's place in the Civil War. There was a time when three knew but it became just Enoch and JD when Irene died May thirty-first, 1889.

*****

During the hours Jenny spent in the ballroom with Enoch, the trinity of knowledge was reformed, and she replaced Irene and became the third person alive and fourth person in total to ever know the secret. She along with the other two knew all about the deal that had its origin at the fictitious corner of Mast and Rockefeller in Cleveland, Ohio along with all the details and as a result was sworn to secrecy by Enoch.

She swore to keep the secret and thought Enoch was like her husband Amos and she was like Irene. The only difference was Enoch gambled and won whereas Amos gambled and lost. Both she and Irene shared the agony their husbands put them through, which, in turn, made Irene like a sister to Jenny.

*****

Jenny was overwhelmed by her newfound knowledge and with it came an intuitive understanding of Enoch. When she asked, "What happened after you took JD's place?" She understood Enoch when he answered, "I became the man on the boat." She knew exactly what he meant, whereas others would have no idea of how his answer fit the question.

He went on to tell her how he became one of the "Roosters" in the Ohio 7th Infantry in the middle of April 1863. Jenny could not help herself and remarked "I can see you as a rooster." Enoch completely missed what she meant, gave her a strange look, and went on how he had missed Chancellorsville, but not Gettysburg. He went on to explain that up till the beginning of July all he recalled were long marches, sleeping in tents, the smell of canvas, eating hardtack and grease but most of all finding the time to write Irene.

Everything he did was focused on writing to her day in and day out. It was not good when he left, her tears were one of anger not sadness. Writing and mailing letters consumed Enoch. Everything else was no different than sleepwalking, which ended on the first day of July. Everything changed when that month began.

During the time up to July he told Jenny how he became friends with the most unforgettable character he had ever known. His name was Royal Marsden, and he wanted to be known as 'Roy'. He would state his name when introduced as Royal' Roy' Marsden with the emphasis on 'Roy' but it seemed to roll off the tongue in such a way that everyone took to calling him 'Royal Roy Marsden,' in one quick pleasant breath, instead of just 'Roy' as he had wished.

He was misunderstood like this a lot. Because of the way he could put things he became one who some thought was a genius, while others thought he was an idiot. The only agreement all could come to was that, if anything, he was always controversial.

Enoch told Jenny he'd sat by many a campfire with Royal Roy Marsden and was mystified by the man. In confidence, and only with Enoch, Royal Roy Marsden would joke about being killed in April at Chancellorsville and they didn't get him off the rolls. His death was being held up by paperwork and he'd have to keep fighting till they cleared him on the records. He was hoping to get killed, again, at Gettysburg so he could move on.

Three things that stuck with Enoch were first, Royal Roy Marsden's theory about dying in your sleep, second his theory about the relatives who attend a funeral. The third and final - the incident in the cemetery.

Once the subject of dying in one's sleep came up and most by the fire agreed it was the best way to go, except Royal Roy Marsden. His reply to everyone was, "Are you kidding me? That's when you hit the ground and feel the pain of every bone in your body exploding. That's what happens right before you die. There's nothing good about it."

He then pointed out how everyone there who had dreamt they were falling woke up before they hit the ground. Most there had experienced what he was talking about. He went on, "Those who died in their sleep will tell you what I'm telling you." When he finished there were few questions, but plenty of conversation about how this might be true even though there was no way to prove it.

*****

"It went on like this every night. Royal Roy Marsden would throw out more things to consider for those gathered around the fire. There was the time he went on to point out when at the funeral of a relative, one who would require the whole clan to show up, the relative, who no one knows, but can talk the whole family history top to bottom to anyone in the room, is the person in the coffin.

"There were those by the fire who knew exactly what he was talking about and were startled by the realization this had happened to them," Enoch exclaimed.

Enoch wasn't aware; he whispered, "There was an incident in the cemetery." Jenny couldn't make out what he said and asked him to repeat it. He did and continued in a stronger voice. He told her during the march to Gettysburg the "Roosters" stopped in the late afternoon of the last day of June to make camp. The camp was close to a church graveyard. After they were settled in Royal Roy Marsden was the first to visit it and had talked Enoch into going with him.

While there Royal Roy Marsden explained to Enoch the importance of getting on good footing with those below the ground. He told Enoch, "In the next dimension cemeteries become towns that don't have graves, funerals, churches, hospitals or orphans, and a lot of other things we have here. The lost at sea and those on land try to make their way back to cemeteries to get their bearings. All the lost have at least one person they know buried in a graveyard; most know where. They're all just trying to get back to town." He went on "It's no different than here. Everyone is always looking for someone, only in the next dimension you have forever to find them."

Just as further discussion was unfolding on the concept of cemeteries turning into cities and towns in another dimension, a comrade, neither liked, who had followed them, interrupted them with a harsh intimidating voice. "Royal Roy Marsden – let's have a chaw! What you say! Get that tobacco over here, now! You hear!" It wasn't a request it was an order.

It was extortion, Enoch was surprised that Royal Roy Marsden, who was a fair-sized muscular man, with dark piercing eyes and thick beard, tossed the chew at the feet of the extortionist, some fifteen feet away without saying a word. At the time Enoch thought it certainly wouldn't be the way he would've handled it. He would have made the man come to him and as soon as he put the chaw in his mouth, he would've blasted him in the hope, he'd swallow the tobacco a long with some teeth and blood.

However, the ultimate surprise came when the largest copperhead in the state of Pennsylvania came from behind a headstone and latched onto the extortionist's forearm when he went to pick up the tobacco and wouldn't let go. The victim violently flailed his arms until the snake went one way and another and ran down the road.

It was as if Royal Roy Marsden and the snake were in league with one another. The snake struck fast and hard and disappeared as fast as it had appeared. The incident had Enoch wondering if he imagined what he saw and if Royal Roy Marsden was behind the whole incident and became the snake.

Their comrade ran as fast as he could from the cemetery, pumping venom throughout his body. On the way back to camp and some distance down the road they found where he had collapsed. Enoch realized he hadn't imagined any of it. Royal Roy Marsden told Enoch, "Now we don't have to worry about him anymore and he doesn't have to worry about Gettysburg. We have to remember to tell the captain he's dead." Enoch was numb and stared at the body, his only reply was a nod.

Enoch asked Jenny to pass him the apple from the fruit bowl beside her. When he had it in hand he took as big a bite as he could and chewed on it for some time as July first, 1863, came back to him. After a hard swallow Enoch began, "We got to Gettysburg late in the afternoon of the first day of July and made camp by a place called Little Round Top. Next day, July second, we were sent to a place called Culp's hill. We were sent to help build breast works, we chopped down trees, gathered dirt and rocks and made walls."

From there Enoch explained how they were sent later in the day to support the Union left but got lost on the Baltimore Pike and returned to Culp's Hill where they again spent the night. The next day, July third, Enoch Mast, the Ohio 7th Infantry, and the Army of the Potomac came into hostile contact with the Southern invaders from the 4th Virginia Infantry along with the Stonewall Brigade of the Confederate Army of Virginia. Neither army would ever forget Culp's Hill.

Enoch looked hard at Jenny, then glanced away at the sea of tables as if they were a vanquished army, the cleared tables were the dead, the uncleared the survivors. He then gave a primal shout, "At the end of the day the 7th held that hill - by God!" Jenny felt his intensity and was aware the "By God!" was not directed at her but the entire world.

He then began to solemnly reflect, "I'd been in some fierce street fights and some ferocious brawls, I thought I knew everything about fighting since I was ten, Culp's hill showed me I knew nothing. I killed a lot of men that day and found it's not a real fight until you start begging for God's mercy for what might happen to you and for what you have done to others."

CHAPTER VII
THE ROOSTERS

Enoch went on to let Jenny know he couldn't recall the exact part of the day, if it was early morning or late afternoon that Royal Roy Marsden was killed. All he could recall for certain was the heat, by the time they heard Pickett's Charge off in the distance the temperature was close to ninety degrees. He told her he had rammed a ball home in his rifle, and as he got up to fire, out of nowhere Royal Roy Marsden took the opportunity to jump in front of him and took a volley of four rounds to the chest. The realization of who the four rounds were headed straight for startled Enoch. What took place July third, !863, never left Enoch.

Enoch told Jenny, "Don't know about Chancellorsville - but I do know about Gettysburg." He went on to tell her he heard the rounds sink deep into Royal Roy Marsden's chest and saw the blood that shot out from their impact,

He told her, four, fifty-eight caliber, rounds thrust Royal Roy Marsden backwards and into him with such force he stumbled over a fallen companion. It was a bad fall; his upper right leg came down on a small stump created the previous day. All the dead weight of Royal Roy Marsden came down on the leg and snapped Enoch's right femur in two.

"I'll tell you, it was the type of fall that had one calamity after another, not only did I break my upper right leg, a bayonet impaled my left hand." Enoch went on to explain that during the fall, he whipped his left arm around so fast, to help break the fall, to where it found the bayonet on a dead soldier's rifle. The rifle had fallen on a log and laid at an angle where the end with the bayonet was close to a foot off the ground.

It went right through his hand. Every bit of the bayonet, up to the hilt, went through his hand and stuck no different than a spike driven into a wet board. It was pierced to where, when the time came, it was first hard to get the bayonet off the rifle and second, once free of the weapon, required a surgeon to remove it from the hand.

Enoch admitted he passed out from his injuries. He let Jenny know it only happened once in his life and it happened at Gettysburg and it never happened again. Enoch was always very sensitive about the only time he was unconscious. He always told it this way to the few who knew, and Jenny would hear it no different. The emphasis was always on the fact it only happened once.

Among the very few who knew, there were some who had their doubts. They all knew Enoch was no stranger to violence. He led the type of life where, at times, one would think total loss of consciousness would have occurred more than just once. However, skepticism of these doubts took root in the fact no one ever saw a case where it happened to him, whereas they had seen it numerous times with those who stepped over Enoch's line.

Just when Jenny believed she had heard all he could recall about Gettysburg, Enoch told her about one more incident. The last event he told her; left Jenny speechless for quite some time. It left her with so many questions she knew would go unanswered. There would never be enough time to ask them, let alone answer them. The last event was on a level of astonishment she had never experienced before. It was on a level almost beyond her comprehension.

*****

Enoch started out by asking her a question, "Know who I saw at Gettysburg?" And then answered his own question as fast as he had asked it, "Alden Sinclair for the first time. Saw him soon after they set my leg and sewed up my hand. When they put the wounded that couldn't walk on a wagon to get us home. Saw him in the field across from us, plain as day."

"He was guarding prisoners. Saw him walk up on one from behind and slit his throat ear to ear with a straight razor. For what appeared to me no apparent reason. Its troubled me over the years. There were people all around him and no one seemed to notice or care. It was as if I was the only one who saw. I saw him and he saw me and smiled. This is how we know each other. There are times I want to think I imagined it – but I know I didn't."

*****

For the first time Jenny felt the exhaustion brought on by her original request. To know everything about Enoch Mast's life one had to cross some rough terrain. To take the journey would leave one short of breath. The more he spoke the more she wondered why fate put her between Enoch Mast and Alden Sinclair and what she came to realize was fate had no answer. The exhaustion brought on her silence which allowed Enoch to go on and on.

No one would be capable of understanding all Enoch said. The parts she did catch explained the ugly manner the two men could display toward each other. Both she and the staff, at one time or another, experienced the unbelievable different people Alton Sinclair and Enoch Mast became in each other's company. Menacing, threatening and explosive, neither afraid of the other. It explained why it always felt it was just a matter of time before the lid would blow off and the outcome brutally messy for one or the other. At times the two could take tension to a whole new level.

Also, it cleared up the many times she overheard Sinclair tell Hardin about Gettysburg like a teacher would tell a pupil. Alden Sinclair spoke and Hardin Lasbrith would repeat what was said as all of their talks on Gettysburg came back to her. As she thought about them, she came to realize what she heard were lectures given by one to the other, not conversations of shared experiences between two veterans.

Over time when Hardin talked to others about the war, he could convincingly make a case that he was at Gettysburg. At first, from conversations she overheard, she did believe Hardin had been there. However, over time she and others figured it out. It seemed to them when it came to the war and Gettysburg, Hardin lived vicariously through Sinclair. They didn't doubt Sinclair had seen battle, but they did have their doubts about Hardin.

The way Sinclair got the message across was the way he would ask detailed questions Hardin couldn't readily answer about the battle. It left Sinclair in the position to answer his own question. It would leave Hardin with nothing to say but "That's right." It was his way to plant the seed of doubt with the staff that Hardin couldn't answer because he wasn't there.

It was his way of tormenting Hardin. It was plain to see Sinclair had little fear when he would ask such a question. He knew half the time Hardin was unaware of the point being made. The times he did, there was little he could do about it if he wanted the common perception everyone had, that he was at Gettysburg, to last.

*****

Without a doubt what shocked her the most was the huge synchronization of past events. She wondered if the coincidences that took form in her mind were even possible. Throughout the history Enoch gave, all she heard, when he spoke about the Civil

War, Gettysburg, the Ohio 7th Infantry, and the 'Roosters,' was 'Royal Roy Marsden.'

It did roll off the tongue. She had to dissect the name. 'Royal and Roy' meant nothing to her but she repeated the last name over and over as if she was on to something. Enoch became background noise to what went through her head.

Through mind numbing concentration it came. Jenny recalled the day Enoch finished the ballroom; she was given a very brief introduction to a man Sinclair hired. He was employed to handle all the garbage the kitchen generated, to maintain the fireplaces, to keep the coal buckets and firewood boxes filled, to sweep out the portico and to make sure the hallway lights were turned on at night and off during the day. A man, about Enoch's age, who came aboard on Enoch's last day. 'Marsden' walked in that day, completely unnoticed, through one door, while everyone sadly watched Enoch walk out another.

In shocking clarity, it was all coming back to her. She had only been introduced to the man once and in the course of her work ran into him no more than twice. She didn't catch his name in their brief introduction. All she had was a face, she now had a name. Marsden was more like a spirit than a person. A soul she would run into on the rarest of occasions and under the strangest light. He was a paradox. Someone, she didn't really know, yet at the same time believed she did. He wasn't threatening, he was mysterious. 'Marsden,' the name that always escaped her whenever they met. She found what she was starting to comprehend, unsettling.

*****

Jenny wanted to ask but was side tracked by Enoch's actions as he continued to talk, she watched him begin to rub his stomach, undo his belt and unbutton his pants, as if she wasn't there. He sighed as his belly began to expand.

He began to consider all he had to eat and drink since he arrived. He let her know how he felt satisfied and comfortable, as he looked back on the times where he waited to get paid under far more Spartan conditions. He no longer looked onto the ballroom floor. Instead, he looked out the window then emptied the ashtray and lit a new cigar. Before Jenny could get a word out, he exhaled a cloud of smoke and sighed "1864 and 1865, in this order - J.D. Rockefeller and Brooks Mast." To let her know he wasn't finished with all he had to say.

Enoch began, "The war ended for me when I came home from Gettysburg. By the end of 1864, I could slowly move around without crutches. I could also move all the fingers on my left hand. Only trouble with the hand, was the limited feeling of hot and cold, which at times was a blessing and at times a curse." He then went into the history of how 1864 ended and 1865 began.

On the first Monday of the first week Enoch was in the Union army a 'benefactor' came to Irene and returned every Monday until Enoch came home and was back to normal. They would ask Irene what was needed in the way of food, clothing and repairs. Irene would give a list of vegetables, stew meat, bacon, soup bones, flour, butter and if available some fruits and nuts. From week to week the list hardly changed. Outside of this she bought the boys new shoes in the Spring and had a broken window replaced end of May. Every week the benefactor was a different person.

Notes sent back with the benefactors informing JD he was home and his condition was improving went unanswered. Since the benefactors were different each week, when Enoch asked about the previous week's note, none could give an answer. One Monday a benefactor came, took the list and then informed Enoch and Irene that J D Rockefeller married September 8th, 1864.

With the news Enoch began to wonder if the work of the benefactor would soon end. He knew how things change when one gets married. It ended mid-June of 1865 when the last benefactor, best dressed and oldest of all, took them to a property by the lake. He handed them a paid-up deed to a five-acre property, on the shore of Lake Erie, with a house and three out buildings, all in their name and told them to take possession. Within that week Enoch, Irene and Seth and Simon were in the house.

This was the last benefactor and the last contact Enoch ever had with J D Rockefeller. Who had become, in a short period of time after 1865, a very successful, a very important, and a very wealthy person, by 1870 he became the richest man in the country. A man who had a bad reputation to some, and a good reputation to others.

Enoch understood their situation. They ran in different circles. However, in his mind the 'circles' didn't take away from the fact, the deal, the two, made on the fictitious corner of Mast and Rockefeller had been met and settled in full on just a handshake and they would always be friends.

*****

Enoch and his brothers sold the old place, took the money and got the wagons and the livestock moving again. Ezra built a room in the forge and Enos in the stables. They had small stoves in their room to warm them and soft beds, tables and chairs, bookshelves filled with all the books, paper, pencils and pens they were denied in the past, along with coffee, tobacco and whiskey. They made their rooms comfortable and every once in a while, on cold nights, when they didn't want to keep stoking their small stoves, would have some overnight female company to keep them warm.

Brooks, on the other hand, built a beautiful rolltop desk and put a small building around it, at the far end between the two buildings. It became the office. He put in a nice large window which overlooked the lake, and a large closet for his clothes and a fold away bed. It turned into the place for whiskey and cigars after dinner.

Enoch's brother, Enos, worked with his brothers and nephews for about nine years then fell in love with the radical Irish woman and ran off with her to unionize the coal fields in West Virginia and Pennsylvania. He still had some of the Civil War adrenalin running through him. He had no fear of the union busters and Pinkertons when compared to who he had fought in the war. In fact, he looked forward to the run-ins and skirmishes. He and his Irish girlfriend lived to give the bosses fits.

They did this for a while but eventually their foes threw enough money at the problem to where they were caught and lynched. Years later Enoch was in the position to play a hunch and hired the Pinkertons. From them he found out about Enos's disappearance. Their investigation gave Enoch the type of information only a culprit would know. He believed that the people who knew the most about his brother's death, were also probably the ones who caused it. It was information worth knowing, even though there was nothing he could do about it.

*****

During the years they spent working together after the war, before Enos went to the coal fields, and Enoch's sons headed west with Ezra. Enos and Ezra liked to tease Enoch and Brooks about their time in the army. In a good-natured way, they would ask how it was the two of them entered the war last and came home first. Whereas, they on the other hand, had fought with the 29th from start to finish, they had seen and done more by far. That they were a nasty boil on the ass of the 'Graybacks' (a term Union soldiers used to describe lice and Confederate soldiers) whereas Enoch and Brooks were just a pimple.

When the topic came up, as it did from time to time, Enoch and Brooks would take an artificial pious attitude and retreat to the parable of the 'Workers at the Vineyard." Found in Matthew 20:8 taught to them by their mother.

It dealt with the fairness of the world. The parable was one of Eve Mast's favorites and she read it to her children often. It was for those who thought they had been short changed. Enoch and Brooks would take turns reciting parts of it calmly, like their mother, to point out to Ezra and Enos the world is not a fair place.

So, when evening came, the lord of the vineyard said unto his steward, Call the laborers, and give them their hire, beginning from the last unto the first."

Then they would end, "According to the Lord we're worth just as much as you – maybe more, since we were paid the same as you but in less time."

What would happen next was a day spent debating the parable and the concept of *the last being first*. Not one of them agreed with Christ on the concept. Yet that was what was found in the Bible and what He said. It was always an all-day debate on what was said and what they felt.

It didn't end there. There were times they'd debate other scriptures their mother had read them. The story of the feats of Sampson a favorite. How in battle he once killed one thousand with the jaw bone of an ass. The story and facts often debated all day.

They calculated and all agreed in what they found. In a ten-hour day Sampson would have to kill one-hundred an hour or more than one every minute of the day. So, it came down to, first, there is the story of Sampson, then, second, there are the facts. And the facts don't support the story. Those days on the wagons filled their lives with good memories of hard work, great conversations and big meals.

*****

Brooks had been away from home the longest and because of this enjoyed these debates the most. He was gone eleven years and returned in the Autumn of 1865 at around the age of twenty-one or two. His was quite a homecoming and the one and only time he told the others how the slavers captured him.

He told them, "It was one like me. But a man not a boy. I'd seen him around Uriah when they be drinking. He waved me over in the store and I thought nothing 'bout it, went to him and ten steps later I'm thrown into a covered wagon with a bull putting a gun to my head. It went fast. Ma chased after me, that's when they snatched her too. They threw her in a different wagon and I never saw her again, all they left me was her screams."

Brooks went on, "I kept asking the black hearted bastard, "Why!?" He answered by telling me this story. "An island catches on fire. A big ole bad fire killing everything. A scorpion comes across a frog and goes over and makes a request. Mr. Frog you know I can't swim, let me ride your back as you swim to the other island. Mr. Frog say, I heard everything about you, all you do is to sting everything. So, the answer is NO!

But in no time the scorpion talks Mr. Frog into it telling him if I did that, we'd both drown. Mr. Frog shakes his head and says "okay." Half way to the other island the scorpion stings Mr. Frog hard and often and Mr. Frog screamed 'now we're both going to die! Why!?" The scorpion answered, "Because it's in my nature."

Brooks never forgot the story or how his captor chose to answer his question. "Why?! The 'black hearted bastard asked and then answered his own question, 'That's why! And added, "Now shut up boy!" Brooks told them from that point on he never spoke to him, or his white partner again, from Ohio to Tennessee. He'd just listen and nod and nothing more. He learned the 'black hearted bastard' was no stranger to the underground railroad, had ridden it several times, and in the near future planned to take it back to Cleveland.

He had a white partner, Charles, and they'd sell the information he got from riding the railroad, names, who they belonged to, where they stayed, where they were headed, to the paddy rollers and other interested parties. It was a good set up, should he get caught, which happened twice, Charles would begin to check the places he would be, claim him, and they'd be back in business in hardly no time.

As the trip continued Brooks didn't expect to find out the 'black hearted bastard' was the brains of the outfit. He was a real mystery. How did he get to be this way? Brooks asked himself over and over. It wasn't his white partner, Charles, giving the orders. It didn't take long to figure out Charles wasn't a partner; he was an employee.

Charles was his ticket to the white world, his passport to both north and south and to the money that he believed made everyone free. Charles was a handsome man, well dressed, and looked important but he was the one who couldn't read or write. The 'black hearted bastard' did all the reading, writing and thinking for the two. The only mystery about Charles was whether 'Charles' was his first or last name.

*****

Enoch went on about Brook's homecoming. It was held in the evening at the new house. In the dining room where a soft glow, from the turned down wicks of the kerosene lamps provided the atmosphere. Enoch spoke of how the light hit the table set in Brook's honor, how he sat at its head, with all his favorite foods before him. He told Jenny it was on the scale of a biblical banquet.

The banquet remembered as the one and only time Brooks Mast spoke of the eleven years, he was a slave. With the help of an ample supply of cigars and whiskey, his account of those years captured the night and invaded the dawn.

He told Enoch, Irene, Seth and Simon, Ezra and Eli along with seven close friends, how he arrived at a thriving plantation called *Eden's Gate*. A place that had over a hundred slaves, five times that number in livestock, with enough crops in the field to feed all the slaves and animals. They planted a little over a square mile or about six hundred and forty acres in cotton and another six hundred and forty acres in tobacco.

These assets were owned by the McArliss family and under the control of Master Felton McArliss, the patriarch. Master Felton was a person that had little empathy towards any living human or beast he owned. To him they were no more than machines in support of the plantation and his family enterprises.

Brooks told of how he called him 'Master Felton' once and as clear as a bell, it was reduced and he was corrected by Felton McArliss himself to pronounce his title as 'Massa Felt'n.' The correction was made to keep Brooks aware of his place. Brooks explained it as "place" training.

Even though he had the ability to pronounce most words correctly he was not allowed to. It was all part of the plan to

217

introduce an artificial stupidity on the slaves and reinforce a self-awareness of inferiority. When he first arrived back in Cleveland Brooks talked the way he had been trained. It took a while to get the grammar back he'd learned from Eve Mast.

Brooks went on how 'Massa Felt'n' then told him, "The one thing I don't need around here is an uppity nigger – you understand me boy?" Brooks answered with a stereotypical smile that showed as many teeth as possible. As it turned out, it was good this incident took place right from the start.

It was at that moment Brooks became acutely aware the McArliss family and those close to them were not the people who would appreciate the fact he could read and write. This type of fact would be way to threatening to them or any owner.

While at *Eden's Gate*, only three other slaves: Abner, Mingus, and Envil figured out Brooks could read and write. Brooks chose to be around these three the most, when he was at the plantation. Brooks traveled, at times, with and without Felton McArliss, to other plantations.

When at *Eden's Gate* he spoke to the other slaves through these three. He didn't need the others to come to the same conclusion. Brooks continually denied the fact to any slave who asked. He maintained limited contact with most and would cordially end many conversations before such an inquiry could be made.

Any information he would, at times, choose to share, through his messengers, always turned out to be accurate. It would be obvious to anyone who spent any time around him, he knew too much about the certain issues of the day to not know how to read and write. He always had access to the sources of information the small population of slaves at *Eden's Gate* appreciated.

Abner, Mingus, and Envil, were 'field slaves,' Brooks was a 'house boy.' Big difference between the two. Not once did the three ever jeopardize Brook's secret. He was the one who made them look smart. They only spread what Brooks wanted, they didn't spread what they knew about him. They kept what they knew about him to themselves. In this respect Brooks was lucky. He knew such information in the wrong hands would have unfortunate consequences for him and all who knew.

*****

As Enoch continued to speak, Jenny, became lost in her own thoughts and Enoch's voice faded into the background. She started to think of Brooks as an exception to the rule. She knew most ex-slaves took up the last name of their owners. Slaves fell into a situation where many didn't have, or didn't know, their original names. Those born on a plantation took their owners last name because at the time there was no other option.

Brooks, on the other hand, didn't 'take' a last name he 'borrowed' one from the people who took his mother and him in, who fed, clothed, sheltered and educated him. His last name didn't come from who owned him but from who helped him.

The realization touched her heart and she blurted out "I want to meet Brooks Mast!" The volume behind her request surprised Enoch for a brief moment. When he gained his composure, he ignored the request, shook his head and continued the history. Acting as if the event never took place. Within a cloud of cigar smoke, he let her know he wasn't finished and she wasn't ready for such a meeting.

Enoch went on to describe what a prodigy Brooks was. He Told her he was first taught to be a carpenter and by age eighteen he was a master craftsman with a major reputation. As a result, he became what Felton McArliss called a 'derby' slave, a quality slave, one that might fetch the same price as a fine thoroughbred race horse. Those who know, wear a derby to the auctions of such fine animals. As a result, Felton always made Brooks wear a derby which was his way of showing others the value of what he owned. The derby was always a major source of irritation for Brooks. He always made it a point to be told by an agitated Felton McArliss, at least once, whenever in his presence, "Get that derby on boy!"

Brooks knew how to read and write; he did not know math. Because of his abilities the second year at the 'Gate' he was taught some complex math that dealt with the calculations of: angles, spheres, cones, cylinders, cubic and linear areas. The methods the Greeks and Romans used to create the shapes used in their designs. The designs of these two cultures were at the time in a period of revival in public and private dwellings throughout the country.

Education in mathematics and the ability to draft and read architectural drawings was all the owners cared about. If the slave's education didn't provide a distinct advantage for the owners it wasn't taught to them.

Math seemed safe enough and didn't offer a direct route to the radical ideas that can be formed by the written word. So, it was provided to some, but not all. Any slave demonstrating above average mental ability had to be exploited to the advantage of the owner. It was understood by slaves that they didn't own their potential, the master did.

Another exception to the rule that Brooks was guilty of was the type of abuse he suffered at the hands of Felton McArliss and his overseers. *Eden's Gate* was a large enterprise that operated, for the most part, on the principle of – "it's not what we can do 'for' you - but what we can do 'to' you."

He had seen field hands beaten within an inch of their life, women's sexual favors offered to the owner's guests, children ripped from families and sold, old people starved if they didn't perform or behave as expected. However, the abuse he suffered was not physical but mental and in many ways the worst of the two. Brooks felt the scars that cover the body are not as deep as the ones that cover the mind.

At a very early age he became perhaps the best craftsman, white or black, in Tennessee. Brooks was a fast study in perception. His teachers couldn't stop the enjoyment they felt and sense of accomplishment they had in what Brooks knew. They didn't buy into the stereotype some wished to perpetuate. He was taught by white men and became close to many of them. Brooks found in general that skilled and educated people had a better attitude towards what one knew as opposed to what one was. That those who share knowledge and those who learn eventually become color blind. Unlike most slaves he didn't hate all white men – just the owners.

What Brooks hated the most was the continued exploitation of his time and skills. He hated the times he was loaned out by his owner to other owners. He hated the skill he had that in the end, paid absolutely nothing for his effort, his work. He hated he was provided cold damp places to sleep most of the time and fed bad food. He hated his skills were owned by his master. Who knew the least but was given the most in praise and pay for work he never did and was incapable of doing. He hated being continually robbed by his owner of his self-worth. But most of all he hated the hatred that was so deep in him.

*****

The evening moved at the same pace as any other evening and the actual time told by the chimes. The origin of the chimes was a large walnut grandfather clock. The Lasbriths stated it was the largest such clock in Cleveland. It stood between two large floor length mirrors in the parlor outside the men's and woman's water closets. It was perhaps fifty feet from where Enoch and Jenny sat.

They could see the reflection of the clock's face in one of the mirrors. The face was reversed and easy to misread. A glance was not enough it had to be interpreted. Instead of knowing the time immediately it took a few moments to turn the face around in their minds.

The first time they noticed the chimes and found the face of the clock in the mirror they determined it was seven fifteen. The candles Enoch had brought over and placed on the table were lit. The next time they paid attention to the chimes it was nine-thirty. "Where did the time go?" each asked themselves without saying it aloud, as all have when caught up in the mystery.

The chimes sounded every fifteen-minutes in longer patterns than the previous as each pattern moved towards the hour. Then a single chime would sound for each hour that had passed. The chimes were designed to be heard and hard to miss. However, they were heard four times every hour, every day and could become so common place as to pass unnoticed and become a 'silent' sound.

What Enoch told Jenny was spell binding. Several such intervals went by unnoticed. They weren't surprised, they were shocked, when they noticed the chimes the third time and how the minutes had turned to hours. The shock that comes when the expected becomes the unexpected outcome.

The time they spent together flowed like clear water in a gently rippling brook. Water that coaxed them to get in and move with the flow. Time at this brook moved to where hours felt like minutes and minutes like seconds.

Within this time Enoch kept his agreement and told Jenny just about all he could recall of his life and most of Brooks. As he did the flow evolved into a current. He felt he was running out of time, being pulled and getting closer to a waterfall he wanted to avoid, the realization he would never have enough time to tell the whole story of the two of them.

He would end by telling her about the things they had in common: two hills, two cities, two objectives, two Confederate Armies and one derby and one cap.

What he didn't tell Jenny was how Brooks entered Tennessee a slave and left it a eunuch. Enoch felt the impact of this information would require more time than he felt he had to explain. So, he left it out. This information would remain private and be held back for another time.

As Enoch went on with Jenny. To legitimatize what he told her, he would often summarize the points he made with "This is all from one who was a slave." To let her know all the information given was first hand.

Brooks was contracted out to other large plantations by his owner, for money or political favors. Not only in Tennessee but other states, as well. These were owned by families who were very influential in the formation of the Confederacy.

He always tried to be thought of as a slave and took on the persona of some sort of idiot savant that could master a craft but nothing else, that he could build, but he couldn't think. He was more than willing to let the owner's prejudices work against them when it came to what they thought he knew.

Often, he'd move their books and papers to make space for what the owners wanted built or changed. What better job for an ignorant slave? In the course of his work he came across copies of the

Confederate Constitution and all types of books, encyclopedias were his favorites.

What he would try to do on each job was to produce at an appreciated level which he could comfortably increase given certain conditions. He would let the owners know he could be far more productive if he were allowed to sleep on site. There were only two occasions where this request to sleep in their studies or libraries was denied.

When he won the right, he always threw a large heavy oil cloth over the largest desk or table in the room. Under what he found he would place what he thought to be the most important books and papers under it in the guise of protecting them. He always left enough space for himself to fit under it as well.

The cloth was heavy enough to conceal the light of four candles. At night he would go "under the cloth," as he called it, and read all he pleased by the unseen candle light. For years he moved unnoticed through the studies and libraries of some of the Confederacy's most influential forebearers.

In his readings he found out the importation of African slaves into the United States was illegal and had been for some time. Yet he knew for a fact it still went on, because the slave importation laws were the most ignored laws of the time.

Soon after, in later readings, he came across a completed copy of the *Confederate Constitution* and found

Article I, Section IX, paragraph IV:

No bill of attainer, ex post facto law, or law denying or impairing the right of property in negro slaves shall be passed.

It became painfully evident the South had no intention of ever ending slavery. They put this right up front and in the first article of their Constitution.

*****

When he traveled to the plantations, to take the monotony of getting there and building this or changing that, he would reflect on what he had read and come to know. How he couldn't use them to his advantage because he was a slave. What he saw in his travels when he was sent off the plantation to work for another owner was a country side of white farmers, most share croppers and the 'outside' trades. The 'outside' trades were made up of teamsters, blacksmiths, and wheelwrights. They were the trades in support of the movement of goods and not suited for slaves.

The 'inside' trades, masons and carpenters were trades that could be taught to slaves that demonstrated abilities for the work. Who were always on site and didn't have to be paid. No need to bring in these types of trades from the outside.

What struck Brooks when he observed the country side was some did well but there was also a fair amount who were living one or two steps above slaves. The only difference was they were allowed to go to the small towns, that had little or no industrial opportunities, and buy their dry goods and food on credit they could never keep current. Fact was one out of three Southern families owned slaves and their labor. The other two-thirds just owned their labor and no one else's.

One third had slaves and two thirds hoped to have some one day. The owners sold the others Article one, Section nine, paragraph four. The Constitutional guarantee negro slaves would always be around and would always be property instead of people. What the one third actually sold the others was the idea they were and would always be above slaves even if they never owned one.

The idea if one fought hard, then worked hard the reward would be the opportunity to take possession of another person's life and become an owner. Becoming an owner was always seen as a possibility, no matter how unlikely. The reality that the owners were not about to let all individuals to become one of them went ignored.

This was the way Brooks had it figured, Enoch told Jenny, and then went into what he had mentioned earlier about the two hills, two cities, two objectives, two Confederate Armies and one derby and one cap.

In mid to late December of 1864, close to a year and a half from the sweltering July of 1863, when Royal Roy Marsden saved Enoch's life and broke his leg, in defense of Culp's Hill, Brooks found himself part of an attack, on a hill, Overton Hill. One hill was in Gettysburg, Pennsylvania the other in Nashville, Tennessee. Enoch fought in the heat of summer Robert E. Lee's Army of Virginia to keep a hill. Brooks, in the cold of winter, fought John Bell Hood's Army of Tennessee, to take a hill. What took place at these hills captured Enoch and Brooks memory and never released it. They would talk about the two hills on occasion, but only to each other.

At the first opportunity after Union forces entered Tennessee, Brooks escaped *Eden's Gate* and Massa Felt'n'. He joined up with the 13th United States Colored Troops (13th USCT) at around nineteen years of age. They guarded the rail yards of Nashville. Mid to late December of 1864 winter was harsh. When the battle for the city broke out the 13th was eventually sent from the rail yards to a place called Overton Hill.

Overton Hill became a meat grinder that Consumed Union Troops. The Union rate of casualties became unsustainable and it was decided the 13th USCT would be thrown into the heart of the battle in relief. They were cut down no different than the white troops. However, unlike the white troops the colored troops did win a huge victory that day.

From their performance on the field of battle several facts became apparent about the untested former slaves. They fought to where General Hood had to take troops from another position on the field to reinforce the hill. No white soldier from either side, could deny the negros could fight. The 13th completely annihilated that myth.

As fate would have it, Brooks was wounded there at the end of the battle. Maybe, one of the last ten rounds fired. It was a wound that stayed with him mentally the rest of his life and in many ways it never healed. The only person who knew about it was Enoch. It was brought up only once and never spoken of again.

A round ricocheted off a rock, tore through Brooks' scrotum and ripped his testicles from him. It spread them on the cold ground about four feet behind him. He went unconscious and almost bled to death. He was rescued from this at the last moment. It took months for him to physically heal. It happened at an age where the physical side effects were minimal. In time he could perform all the primary functions, but one. The psychological side effects never left him.

After the battle and for the record, it was written in the report that the 13th USCT distinguished themselves at Overton Hill. General John Bell Hood of the Army of Tennessee signed the report which in part stated.

Yet in undertaking this task as if with "a charge into hell itself" these freed slaves, untried in fierce combat, won in their deaths the admiration of friend and foe alike… Two articles were unpacked for Jenny from an imaginary suitcase that held what belonged to Enoch and Brooks over the last forty-nine years. One article was a painting that belonged to Enoch, the other was a blue cap that belonged to Brooks. Jenny knew about the importance of the painting and was about to find out about the cap.

*****

The last event to be told to Jenny, was about the derby and the cap. In December of 1867, and the forty-six Decembers that followed, Enoch and Brooks would take a derby, the type Felton McArliss made Brooks wear, to the shores of Lake Erie. They would put up a post and place the derby on top. They would fire at the derby with a fifty-caliber breech loading Burnside carbine. The first year the range was sixty feet. The range was increased five feet each following year to where the target was over five times the original distance the last time they were at the shore.

They wanted to start the tradition in 1866 but it was at the end of 1867 when they made enough extra money to buy the carbine an along with it an expensive derby. Both had seen what a carbine could do in the war and both wanted to get their hands on one. The end of the war didn't change their desire to own one. The Burnside carbine they bought was central to their tradition.

The rifle was never cleaned at the end of these events, it would be cleaned twice in the following November. One would become aware December was coming and clean it. Then the other would become aware, take it down, and clean it again, paying no attention to how clean it was when they retrieved it. By December of each year the carbine would become the most operational breech loading fifty-caliber carbine in Cleveland.

They did this the last month of every year, but never on the same day, any day in December was fine, any day but Christmas. They'd ride out on horse back to their remote spot, and execute the derby one more time.

As the years rolled by and the target moved farther down range it also became smaller than the year before. Add to this each year their fading eyesight. The derby had been hit over forty-six times with a fifty-caliber round. Every year it became more of a challenge to hit what was left.

It no longer sat on a post. What was left, part of the brim, was carefully pinned to the white background painted on the top of the post down range. They would leave when Brooks hit it. To accomplish their mission took more and more determination from one year to the next. Both were of the same nature; they would stay until they hit it.

They began to dress more appropriately for the increased time they would spend in the harsh elements of an Ohio winter on the shores of Lake Erie. Each year they became more comfortable in the winter environment. They also increased their rations of whiskey, cigars, and fine beef jerky. Of all they took with them, the item that saw the biggest increase from year to year was ammunition.

They would make a day of it. They had no choice, the trouble each had to properly sight in the target consumed a large amount of time and ammunition. Brooks would fire and Enoch would look through the binoculars and guide him in from there, he'd tell Brooks "Put the next round a little to the right and up a hair,". Each year the time to hit what was left of the derby took longer and each year they ate and drank all they had. What had the greatest effect on them was the alcohol and it brought on the non-stop chatter drunks are known to have.

They spent the time between shoving a round in the breech and sighting in the target making fun of and insulting the Confederacy for laughs. Not so much their soldiers – they could fight but the system that created them. On second thought they did make fun of the soldiers for buying into the system where two thirds did all the fighting to benefit one third. Enoch and Brooks knew about all the things the South didn't want to talk about when they would bring up their "The Lost Cause."

Enoch told Jenny the more the two drank and smoked the more they tore into who they had fought. The fiction of the noble south fighting for everyone's states' rights and the righteous antebellum Southern way of life where all were unafraid of Northern aggression. Their Lost Cause which ignored how the institution of slavery played the central role when the curtain went up on the first act of the Civil War.

Enoch and Brooks took perverted joy in the fact the South had to draft every year of the war and how each year the interval of ages increased. To where in the last year the range was fifteen to forty-five. By the third year of the war they had bread riots in Richmond, the capital and they were brought on by the women the men left behind.

They didn't know how to use their railroads or their telegraphs. That they could fight but they sure couldn't think. When they did, both Enoch and Brooks agreed, they thought about the day they'd take full advantage of their constitutional right to own slaves. Two thirds of them fought hard for the owners who told them this right was God given and they also would one day own slaves. The day it could happen being right around the corner. They just had to keep up the fight.

Tradition called for the day to end with the biblical synopsis of what Brooks had read while under the 'table and tarp.' Back when he worked on some of the founder's libraries and studies. No one was aware he had been undercover in their mansions when the South was impregnated with a host of uncommon ideas that brought on the birth of the Confederacy.

Enoch told Jenny, Brooks told him, one of these ideas came from Benjamin M Palmer a pro-slavery Southern Intellectualist who wanted to give the institution some biblical depth and justification. He put forth black Africans were under the curse of Ham. The curse can be found in the *Old Testament* in the *Book of Genesis.* Ham is one of Noah's sons. Those under the curse are subject to a life of servitude and they are known by their black skin.

A grin turned into a big smile accented by a chuckle. Jenny heard Enoch mutter "Brooks can sure tell you about the curse." He went on to tell her how Brooks always pretends Mr. Palmer is there in front of him as he explains the way he sees the curse. Enoch pointed out by this time of the day both were pretty drunk and there would be parts she wouldn't understand. It was okay because he didn't understand them either. He then went on to tell her about the types of conversation Brooks and Mr. Palmer would have. Enoch let her know what she heard from him was second hand. That Brooks was the only one who could tell this story right.

Brooks would tell the imaginary Mr. Palmer this was what he got from the Book of Genesis, in the Old Testament about the curse. First off, the curse Noah made wasn't even put on Ham. It was put on Ham's son Canaan, for the sake of accuracy should it not be the curse of "Canaan?"

Brooks would go on and let Mr. Palmer know he knew the background of the curse. That what brought it on was a blanket. That one day the prophet Noah got drunk and naked and then fell asleep or as some would say passed out. One of his sons noticed this and told his brothers and they covered him up with a blanket because they found the situation their father was in embarrassing.

Noah noticed what they had done as soon as he woke up. For some reason the blanket angered him no end. Perhaps he preferred to be naked but his sons preferred him covered. That a changing of the guard was taking place. People have put forth several reasons as to why it angered him but the reality is no one knows why.

Enoch told Jenny That in this imaginary conversation Brooks would also let Mr. Palmer know that Ham in Noah's mind was the culprit behind the blanket. Next, Noah makes his servitude curse but puts it on his grandson and then asks Mr. palmer "Why?"

In short Mr. Palmer you found this biblical curse that dealt with servitude manna from heaven for your purpose and stitched in the color and slavish characteristics on your own. Characteristics that are not found in the scriptures. You chose Ham and his decedents who become black to take the blame and for what? Placing a blanket on Noah?

By doing so believe you have biblically legitimatized the institution of slavery. In the end the synopsis would read, "People are black because of the curse made by Noah found in the *Old Testament Book of Genesis*," and for most this would be all one would have to say. After it is said it would become apparent those who go against this biblical decree and try to abolish slavery go against the decrees of God.

As the years rolled on the synopsis from under the tarp and the curse of Ham got more and more humorous and profane. It seemed any scripture that had Noah, his son's and alcohol in it left the door wide open for blasphemy.

They called it "Cap Day" and it became a very important day of the year. As they would say, "shooting the derby," became a very therapeutic tradition. Over the years the sentiments of the day made them drink more and talk less. However, their sentiments when they did talk didn't change. They didn't buy the South's "Lost Cause" explanation for what they did, they made it a point to make fun of it at least once every year if not more.

Enoch went to the depth of the day to let Jenny know the role the blue union cap, with the shiny brass thirteen in the center of it's top, played in Brooks Mast's life. From the day he joined the thirteenth he took off the derby, but kept what it meant as a reminder, and put on the cap. He never took it off, he slept with it on. Inside the cap, wrapped in fine supple leather and held together with an expensive purple ribbon was a picture of his mother taken the year before their recapture.

Brooks wore it every day probably the first year in Cleveland until he noticed the wear, he was putting on it. When that happened, he immediately retired the cap and worked on returning it to a perfect condition. He tried his hardest to keep it in the best condition he could to let his mother know that whenever he put it on, she was under the cap of a free man. The way he felt the one day a year he would put the cap on was beyond how he felt on any real holiday.

The Union Blue Cap worn in the field was Brooks Mast's Gulf Stream and it kept all he'd experienced under it and in order. Over the years only family members and a very small and select group of his friends, the ones who would have loved to have heard what Brooks confided to Mary Irene, were allowed to call Brook's "Cap," the ultimate term of endearment for him. Only his inner circle knew of the nick name and were allowed to use it. Mary Irene didn't know him by any other name.

It was almost eleven when Enoch ended all he had to say telling Jenny, "I know he will let you call him Cap too." He said it to let her know she was in his future. Jenny got up gently smiled at

Enoch then kissed his forehead and whispered, "I'll be back soon, I'm going to find us a room."

She kept to herself she was also going to look for Marsden. Enoch, smiled and stood up, pulled the candle labra towards him, took a candle from it and handed it to her, "We might need this." The gesture panicked Jenny, she controlled it with a smile and quickly told him, "You're not coming with me – you need to stay here – We don't need to risk being seen together in the hallways – I will come back for you later."

Her response upset Enoch but not to where he would go against her wishes. He sat down, sighed through a smile, "Make it fast, you owe me a story." She raised the candle in response, in its light she smiled, nodded yes and left.

She left with two goals in mind, to find a room and to find Marsden, but she couldn't decide which was to be first. She had too much whirling around in her mind and had trouble organizing her thoughts. Overwhelmed by the response given to her request to know everything about Enoch Mast.

CHAPTER VIII
RACHMANINOFF'S, PIANO CONCERTO NO 3

Jenny gazed down the long hallway, the lights behind the crystal sconces were off. She stood still in the moonlight for a few seconds and thought how there's a first time for everything. For a moment she thought the person in charge of the lights had neglected to switch them on. Or perhaps they did, but there was a malfunction.

For one brief moment she found it odd how she could come up with reasons why the lights were off. She realized her thoughts were out of character, but they didn't last long enough to establish any real concern. She was enchanted by the moonlight; it was something new. If she was upset about anything, it was she wasn't disturbed the lights were off.

The type of life the Lasbriths led made them very paranoid. As a result, the lights in all hallways were to be on at least a half hour before sunset. No mansion on Euclid Avenue gave off more light at night than the Lasbrith estate. For safety and security concerns, such as fire, or intruders, or both the hallway lights went on before sunset and off after sunrise. Of all the mandates made by the family, the hallway lights became the only decree to have never been violated.

There was no way to know the penalty for unlit hallways. It never happened, should it happen, all the staff needed to know was the penalty would be severe. The family was very firm about the edict. Not once in her tenure had the hallway lights not been on. The fact the moon was the only source of light in the hallways should have concerned Jenny, but it didn't.

She whispered under her breath, "Marsden – he's in charge of the lights!" The fact hit her hard and she couldn't overlook the notion he was behind all that went on. She would find him. Even if she had to look in all forty rooms and every part of the cellar, she would find him. When found, the hall lights would be the last matter to be taken up with him. She had a long list of questions way more important than the unlit hallways.

There was enough moonlight coming through the windows to allow the furniture to cast faint shadows on the walls and carpet. The lit candle more than enough to help navigate to where the rooms were much smaller and intimate. She would gaze into every room she passed for Marsden on her way to the dining hall, from there she would begin her search in earnest.

*****

As soon as Jenny faded from view Enoch moved the candle labra to the window sill and began to carve. The mixture of moonlight and candlelight provided just enough illumination to continue the work. He thought about how Jenny left without a word, only a smile and a nod. He thought about how she took the candle and by doing so, for a brief moment, created a vision neither would forget. In the light of a single candle, they looked into the soul of the other and were captured by a beauty neither could escape.

As he worked, he was bombarded with the thoughts of the past, present and future. One irrational thought surfaced from the future and wouldn't go away. She took her light from him when she stepped away with the candle. The notion he would never see her again in this world overwhelmed him and he couldn't explain to himself why?

*****

236

The soft moonlight fabricated a fantasy atmosphere. Jenny wished it to be real but knew it was a mirage. Even so, the hallway captivated her, she looked around, and like a young school girl, slipped off her shoes and stockings and let her feet sink into the plush carpet. She pretended she was on some grassy path which would lead to an imaginary meadow of beautiful wildflowers, instead of some dining hall filled with buckets, rags and spent people.

She walked slow with her stockings and shoes in one hand and the candle in the other. Every so often she stopped at a window to bathe in the moonlight. When she did, Enoch's last words came back to her how she owed him her story. She began to think of how to tell it, instead of getting a room or finding Marsden. What jumped in front of them was the fact she had no *Gulf Stream* painting to eloquently illustrate what she had to say about her life, and it bothered her.

The thought of how the day began, who had filled it and all that was said and done passed through her mind. Each notion picking up tempo and gaining momentum to where she could hardly get a grasp on any of them. It all changed when she thought of the Kolten family, followed by another thought, the concerto. Their arrival and the concerto brought on a huge smile and a colossal revelation.

The Kolten family became her compass and pointed out the direction she needed to take to tell Enoch her story. They were the family she worked for, prior to the Lasbriths. She wanted to stay on with the Kolten family forever, but Spring of 1910, in Cleveland, brought with it charges of embezzlement and bank fraud against the family. When they surfaced the hope of 'forever' came to an end.

On May fifth, 1910 the Kolten's left for Saint Louis. It wasn't known by their staff if their trip was for business or pleasure.

It was neither, it was an escape. Later it was found they traveled under assumed names. All that was known and treated as fact, the Kolton family never returned to Cleveland, they disappeared. Some say they perished on the Mississippi River while at a dance on a steamship called the Saltillo, that was headed for Waterloo, Alabama.

What got back to Cleveland was the Kolton's, on May eleventh, 1910, a Wednesday, around nine in the evening were on the *Saltillo*. The ship ran aground outside Glen Cove Missouri. The impact caused its boilers to explode, killing thirteen people. The theory was the Kolton's were on the Saltillo and killed in the explosion.

The origin of the rumor came from the baggage left in their room bearing the Kolton monogram with city and state identification. There was no such name on the passenger manifest and the luggage went unclaimed. It was a thought, not a fact, they were killed. The thought gained enough strength to be referenced as the date they vanished in all legal matters, announcements, and filings.

*****

Jenny stood in the moonlight as it streamed through the open window. Long enough to recall the Kolten family hiatus to New York City in 1909, to celebrate Thanksgiving, which, like Christmas, was on the twenty-fifth that year. A little over five months before the family disappeared.

They took practically the whole staff with them. What she remembered the most about Thanksgiving of 1909 was three days later, on the twenty-eighth, she was part of the entourage that accompanied Mr. and Mrs. Kolten to the world premiere of composer Sergei Rachmaninoff's, *Piano Concerto Number 3*.

The debut should have been in Russia, but Rachmaninoff chose America. He had his reasons, there were some prejudices in Moscow he was opposed to. His opposition was to the benefit of The New York Symphony and its director, Gustav Mahler. The composer was the soloist. It was said Rachmaninoff treasured the night of his *Piano Concerto Number 3* debut, the rest of his life.

He was not alone. The music of that night never left Jenny and as she moved over the plush carpet to the dining hall, it began to play in her mind, it came to her no different than it did on the last Sunday of November 1909. Every note heard like every word ever spoken to her. Every instrument played like the voice of every person who ever spoke them.

The mission to find the perfect guest room, or Marsden, faded as she thought of how Rachmaninoff's concerto was her *Gulf Stream*. She would start out on how the piece moves from harmonious to frantic to stunning and how it ended as beautiful as it began.

The movements of the concerto ran parallel to the emotions of her life when she felt love, loss, redemption, disappointment, sorrow and joy. She would begin to tell Enoch her story by asking him if he had ever heard the concerto? His answer wouldn't matter, yes or no, either way she would inform him the concerto was the musical interpretation of her life and just as it was incumbent on her to one day view Winslow Homer's *the Gulf Stream* to understand him, it was also incumbent on Enoch to have heard *Sergei Rachmaninoff's Piano Concerto Number 3*, to understand her.

She wished Enoch was with her, instead of the ballroom, the moment the memory of the concerto came to life within her. All the things she would tell him as the concerto played on in her mind. As long as she could recall the evening, the composer, the soloist, and the piece, she would be able to tell Enoch everything. The problem of how to tell him, solved. The weight of 'how' lifted from her. She breathed better and was ready to move on, to find Marsden, the room, and a new life.

*****

The concerto continued with every step she took toward the great dining hall. It stopped when she turned a corner and noticed a far-off glow. When she arrived at the dining hall's entrance, she found the lights were on when they should've been off. The hall was empty, she should have been aware there was no noise as she approached it. She thought for a moment, but had there been noise there was a good chance it went unnoticed and over-ridden by the concerto that played in her head. Her thoughts stopped her in her tracks as she said out loud, "What is this? Everything is backwards, what is to be on is off and what is to be off is on, and a whole bunch of other things!"

The thought came to her, it could be the person responsible for throwing the switches handed the responsibility to another. A new person, who managed to get everything backwards. It was hard, but not impossible, to believe this was the case. The thought was more of a rationalization than a reason for the unexpected outcomes of some of the events that took place.

Jenny stood in the entrance and stared at the paintings and mirrors and for a second time saw a failed decimation that was brought on by a smudge and a cobweb. Saw those who would clean the dining hall as many times as told. Saw those who wouldn't. There were those who followed what they were told to do out of blind loyalty and those who chose to refuse in that what was required of them made no sense. Each believed they had the best reason for the actions they took.

What struck her the most was where were they? The place was completely empty. She could feel a change coming, everything from that moment on would be different. Where were the people? After Sinclair told them to 'carry on' and left, an hour or two later so did they.

The events of the morning finally got to all of them. They couldn't work with the conditions the division caused. Both sides cleared out. Some left what they had behind and went to town and stayed. Most packed up what they had and went down the road for good. It wasn't a desertion; it was an evacuation, no one wanted to be there for the return of Hardin Lasbrith.

Jenny had no idea that for the most part the staff was gone. There were no buckets and rags left behind as she had expected. The dining hall was in perfect shape and no one would be able to know if it had been cleaned once or a hundred times. Hardin Lasbrith could come home and all would be safe. She felt, a false, sense of relief.

She sat down on a nearby couch in the hallway and should have kept her view fixed on the well-lit dining hall, and return to her thoughts on the selection of the best guest room. She had several to choose from, but there were three, with views of tree lines, sky lines and Lake Erie the other rooms couldn't surpass. She should have been making choices.

Instead, her thoughts drifted towards the little country she had made up in her head during the morning's upheaval. The disorder that took place right before she left for the kitchen and then Enoch. Jenny sat there believing the country survived its civil war and had held together when it hadn't. She wanted to believe they were all still there and in bed.

The pattern of thoughts that ran through her head were like looking through a kaleidoscope where the slightest movement changed the view of everything. She was transfixed on the dining hall and all that had taken place. It came to her the day's Decimation was one for the ages. The people who were there and the things they said and did etched in her memory.

She sat there for some time. It was strange there was not even a sound, let alone, a glimpse of anyone. She tried to remember and couldn't, a time the house seemed so empty, there was always someone moving about. She knew it was late and murmured 'but even so.' Then Jenny thought of Sinclair and slowly ask herself, "Where has he been all day?"

*****

It was well known by the staff; Sinclair would disappear for a few hours after lunch almost every day. The days Hardin would leave for downtown Cleveland, or go out of town, which was often. Jenny's guess was to take a nap, aware of what most of the staff knew, but willing to give Sinclair the benefit of the doubt. No one minded or complained about the fact he would disappear; all knew the atmosphere was better when he wasn't around.

She slowly shook her head and whispered, "He's never been away this long." He hadn't tracked her down, even once, to irritate her and that was always a big part of his day. Things were out of balance. She began to wonder more and more about what was going on.

She knew for a fact the last time she saw him was when Sinclair told the staff to "Do it again," Phase Two, of the instructions they were all given by Hardin Lasbrith. Jenny had no idea where Sinclair drifted off to that day. She would have not guessed Olivia's bedroom. She would've also not guessed he spent the whole day there. Jenny didn't speculate on the two, not because she couldn't, but because she didn't want to, they meant nothing to her. She chose to stay unaware, when it came to Sinclair and Olivia.

It would and wouldn't surprise her if the rumors were true. She was the one who deep cleaned Olivia's room every Wednesday and she never found any hard evidence Olivia was keeping company with another man. There was, however, plenty of circumstantial evidence she was, which Jenny chose to disregard.

Olivia had quite a collection of strange religious artifacts. Cleaning Olivia's room was the one part of her job she hated the most. The thoughts she would have about her and all the items the room held would overwhelm her every time. The items were even too bizarre for Sinclair, or so she thought. The fact Jenny overlooked the most, Sinclair was no stranger to Olivia's room.

What was different from all the past days was Sinclair never spent almost the whole day there and a good part of the night. It would turn out to be the longest period of time Sinclair and Olivia had ever spent with each other. It would also turn out to be toxic enough to be the last time the two would ever share the company of the other.

Jenny was wrong about Sinclair; he appreciated all her artifacts. To Sinclair, Olivia's room was a shrine to the exploitation of gullible people who deserved everything that happened to them. The ones who want to buy their salvation. The ones who don't understand it has to be earned by word and deed. He knew firsthand selling salvation to those who want to buy it instead of earn it is easy.

There were clear and tinted vials of water said to be from the Holy Land in Olivia's room. No matter how much money was put into their display there was no way to hide how cheap and tawdry they looked. Olivia's room was the perfect attempt to make a silk purse out of a sow's ear.

Jenny knew Olivia paid top dollar for every item in it. In the case of the vials, where the water was said to come from, and its true origin, were always two different places. The vials proclaimed to be filled with the waters from the lost rivers of the *Garden of Eden,* when in fact, they were filled with the polluted waters of the Cuyahoga River. Every time Jenny gazed at the vials, she felt embarrassed for Olivia.

There was a large collection of splinters of various sizes and shapes that were said to have come from the table of *The Last Supper*. They were in small boxes lined in green velvet that were all the same size and looked like miniature coffins. There were fifty boxes to a row and twenty-five rows displayed. She had purchased twelve-hundred-fifty splinters from the table of the *Last Supper*. Olivia believed she owned a good part of the table and was the only one in procession of the splinters.

Each splinter a different size than the one next to it, not unlike different sized humans shown in their coffins at a mass burial after some catastrophe. They were all on an expansive dark walnut Chippendale table that was under a crystal chandelier. The décor chosen for the display, similar to what is found in a funeral parlor.

A large collection of worn and filthy cloth remnants, each said to have mystical powers, each worn at one time by some prophet or saint. They were displayed in the shape of a fan on a white marble wall, like the flags of knights who created some important council.

The largest display were the seeds. They were all from the Holy Land. One seed glued to a one-inch square on a six-foot by eight-foot expensive white silk sheet with purple and gold embraided edges. Olivia provided the sheet. Each square on it cost an unbelievably large sum of money.

If the actual cost of the seed was a penny, she bought it for one hundred dollars. Next, she would turn around and again pay, not just anyone, she would pay a top rate craftsman to mount the seed on the sheet. She thought she understood what most didn't. That the seed of faith that provides salvation has to be bought from the right person. The seed can't be sold by just anyone or given away. Those selling salvation let themselves be known to all but only a few are intelligent enough to take advantage of what they offer.

Seeds, the first product anyone seeking salvation has to buy and anyone selling salvation has to have. Everyone has to plant the seed of salvation. May have to plant it more than once. May have to plant it several times. May have to try different seeds. Every time one plants a seed, they have to water it with faith.

Each time a seed fails it's because one didn't water it with enough faith and the water of faith is money. Failure to grow is never the seed's fault. Failure is always the planter's fault. The seed didn't get enough water because the planter didn't have enough faith. The planter will have to go back to the seller of salvation and buy another seed, plant it, and water it better.

And what is faith for those who want to buy their salvation? It is theological money. Back by a seller's theology, to get the gullible to believe the more one buys from the seller of such things the closer they are to salvation. Jenny was wrong about Sinclair, he was comfortable there, because he believed in the theology of Olivia's room, he had always admired the work of charlatans and her room was a shrine to them.

*****

Sinclair and Olivia were at the point in their relationship where they began to abuse each other, the only common thread that held them together was alcohol. The times they were in each other's company soured, each looked at the other as someone to drink with in order to make their sexual activity more tolerable, nothing more.

Heavy make-up invaded Olivia's natural beauty. Her hair was dyed and done up in an attempt to show maximum volume. An artificial beauty started to overtake what was once natural. All she had left was her figure, which sooner, rather than later, would also wither. In a way, time, became as abusive as Sinclair.

Sinclair's stature was as thin as the volume of hair on his head. He was once a wiry man of muscle and bone, but no longer. He was skin and bones and on the edge of looking unhealthy. His hair was always glued down with hair tonic. Any way he tried to comb it made him look ridiculous, which he knew, but continued the practice in order to appear groomed.

By virtue of being a male he believed he was entitled to any female he desired. In return, it never entered his mind, what a female was also entitled to. He didn't understand, or care, what it would take for him to be desirable to them. For example, to cut off all his hair and to stop playing around with something he didn't have. A woman would tell him it sends a bad message. The fact he had the dead eyes of a shark with unattractive bags under them made him even less desirable, but in his world all these things shouldn't matter or get in the way of what he wanted as a man.

The only compensation Sinclair had for his appearance was the suits he wore were always cleaned and pressed. Other than his physical features, he looked good on the outside and at a distance. Underneath his clothes he wore what he slept in. A set of underwear he changed at least twice a month. He masked any odors from his body with the toilet waters he took from Hardin's bathroom.

Olivia's attire never changed. She always wore a sheer black robe trimmed with fur on the cuffs and hem. She wore nothing underneath and left the robe unbuttoned. Sinclair would strip down to his suspenders and would have to ask her permission to take off the rest.

They would drink expensive bottles of wine, she would make him beg, they would have deviant sex, when it was over, he would insult her and she would ignore him. They would drink more wine and repeat the pattern day in and day out.

The day of the failed Decimation, as always, Sinclair stopped by the wine cellar. Only this time instead of two bottles he brought four to Olivia's room. Midafternoon he went back for four more. They skipped dinner and Sinclair made another trip. There was a trip after the dinner trip. As midnight closed in each had about ten bottles of wine. Between each trip, they had sex and Olivia would make Sinclair beg harder and Sinclair became more insulting.

Before the last trip to bring each to a dozen bottles of wine, about a bottle an hour for each, Sinclair's insults were the harshest of the day and more ruthless than in the past. He told how her life was nothing but a genuinely cheap carnival always searching for the worst part of town. A carnival filled with bad acts performed not for, but on, any slick dressed, fast talking conman selling a ticket to salvation and immortality. He would remind her of the tricks she pulled for every evangelical imposter to get what they said they had when everyone but her knew they had nothing.

He brought up the snake handler George Wendt Hensley and told Olivia he killed all his snakes and that was the real reason she and Hensley never met. That he wanted to kill Hensley too but he got away. Sinclair told her, "Hensley was insane! Paused for a second and then continued "But not as insane as you." Sinclair knew how fragile Olivia was when it came to her own sanity and always told her she and everyone she knew was insane.

He'd tell her there was nothing normal or good about her or any of them from the nickel/dime bible thumper on a small street corner, to the seedy ones who moved up to store fronts, clear up to the big time/big deal evangelist up on the stage of some giant auditorium he could either afford to rent or build. Sinclair would end, "You're all fakes and you all know this. You're all false profits that won't or maybe so morally weak you can't stop being what you really are. Fake!"

Olivia had no way of knowing if what Sinclair told her about Hensley was true or not. When she felt this way, she would always go with her first assumption, which was he was lying. Nine times out of ten she would be right; it was no different this time. George Went Hensley and his snakes weren't dead and Sinclair couldn't have gotten away from them fast enough. Hensley's brother witnessed Sinclair's departure and it wasn't even close to what Sinclair told Olivia. It didn't matter she had no way to know.

What Sinclair would get in return from Olivia was a cold silence and the most menacing look a female can make. A look that said, "Maybe you're right…maybe I am insane." She would stand by her dressing table and file her nails with a file that could easily pass for a dagger. Everything about her was reminiscent of some extremely venomous viper coiled in a corner trying to decide whether or not to strike.

It would spook Sinclair to where he would back his way to his clothes and then the door. He put on his pants and pulled up his suspenders. He would back out of the room bare chested and barefoot. Once int the hall he would walk forward to the wine cellar. Olivia would slam the door and lock it as if she were through with him. Sinclair would chuckle when he would hear the click. He knew when he returned, she would open it back up in a second for the wine. It didn't matter who had it.

Although it was supposed to be, it was no secret to either the staff or the Lasbriths that Sinclair and Olivia were functional drunks. They both could drink phenomenal amounts of alcohol and walk straight and stumble no more than a normal person. They did slur their words, on occasion, to draw one's suspicions, but it didn't happen often. Both trained the staff to read their facial expressions which the staff picked up in no time. It was when a staff member would cause them to speak that the staff found themselves in trouble. It turned out all knew both drank, but no one had any idea how much.

*****

The late night brought on an unusual volume of moonlight. The mystical glow it created made the imposing Lasbrith mansion appear enchanted. Moonbeams poured through every window. They put a silvery cast on everything, to where one could become hypnotized by the soft radiance and unaware of what dangers lurked in the hallways and doorways of the Lasbrith mansion.

Enoch gazed at the mark on the sash and sill of the window. The mark left behind for all to see, by day, month, and year, who was to be credited for the beautiful room they were in. He gave the ballroom a date of birth and an illegitimate father.

Those who found the mark, could age the ballroom in no time, with little effort. However, it did take some time and effort, for the bankers, lawyers, agents, and those who studied the mansions on Euclid Avenue, to figure out who the real father of the ballroom was, or catch Enoch Mast's inside joke on the Lasbriths. It came to pass the mark left by Enoch accomplished all he had intended it to.

More and more, with each second that passed, Enoch believed the mark's completion to be the true reason behind his return to the ballroom. Its importance greater than getting paid. Fate gave the mark purpose. Purpose, let him know he returned not to receive his pay, as he first thought, but to leave his mark.

*****

Enoch etched June twenty-eighth in his mind as well. The day he captured and marked the Lasbrith Ballroom. Unaware the episode would be severely overshadowed by an event on the world stage of far greater significance. Even though his invasion of the Lasbrith estate and capture of the ballroom would surface first in his mind, others would have a completely different reason they remembered the date.

He moved to the overstuffed chair, lit a cigar, and gazed at the ballroom in the moonlight, and thought how his work had been seen by him in all different shades of light a day has to offer. In all the diverse shades, not once, was he disappointed in what he saw.

He could see the influence of their best past works in the ballroom. He saw the ballroom as the best example of the Mast Brothers capabilities. Once the mark he left behind was discovered, all would know who to credit for the beautiful room they were in, The Masts, which Mast would become another matter.

The objects of his design, the sculpted banner, on the window's sash, which read, "June 28th,1914," and the fashioned shield, to where it looked like the badge of an important official, with "Brooks Mast" name on it, couldn't have been made any better. All the finished letters and numbers where the right size and depth to almost pass as machined work. All that remained to be done was the hand-rub, where the oils from Enoch's hands would forever expose the beauty of the wood.

There were more than one or two occasions, visitors noted the date given Enoch Mast's ballroom was the same for the event that gave birth to the First World War. It occurred over forty-seven-hundred miles from Cleveland in Sarajevo, Bosnia/Herzegovina. The day, month, and year tattooed on Enoch's ballroom, also turned out to be the date Archduke Franz Ferdinand was assassinated by Gavrilo Princip.

*****

Enoch stopped to smoke a cigar and rest his eyes. He smoked half, placed it in the ashtray and began to drift off to the no man's land between two states of consciousness. The state where one is awake and the state where one is asleep. While in this no man's land he began to reminisce about the Osstill mansion, Irene, Saint Dorwin, Saint Bedmir, Crandell Poachfield, John D Rockefeller and a host of others. They would all be part of a dream that was yet to arrive.

The no man's land between what was real and what was imagined at times plagued Enoch and if one were to enter it, it was best for them to keep moving. There was a time Enoch got stopped and the time spent in this land was not good.

Because of this, what happened next in the ballroom, would lead to a situation where he was stopped in no man's land for the second time in his life. Again, unable to tell if the event that took place was real or imagined. He would have an experience not unlike what took place at Gettysburg. Where Alden Sinclair slit a man's throat for what appeared to be no reason at all.

That turned into an event he could never say there was no doubt in his mind that it happened because there was some. However, it was quite small and in a very deep recess of his mind. He knew the address but hardly ever visited the doubt. For the most part Enoch was certain the Alden Sinclair incident did take place, but every once in a great while had to convince himself.

As he drifted towards his dream, Sir Carl interrupted and again was down by the stage. He was at the farthest part of the room from Enoch but felt closer in Enoch's mind. Only this time the bitch climbed the stairs to the stage and began to walk across it instead of in front of it as she had in the past. The view of the dog from where he sat was as impressive as it was frightening. It was the full look of a large domesticated dog that had somehow returned to the origins of a dangerous wild beast.

As usual Sir Carl entered from the door on the left of the stage and exited the ballroom from the door on the right. She went down a set of steps and through the door, or did she? It seemed; she didn't do what was expected. It seemed she disappeared into thin air. It became a question in Enoch's mind, did she disappear or did she go through the door? He couldn't decide.

The dog put on a very short, yet, threatening one act play. Where an actor transforms from a tolerated character to a dangerous one. The one everyone in the audience keeps their eye on.

The one act play was a horror story that drove Enoch inside his right pocket for the switchblade. He got it out in one brief smooth fluid moment, pressed down the button and the knife snapped from closed to open in less than a second. He did this just in case, out of instinct. He would put a six inch very sharp blade of steel between him and the dog and open Sir Carl up if he had to. There was not one thing normal about the dog's behavior. He knew the dog could cover a lot of ground fast if it wanted to. If he was spotted, he would be unwelcomed in what Sir Carl believed to be her territory and she would treat it as an invasion.

Enoch kept his eyes on the stage watching for any movement that would tell him Sir Carl was back in the area. He didn't trust the dog at all and from what he had recently seen wanted to be aware of where the dog was at all times. He stared at the stage area more than what was necessary. To where it became counterproductive and he began to imagine movement that wasn't there.

When he finally did turn away, his eyes became fixed on the entrance to the ballroom. The entrance had the largest area of exposed hallway. Next, he saw in the light of the moon Alden Sinclair, with a candle in hand, walk across the entrance to the ballroom, no different in mood and manner than the way Sir Carl moved across the stage.

Enoch quickly blew out his candle so as not to be discovered and began to wonder from who Sinclair might have gotten his candle. It didn't matter, Sinclair walked by the ballroom with no intention to enter. It was as if he was in a daze. Enoch wondered what Sinclair was up to and where he was headed.

He got caught up in how Sinclair was barefoot and bare chested. All he had on were pants and suspenders. How he looked unaware and weak, how he seemed to be detached from everything around him. With his switchblade in hand, for a moment, Enoch thought about coming up on Sinclair's blind side and slitting his throat. To surprise him just as he once did to some poor prisoner. He thought why wait for Alden Sinclair to come after him?

Enoch didn't wrestle with the thought for long, and decided to act on it, as he watched Sinclair move down the hall. In his mind he turned the hallway into an ally and stalk him no different than he had stalked others down some backstreet. A premonition came over him that someone or something was behind him and he turned to look.

In the distance it was Sir Carl and Enoch fell back into the dining hall, again unnoticed. He thought, "One moment he's by the stage, next he's in the hallway," wondering how it was possible. The stage door led back to the kitchen then the dining hall, he'd have to go through both to get to where he was. There just wasn't enough time for the dog to appear as he did. The dog looked as if he was tracking prey and Enoch kept still as Sir Carl also drifted from sight in the direction of Sinclair. Enoch began to dream and saw himself return to the overstuffed chair. He saw all this take place just before his dream came and he fell asleep.

*****

The couch Jenny sat on in front of the dining hall was in the middle of the hallway. Traffic coming down the hall from the large Fourier at the entrance or from the upstairs ballroom could walk behind the couch as easily as in front of it.

The mahogany table behind the couch ran its length but had a thin width. The table served as a collection point for those who wished to place their finished and half-finished cocktails on before entering the hall. The couch and table were like an island in a river. It separated the flow of people entering the dining hall. The couch and table were there to assure both sides, of the highly polished, expansive mahogany dining table, which had six very large candle labra, spaced close to five or six feet apart, would be filled equally.

Jenny was too transfixed on the dining hall and the day's events to take notice of the two strange hands on her shoulders, which were neither warm nor cold to the touch. Her preoccupation with the hall and the day's events the reason why it took her more than a second or two to become aware of them. When she became aware of the hands on her shoulders it struck her like a bolt of lightning that her neck was between them.

Fear rippled through every part of her body for a moment. The possibility of a move towards her neck made her lunge forward to get out of range. She didn't scream. She confronted the situation by immediately turning to see who had come up behind her and looked them straight in the eyes. It was Marsden, and a moment of true irony, when she realized he had found her before she had found him and she thought it wasn't supposed to play out that way.

He was surprised there was no scream, he was prepared for one but was pleased he didn't have to put his hand over her mouth. It didn't come to that and Jenny's composure impressed Marsden. Nothing was said for a few seconds, Marsden gave her the opportunity to speak first. She became a whirlwind, "Why would you come up on me like that?" Marsden didn't give an answer, he gave an apology. As he gave it, she began to drink in everything about Marsden as one slowly consumes an elixir and waits for it to take effect.

An interesting side effect was that with each second that passed she became less tense and more relaxed and less frightened. Each second that past she became more secure in his presence. Marsden had a reassuring manner and affable personality. He looked old and strong at the same time. Which made his appearance a paradox in that the two hardly ever complement one another.

Marsden had a shock of thick white hair, the darkest brown eyes, square shoulders, long arms and was slightly bowlegged. He wore a tan cotton shirt with the sleeves rolled up. A darker brown leather apron, that went a little past his knees. His navy-blue trousers were tucked inside a pair of well-maintained black leather boots. He had more the appearance of a blacksmith than a custodian. When he walked there was a faint and pleasant jingle from the key ring that hung from his belt.

He had a pass key for every guest room that had a fire place. All of Hardin Lasbrith's guest rooms had locks that required a key. There were no drop latches or dead bolts as backup security. The guests were given a key and none ever questioned or requested any type of backup system.

Hardin had it this way so he could enter a locked room any time he wanted and for any reason: to search it, to rob it, or to take advantage of the occupant. The way the locks worked on these doors Hardin Lasbrith could confine a guest for as long as he wanted. Visitors assumed when they locked their rooms, they were safe. Given the two-way mirrors and the way the locks worked, no guest at the Lasbrith estate ever had a secure and private room or was safe.

Hardin visited several guest rooms the day of his granddaughters wedding reception. He took things that weren't his, read things he shouldn't have, and locked the young woman he captured at the reception and slept with, in the guest room above Olivia's bedroom. Hardin, Marsden, and a safe held the pass keys to the guest rooms.

Marsden had a set because he tended all the fire places, he cleaned them out, filled them with wood, and made them easy to light for the guest. Those who came in contact with him found he was humble and noble in almost everything he did. Even Hardin Lasbrith fell under his spell. Against his gut feelings, the man who trusted no one, allowed Marsden to have a set of keys. He rationalized if one couldn't trust a person like him, who could they trust?

Marsden spoke and he asked if she knew why the hallway lights were off and the dining hall lights were on? He shared a theory with Jenny that the one responsible for turning the lights on and off may have shared the same fate as the person he found in the wine cellar. He had a suspect in mind. A still at large suspect. Jenny didn't answer him she shook her head "no" to his question of if she knew why the lights were the way they were.

Jenny finally spoke and wanted to answer, "I was about to ask you the same question!" However, she was unable to do this. Instead, what came out of her was, "I know all about you Royal Roy Marsden!" and she proceeded to tell him what she knew and who told her and how he -Marsden - should be dead. How she knew about the "Roosters" of the Ohio 7th Infantry, the cemetery, the copperhead, Culp's Hill, Gettysburg and the four rounds he took to the chest and whose leg he broke, she tried to tell him everything.

She spoke like a runaway train. Her words were rushed as if she had finished a race and was out of breath. She tried to tell Marsden everything she knew about him in one world record-breaking run-on sentence. A sentence capable of sucking up all the available oxygen in the room if allowed to be completed.

Marsden gently raised one finger to his lips in such a manner that when Jenny saw it, she stopped in the middle of all her rapid-fire questions and waited for him to speak. The only question he answered was "Where is everyone?" He told her of the mass evacuation that occurred soon after she left for the kitchen. It didn't come as surprise to her that she knew nothing about it. What unsettled her was how Marsden knew she went to the kitchen. She knew how cautious she had been about who was around her. In silence she said to herself, "How could it be he saw me and I never saw him?"

*****

By virtue of the fact she didn't scream, Marsden decided to leveled with Jenny. He told her the unvarnished truth, "There's a body with no left arm in the wine cellar, it's Alden Sinclair's. Sir Carl ripped his arm off and he bled to death. It was bad; Sinclair broke a wine bottle and he held it like a knife in his right hand, the beast charged and they fought. There was a lot of blood, Sinclair is dead, Sir Carl is wounded, and the one I put in charge of the lights is missing."

He went on to tell her he was in the hunt for the new person, Alton Sinclair's arm, and Sir Carl. Marsden told her he didn't care in what order they showed up. He walked to one of the fire places in the hall and grabbed a fire poker and began to swing it around as if it were a saber to get acquainted with its balance and weight. He informed Jenny, so far, he had found nothing but it was just a matter of time.

He also informed her Sir Carl was no longer a dog, he was a very large and very rabid wounded beast on the loose inside the mansion. The worst place to be was in an unlit hallway. They needed to find a room with a thick door and strong lock to be safe.

Marsden took Jenny to the room he had in mind. He told her she would have company and that he had already put Hilda the cook in it. He explained to her there was safety in numbers. It was as if Marsden knew of all the household staff Hilda was jenny's favorite. It was a pleasant large room filled with heavy furniture, thick rugs, nice mirrors and had a large window with an excellent view of Lake Erie under the moon light. It was the room Jenny would have picked had she not become lost in her thoughts. For a moment it struck her as ironic how she didn't find Marsden, he found her, and she didn't find the room but was taken to it.

Once inside Jenny told Marsden that Enoch was in the ballroom and in an effort to muzzle the panic that ran through her whispered "We have to go get him." She said it in a very determined low voice.

Marsden informed her there was no "We" in his plan and it would be his plan that would be carried out. He, and he alone, would go get Enoch and bring him to her. He explained his plan as he backed up to the door of the room. The whole time he gently blocked her attempts to rush the door and get out of the room.

Once outside the room Marsden gave her one last shove and she went into the arms of Hilda. He quickly closed the door, went to his key ring and locked it. He was locked out and she was locked in. The door was between them. On his side of the door Marsden wondered if he should come clean and tell Jenny the truth. That he wasn't going to bring Enoch back.

The thought came and went and he decided to say nothing and headed for the ballroom. Locked up on her side of the door, the thought that she couldn't abandon was the dog had already killed and would kill again, to add two more to the list wouldn't be a problem. That there was a good chance Sir Carl could get both of them.

As Marsden walked towards the ballroom. He began to evaluate the decision he made not to tell Jenny she would never see Enoch again, maybe in another dimension, but not here anymore. He began to go over some of the parts he hadn't told her. That he was in the wine cellar when it happened, back in the racks where he could see Sinclair but, Sinclair couldn't see him.

Sinclair could no longer read the labels on the bottles. He groped the rack, no different than a clumsy drunk would grope a woman, knocking some bottles to the floor. It seemed the out of reach bottles were the ones that fascinated him the most. He swore a blue streak every time he broke one. The racket made by the shattering glass, and his loud, harsh, and profane soliloquies, had a negative effect on the audience of one that lurked in the doorway.

The racket came to an end when Sinclair looked up and saw the large rabid dog. The monster filled the doorway of the wine cellar. There was no escape. The beast kept its place in the doorway. Sinclair decided to stay behind the racks for protection and wait for Sir Carl to make the first move. It was as bad a situation as one could have.

For a few moments, which seemed like forever to Sinclair, he and Sir Carl stared at one another. The beast stood there with fluids dripping from its eyes, nose and mouth and one couldn't tell which location irritated Sir Carl the most. He would shake his head and the fluids flew from him in all directions. It brought on the most menacing growl; any creature could have.

Sinclair used the time to grab the nearest bottle. He brought it down hard on the edge of the rack. The move changed the dynamics of the situation and the tension between the two hit the breaking point. The bottle broke perfect, with one long shard no different than the blade of a large hunting knife, just as long, just as sharp but not as strong. For a brief moment Sinclair smiled at the weapon in his hand and looked to grab another bottle and repeat the process to fill his other hand. When his other hand was filled, he would be ready to fight. The exact moment he went for the second bottle, Sir Carl charged him with the lethal velocity of a bullet.

It happened much faster than Sinclair had ever anticipated. He tried to fend the bitch off with his left arm. As he sacrificed his left arm, his right arm was able to bury the glass shard into Sir Carl more than once. When the shard broke off in the dog it was replaced by a large tuft of fur where the shard had been. It left Sinclair defenseless. Sir Carl viciously pressed on with the attack and eventually rip Sinclair's left arm from his body. It remained in the dog's mouth as it walked out of the cellar.

Sinclair writhed in tremendous pain on the floor. He went into shock and bled out. Through it all Marsden did nothing to stop the attack or aid the victim. It was his job to witness the event and nothing more. Marsden was right behind Sir Carl when he left the wine cellar. As he reflected back on Jenny, he was glad he left that part out of what he told her.

*****

Enoch was asleep when Marsden found him. He was in the middle of a dream, where he dreamt, he woke up. However, what Enoch thought to be a dream turned out to be reality, he did wake up. Why it seemed to be a dream was brought on by who stood before his eyes, Royal Roy Marsden. The only time Enoch ever saw him, over the last fifty years, was in dreams and the reason he thought he was still dreaming.

Despite the years Enoch recognized him right off and called out his name. "Royal Roy Marsden!" Enoch was quick to add, "But you're dead!" He spoke out loud to the dream he believed he was in. Marsden made no attempt to deny what Enoch said, instead he smiled at Enoch and fired right back, "So are you."

Marsden then put his one finger to his lips, shushed Enoch and directed his eyes to the stage. His long right arm pointed out the character that occupied its center. Enoch looked straight down Marsden's arm, no different than a surveyor looks through a transit at a far-off object. Enoch focused on Sir Carl. She stood long enough for Enoch to clearly see, not only her, but also the arm in her mouth. Long enough for Enoch to get a good look at the stage, dog and arm. As soon as it registered in his mind, what he saw, the dog collapsed, and was dead before she hit the floor. Enoch thought for a moment about waking up, again unaware he was awake, but the thought left as fast as it arrived.

What Enoch took in surprised him more than frightened him. Marsden asked, "Whose arm do you think it is?" Enoch replied in relief, "Well it's no woman's arm" and Marsden nodded "Its Sinclair's." Enoch had to fight off his urge to smile.

He didn't mention that he'd seen Sinclair pass by the ballroom earlier and at the time was going to slit his throat. He would have too if it hadn't been for Sir Carl who followed Sinclair down the hallway. He backed off because he didn't want to be between Sinclair and Sir Carl, he thought it was a bad place to be so he slipped back into the ballroom unseen by the dog. As he did, it came to him he would have to kill Sinclair another time. Had Enoch mentioned it, it wouldn't have mattered, Marsden already knew and was the one who set it up so the dog, not him, would kill Sinclair.

*****

Marsden told Enoch; Sinclair was on his way to the wine cellar to get some bottles of wine for Olivia and him. He too was looking for a bottle wine when the attack took place. Through it all Enoch was totally satisfied with what he was told and didn't ask Marsden one question. He did, however, make a request for Marsden to repeat the part where Sinclair's arm got ripped off, moving his head up and down unable to hide how he felt about the news. After Marsden repeated the part, he had to ask Enoch, "No words of sympathy, huh?" Enoch answered, "None."

Marsden turned from Enoch and walked to the ballroom entrance, he returned with a fresh box of cigars, full bottle of bourbon and two clean glasses. His trek to and from the bar gave Enoch time to think. He found it hard to ignore how familiar Marsden was with the ballroom. He didn't have to ask for anything he wanted. He knew where to get it right away.

It was pleasant and strange at the same time. It seemed Marsden was as familiar with the room as Enoch. As Marsden got closer to Enoch, maybe thirty feet, he began to speak and spun around a few times to take the room in. He raised his arms above his head, one hand held the bottle, the other the cigars and proclaimed, "This is a handsome room, full of balance and character. You know what they say, your 'work' reflects you. This is a fine room."

Enoch was overcome by the compliment and didn't know what to say and pretended Marsden was just out of range for him to hear all that was said. He didn't know how to acknowledge Marsden. It didn't matter Marsden phrased what he said to get such a response. It was the part of the job Marsden enjoyed the most, never being wrong in the direction he chose when he took one 'up' or 'down' the road. He loved to be the first to deal out the revenge or reward one deserved.

When Marsden returned, he emptied the ashtray out the open window and moved a table and chairs in front of it. He set it up to where they could enjoy any gentle warm breeze that came along. He set it up to where they could take full advantage of the moon light from the outside and the candle light from the inside to see each other, not in the best light, but in the right light for the drinks, smokes and conversation they were about to have.

Enoch didn't want to get up and move to the table, he was too comfortable in the overstuffed chair to make the effort. He made the move after he was coaxed in a firm manner by Marsden that it would be in his best interest to move to the table.

At the table Enoch stretched and shook his head while Marsden poured him a drink and then one for himself. Marsden lit a cigar and a breeze captured the smoke and moved it past Enoch's nose and he opened his eyes wider to all that surrounded him and lit a smoke too. He was still unaware of his true condition. He didn't believe he was awake and what made it peculiar was he didn't believe he was asleep; he was somewhere between the two in a very unfamiliar place.

Both settled in at the window and table, with drinks and smokes in hand, Marsden told Enoch, "No easy way to tell you this – but you're dead." Enoch replied, "I don't feel dead." Marsden fired back, "Well you are! And don't be someone I have to prove it to, just accept the fact and let's move on."

Enoch told Marsden, "I'm just telling you how I feel and it isn't dead." Marsden shook his head and sarcastically asked "Oh? And you've been dead before?" It was a point of departure. From that point on all Marsden said proved how wrong Enoch was about how he felt. What he felt and where he was were two different states, one false and one true. What he felt was false, where he was, true. The fact he felt no different, wherever he was, didn't change the reality he was dead. Marsden knew when the fact hit, Enoch would be scared – everyone is.

*****

At the table their conversation deepened. Enoch asked Marsden if he was some type of spirit, aberration, haint or ghost. Marsden didn't answer. What he did do was fill in some blanks that only such beings are capable of. For example, Enoch learned Marsden was like him, a replacement. It was how they came to be at Culp's hill, when in fact it should have been Hardin Lasbrith and John D Rockefeller. Marsden footnoted the information with, "It was supposed to be those two but it turned out to be you and me." Fate is just as odd as eternity.

Marsden continued, "Know the Lasbrith's had quite the wake for me when they found out. Hear it was quite a tribute to the Union cause and the life sacrificed. Through it all my name was never mentioned once, but Hardin's was. Then you had Sinclair who coached Hardin all the time about a place he never went and the things he never did." What Enoch saw between the lines of what Marsden said was enough animosity to explain his behavior in the wine cellar.

They were both okay with Sinclair dead and the way he died. However, Enoch told Marsden he didn't think it right he had to die on the same day. Marsden sighed and told him, "Look at the way he went and the way you're going! What's wrong with you?" Enoch couldn't hold back and asked, "Am I going to have to deal with him again?" Marsden answered, "I don't know! But its eternity, thinking eventually you're going to deal with everyone, good and bad, that ever was, is, or will be, at one time or another. It's eternity – you'll have the time"

*****

To avoid an onslaught of questions, Marsden finally leveled with Enoch, "Look, I was dead before I got to Gettysburg. Like I told you then, I got killed at Chancellorsville, you thought I was joking, but I wasn't. For some reason it never got recorded, the documentation either never came through, or what did was wrong. I think because the 7th Ohio couldn't account for me, I had to come back and do it all over and go get killed again at Gettysburg to get the record straight. Oh, and I'm not the only one this happened to, a bunch of us showed up at Gettysburg, I'd say a platoon of us were sent back for one reason or another and were spread all over, both sides."

The expression of amazement never changed on Enoch's face as Marsden continued, "I went fast both times. The first time, I woke up in a 'new' dimension. The second time was when I was sent back to save you. Which I did. You were my ticket back to the new dimension. It's really nice there and I was told, all I had to do, to stay, was watch over you, to be your guardian angel.

To be honest, after Gettysburg I got sidetracked by many delights and pretty much left you on your own. The few times I did check I found you've almost always landed on your feet, sure there was maybe a time or two, I could've jumped in, but you survived. You done more than most and surprised many, which, in the end, would mean I did a pretty good job."

Marsden went on, "I admit I was lax, but you'll find it's easy to do here, besides didn't it turn out for the best. In fact, I'm only one or two steps and a couple of lessons in front of you. Fifty years to you is like fifty seconds to me. So, I'm new at this. I can do things in the new dimension I couldn't do in the old one. These powers from the new dimension are light years beyond useful. I travel to both dimensions all the time. Simply put - I go to the new dimension to get my powers and I go to the old dimension to use them – and its great!"

Marsden went on to explain how he had adjusted to the new dimension and liked what he did. How he gets sent places to do things, to get someone, provide a small miracle, heal a wound. To take care of problems for the living. How in between what he does, he gets a lot of great food and rest. How, all in all, he's pretty satisfied. Enoch at once asked Marsden about the sex and Marsden told him, "Haven't had any yet but if it's like the food and sleep it'll be great. Thinking it's up the road or around the bend, bump into it eventually – this is eternity – so I know it's just a matter of time."

Marsden's happiness began to frighten Enoch in a strange way, it made him want to be dead but he fought the desire because 'living' was all he knew. Marsden told Enoch to take out his pocket watch. Enoch tried to get in front of Marsden and told him. "I know

266

it stopped the moment I showed up at the kitchen door. If that's your surprise."

Marsden answered, "Stopped? No, here's my surprise, your watch is dead, like you." Enoch, smiled at Marsden as he popped open his watch to show him, "And according to my watch I ran out of time the moment I arrived here. Right? Which was?" He looked away from Marsden and down on the opened watch. He was certain the watch would show seven forty-five, the hour and minute he arrived at what would be the scene of his death.

Somehow the information he thought he had would prove to Marsden that he wasn't the mistaken party when it came down to the condition of dead or alive. That since the concept of time was still with him, he was still alive. Instead, Enoch said nothing and gave a short gasp, when he looked at the face of the watch and found it had no hands, tic marks, or numbers. Its face was blank. The symbolism overwhelmed and frightened him.

Enoch began to mount a case to put a stay on his death. But for a moment was curious to know, "Will I get what you have?" Marsden answered "I don't know, I only pick up and deliver." Enoch liked the fit robust figure Marsden cut and believed he did more than pick up and deliver. He lit a cigar and told Marsden, "Think of it this way. I've only really lived a minute and fifteen seconds, if you count each year at one number per second. Any chance I could get a minute and a half?" Marsden's answer was at first a blank stare followed by a very dry voice, "Hardly anyone gets a minute and a half and I can assure you; you aren't one of them."

His answer didn't stop Enoch. Enoch went on to tell Marsden, "I understand it's a good time for you but it's not a good time for me. I have a few things to finish before I can go anywhere." He went on to point out, first, he had to collect from Hardin Lasbrith so he and Brooks Mast could develop their concept of the 'pick-up truck. He told Marsden, "No one has in mind what we want to develop." He went on, "I also have to finish the mark on the window and hand rub it, that'll take some time too." Enoch went on and on until Marsden finally yelled, "Stop!"

Marsden wasn't at all sympathetic and answered, "What makes you think I can bend the rules for you? Everyone I pick up has something to finish! No one is ever finished! You think I haven't heard this time and time again! Everyone leaves with something undone!" He then told Enoch to look at his pocket watch again to see 'exactly' how much time he had left. He told Enoch, "The time you know is gone, the new time will be different."

To get off the subject of more time, Marsden told Enoch to recalled the graveyard, they visited the day before the battle. Enoch nodded, it was the time he asked Marsden about the souls under the tombstones, "Is it true, whatever isn't heaven, is hell?" It was there Marsden told Enoch about the other 'world' and how cemeteries were actually towns in another dimension.

Marsden informed Enoch he passed through some of these towns shortly after several more bullets blew through him the second time he was killed, "The moment it happens, in so many ways, you'll be off on the journey of your life, you'll travel to a state with no boundaries on continual amazement. But keep in mind 'amazement' comes in two forms, good and bad."

What Enoch heard puzzled him more than the changes on the face of his watch. What frightened him the most was he had far more questions than could possibly be answered, on what was happening to him. Or so he thought, again, he forgot he had entered eternity.

*****

Marsden patiently again informed Enoch he was no longer in the world he had known all his life. The world that began on July 8th, 1839, and ended seventy-six years and ten days later, on June 28th, 1914. With his allotted interval of time completed that world was over. Enoch didn't make the transition easy and had to be told, over and over again, his situation had changed.

Marsden let Enoch know the truth, the world was no longer between heaven and hell. There was no longer a buffer between the two and in his journeys from here on out what ever wasn't heaven, was hell. Marsden ended, "A bad day here will never be followed by a good day."

Marsden then gave Enoch a huge tip for his trip to the other side, "Some towns still use and worship money, because it is still their god. Some don't, because they know better. He continued, "If the towns you get to have, banks, hospitals, churches, funeral homes and cemeteries they use money and you're not in the 'new' dimension. Be careful not to get caught in your escape from the 'old' to the 'new.' It has happened to many." He went on, "If you do - you're 'ghosting' and haven't moved on to the 'new' dimension." Marsden paused, for a few moments and asked, "Is any of this getting through to you?" Enoch answered with a blank stare and a nod.

Marsden ended, "The hell in these towns is worse than the hell you ever saw in any town when you were alive. The ones who were too much of the world find they can't leave. The one's who dealt from the bottom of the deck or had a card up their sleeve, who lived to take advantage of others. Because of who they were, and how they were, they get imprisoned by their own desires in these towns and can't escape. They become ghosts; ghosts are the prisoners of the old dimension."

The information continued, "The towns you'll go through will have all types of people of all ages and shapes along with the animals they looked after. The population will be made up of heroes, villains, and victims. All arrived in these towns many different ways. Some were murdered, some drowned, others had horrific accidents, some killed themselves, others died fighting a war, some died of diseases and some died in their sleep, some died of hunger, there are so many ways." Marsden told Enoch he would recognize many people and many buildings in the towns he passes through and recall the buildings were burned, blown or torn down during his life. Pets and buildings die too and follow the people who kept and built them.

Marsden told Enoch, "The towns that have no money worship knowledge, they won't have what the towns with money have. They'll have first class homes, libraries, museums, art galleries, parks, beaches, lakes, pools, theatres, restaurants, cafes and taverns. The weather will always be perfect, the rain will always come along when needed and the amount of sun light favorable, all that's planted flourishes and all the natural resources well managed and renewable.

The lust for money, the root of all evil, is absent in these towns and so are all the institutions related to death. The atmosphere is such that it will take a while to notice there are no banks, hospitals, funeral homes, churches, and cemeteries when you're in these towns, they're absent and not missed."

He went on, "The people here have an almost undefinable level of cooperation with one another and work towards goals that are to everyone's benefit. They learn new things, build great things, they eat and drink the best and sleep well. They are the faithful who always believed in the dimension they had reached, the 'new' one, and in their conception of the God that gave it to them.

The last tip Marsden gave Enoch to look for in these towns involved mirrors and windows, "Some towns will have more mirrors than windows and some will have more windows than mirrors. In some towns the people want to look at themselves and in some towns the people want to look at others."

Marsden told Enoch a little-known secret, "The real hope of any mirror is to one day turn into a window. Every time a mirror breaks a window pops up for each piece, and the reason why there's more windows than mirrors. The idea, a broken mirror is bad luck, is a myth."

He expressed to Enoch, to make up for the shortage in numbers, mirrors possess strange powers and many uses. Marsden told Enoch to go stand in front of the mirror he and Jenny had gazed into earlier. He did as he was instructed, and saw the mirror reflected him in the foreground, and in the background the empty overstuffed chair and Marsden.

Marsden called out to Enoch. Enoch looked away from the mirror and directly at Marsden. Marsden did nothing to hold his attention and Enoch returned to the mirror. What he saw had the same impact as his watch. He saw his full image was gone and so was Marsden's. The mirror only revealed Enoch asleep in the overstuffed chair, no different than when Marsden first came upon him.

Enoch watched Marsden walk over to the overstuffed chair and heard what he whispered, "This is where Jenny will find you tomorrow and you will be dead to her and everyone else in this dimension." He continued, "There are so many decisions that have to be made. Basically, all you need to know is only when it is determined that the mirror of your soul has evolved into a window, and you no longer see yourself but others, will your new life in eternity begin. Remember this."

Enoch was also informed by Marsden, "We will begin to see each other more often. The trigger to set up a meeting will be when we both think of the same place at the same time, like Brooks' office. We'll have to work up a system and a schedule."

Enoch nodded as if he understood. He didn't and it was apparent by the unrelated question he asked, "When will I know where I wind up, heaven or hell?" Marsden laughed, "When you have an absolutely perfect day and the next day is better. Or when you have a devastatingly horrible day and the next day is worse. Knowing where you wind up won't be hard."

Marsden left the ballroom and Enoch went into transition. He found himself on the borderline between awake and asleep, he was neither conscious or unconscious. He saw himself fall off a high cliff and move at the speed of light toward the ground. He expected to splatter all over, but that didn't happen. What happened was every joint and organ in his body felt like they had broken loose from what held them in place and what exploded in a pain, that defies description, inside him was every sin he ever committed. The unbelievable agony was a very brief and equally unforgettable episode. The memory of the sting eternal.

The moment it ended he was on his feet, and felt a charge surge through his body that strengthened every bone, joint, muscle and organ. With it came an awareness he stood in a place he had never been before, it was different, yet he was familiar with all that surrounded him. The place was a paradox.

*****

Enoch stood at the intersection of two roads, one ran north and south the other east and west. He was struck by the fact he had no answers as to what to do next. He felt like the time he was at the intersection of Mast and Rockefeller, when the other big change in his life occurred. Only that intersection never existed, the one he stood on did.

The crossroad he was at gave four choices and one question. The question, "Is there just 'one right road? Or are 'all roads, right?" With no idea where to go, it seemed any road would lead to somewhere or something. At that moment All he had were four choices and choices are selections not answers. He had never stood at such an intersection, it was different.

As he gathered his thoughts, he put his hands in his pockets. He felt his knife and watch, he ignored the knife and began to rub his left thumb over the smooth cover of the watch. He took it out and opened it. What he expected and what he saw again caused him to gasp.

The blank face of the watch, with its missing tic marks, Roman numerals, sweep, big, and small hands, was filled in with the full face of a compass. The numerals replaced by the directions: North, East, South and West, the tic marks that measured seconds returned to measure the degrees of a circle. At the center of the face, a half red, half white magnetized needle sat atop a metal stem, at the expense of the watch's hands.

Enoch aligned his four choices with the four directions on the compass. In the far-off North, he could catch a glimpse of a lake, in the far-off East some small towns, in the far-off South the distant silhouette of a plantation. Finally, in the far-off West, Enoch could catch the faint glimpse of a horse and buggy. Each direction shared an interesting vision of what was down the road for him. He could always return to the origin if he wanted to change directions. The glimpse of the lake won first choice, and Enoch decided to head North.

CHAPTER IX
THE RED CATS

Late winter of 1914, in Cleveland, Ohio, the first heavy lake effect snow fell on the Mast home. A property Jenny took over, in much the same manner Enoch Mast seized Hardin Lasbrith's ballroom. From the moment she and Hilda set foot on the five-acre property and marched forward, past the outbuildings, into the house, she was determined to make it the place they would stay, and when the time came, die.

One winter night, as Jenny continued to put her broken heart back together, a random and vivid dream about Enoch's death came and stung her again. A few months had passed since the funeral and the dream caught her off guard and ripped open in her mind, a mixture of events, that did and didn't happen and she had trouble deciding which were true and which were imagined. The dream haunted her for days.

Many dreams are difficult to explain, the one she had would be more recalcitrant than most. She saw many luminous colors she had never seen before in the form of a mist. The mist filled a locked room and began to escape through a keyhole. She became like it and the mist beckoned her to follow. She did and the mist showed her the way to Enoch Mast's home.

When they arrived, Jenny's normal appearance returned. The mist took the shape of a woman. The woman spoke to Jenny, not with her lips but with her eyes and Jenny heard, "It is up to you to hold on to this place for us, we are one now." Jenny found the woman to be a likable, non-threatening entity. Even though she had no way to know, Jenny believed the stranger to be Irene O'Flynn

Mast, and she came to her as a sister with a message not to be ignored.

In her dream she and Hilda notified a mortician, who went to the ballroom and removed the body. He put Enoch on ice, tapped a team of white horses hitched up to a black hearse and took Enoch Mast home. The glass sided hearse slowly moved through the heart of Cleveland, people asked who was in the hearse and the answer they got spread throughout the city.

A sequence of events took place in the dream where she and Hilda prepared the stable/garage for the viewing. The whole time they worked on it she told Hilda, more than once, how much Enoch would appreciate the location. A large crowd showed up for the funeral three days later. People from all walks of life, formed an almost endless line, each had their own story about Enoch Mast. They all crossed her path and it seemed she listened to all the stories, but one. The one she wanted to hear most.

*****

After the initial shock, what actually took place, was Hilda and Jenny, wrapped Enoch's body up in a silk sheet they took from a hall closet adjacent to Olivia Lasbrith's bedroom. They placed his corpse in the back of his pick-up truck and drove him home.

Before Hilda could ask, Jenny began to explain how Enoch had taught her how to drive and that was how she knew the way to his place. From that point on, what she told Hilda, about her and Enoch's relationship kept Hilda's eyebrows raised the whole way.

She told Hilda, "During the driving lessons Enoch told me everything. I never asked him about any of it and when I would tell him to stop! He would joke, 'Even though Cap knows, I feel the need to tell someone else – and that 'someone,' might as well be you. You need to listen – your name is on a lot of paperwork. I don't know if it's true or not but that's what he told me."

She informed Hilda she knew where all his important papers and treasure were. The hiding place for the will, bank accounts, insurance policies, deeds to his properties, stocks and bonds, plus two-hundred-fifty, twenty-dollar gold pieces, all the items that belonged in a safe were in the fire proof compartment inside the Wooten Desk found in his bedroom. All one had to do was slide a piece of molding to unlock and reveal their location. There wasn't much Jenny didn't know about their destination. Jenny even told Hilda how the 1912 Runabout they rode in was to eventually go to Jesse O'Dell's family.

As they went down the road, she asked Hilda, "You know about Wooton Desks?" Hilda nodded, "Everyone does." Jenny continued, "Well around the late eighteen-sixties Enoch told me he built a desk with over a hundred drawers, twenty-four pigeon holes, one for each year's current and past month, a slide out desk top with an inkwell, a desk that when you were done, folded up like a trunk. He built it more as an exercise in joinery than a concept in organization and storage."

Jenny went on, "No one knows what actually took place, but a patternmaker Enoch met and liked, named William Wooton, saw the desk and realized its possibilities. Around 1870 they entered into a secret agreement and Enoch became both a silent and invisible partner in the Wooton Desk Company. Both did well, the desk caught on as the fountain pen and typewriter went into mass production, and the American office changed. The desk provided organization and storage for the ever-increasing amounts of paperwork the pen and typewriter created. J D Rockefeller, on up to the White House, and everyone, in between and on that level, had one."

Although Jenny was never in Enoch's bedroom, the one and only request she ever made to him was to describe it to her. She passed the description on to Hilda. Who, the first time she saw the room, found it to be exactly as Jenny said. Hilda drew on her imagination as to how deep Jenny and Enoch's relationship was and what the nights they spent together must have been like, unaware they never took place.

*****

After they arrived, they put his body on the first bed they found and opened every window in the room. Jenny and Hilda emptied Enoch's pockets. The knife, watch, wallet, business cards and wedding invitation went into Jenny's purse.

She read the business cards and the invitation, impressed by the card for William S Rowe, Cleveland's Chief of Police, and the card for the owner of the *Cleveland Plain Dealer* newspaper Liberty Holden. She didn't know what to make of the Pinkerton card, after she saw the picture of the 'eye' and read the slogan below it, "We Never Sleep." Other than it was some type of a warning.

As she closed her hand bag, she wondered how the items found their way to Enoch's vest pocket. With his pockets empty and her purse full, the two left the room and closed the door behind them. From there Jenny and Hilda began to explore the rest of the house.

The two wandered into the kitchen, found the note Enoch left Brooks the day before and began a search for two people who should have been back from their buggy ride way before her and Hilda's arrival. Where were they? Jenny and Hilda had searched every room in the house and every building on the property. Hilda asked, "What if we put the body in one of their rooms and they come back and find it before they find the two of us?" The question caused a blank stare from both followed by a stifled chuckle. It was all they had left after they thought about the situation, they found themselves in.

The next day Hilda stayed back, in case they showed up, and Jenny drove into Cleveland. She hired a mortician, gave him directions to the place, told him who to see, and instructions on how and where to lay out the body. The mortician phoned in an order for ice to be sent to the address she gave him. He next proceeded downtown to process the death certificate and from there, Enoch's residence.

From the mortician she headed to the newspaper to put in a "Death Notice," for the record and any legal matters that may come up. She was directed to where she needed to go and gave her information to a young clerk. As the clerk wrote it all down, Jenny gazed at her desk. The "In and Out" baskets held her interest.

The clerk read back to Jenny the information she had given, the full name, age, date of birth, date of death, occupation, there were no problems and Enoch Mast's death notice would be published in the following day's newspaper. As Jenny thanked the clerk, she asked her, "Has it been an interesting morning?" The clerk answered, "Why do you ask?" Jenny then nodded towards her Out-Basket and the title on a very short memo which sat on top of all her outgoing work. The title of the memo read, "Two dead bodies found on Lake Erie shore."

The clerk told Jenny right away she couldn't discuss the memo but her body language said the opposite. It wasn't hard to see she was filled with the desire to tell Jenny everything because there was a lot to talk about. The short memo had the perfect recipe for some salacious gossip.

All the clerk needed was a gentle nudge. Jenny began to coax her and assure the clerk it would be okay to tell her what she knew.

She had a card to play, she had Liberty Holden's. She reached into her purse and showed the clerk as she explained Holden was a good friend. She also showed the clerk William S Rowe's card for good measure. She told the clerk in a very pleasant and persuasive manner, "There you have it! What better references do I need! The owner and the chief of police."

The cap blew off and the clerk gushed out all she knew. What was in the memo, the police report, which was for the record, not publication. The police didn't want the news out before they completed their investigation. The facts were, one body was a male negro, the other body was a white woman. Both were shot through the right temple. The male was found in his underwear, the woman was nude. There are no suspects, no weapons. Both are unidentified and at the city morgue.

The clerk continued, "The 'unidentified' at the morgue usually wind up with the 'Red Cats,' that's what the cops call them. They're who the cops sell the bodies to." Jenny tilted her head to show her bewilderment. The clerk went on, "You know, where the college and hospital are off Chester Avenue? Well, there's a medical school and morgue up there. More often than not the 'unidentified' bodies in the city morgue wind up in that morgue and then in an anatomy class. The clerk laughed, "It's a good day for the Red Cats and the cops when they get to pick up the unknown – it's the best-known secret in Cleveland"

The clerk got the reaction she wanted from Jenny. The revelation stunned her. She politely nodded and left. Her first assessment, as she walked away and from what the clerk told her, there was no point in going to either morgue. She had never seen the two, she couldn't identify them. There would just be a lot of questions and no one would know anything. If the two, in the note, who she believed to be 'Cap' and Mary Irene, weren't back when she returned, she had a pretty good idea as to why, and where they were. What she didn't know, or anyone else for that matter, was who shot them. She would have to tell Hilda all she knew, and what she thought.

*****

While preparations were made in Cleveland, in the new dimension, Enoch Mast headed north on a dirt road. The road eventually turned to sandstone and what came into view were buildings and the landscape of a large city, along with the people who went in and out of their shops, offices, taverns, apartments and houses. There were all types of people, traffic, noise and commotion and as he moved on Enoch became another face in the crowd.

Enoch moved with the flow in the new dimension and turned his head every moment he thought he saw someone he knew, which was often. Those around him were able to see he was a stranger. Most, but not all, smiled or nodded as they passed. There was a pleasant and even pace to all the activity that took place as he slowly moved through the crowd. He didn't know for certain, but felt if evil existed there, good prevailed over it. Yet in the back of his mind, he doubted if all evil could be absent from anywhere. It was hard for him to imagine he'd be in such a place.

It wasn't a person, but a building that stopped him in his tracks. He came upon the Gerhardovitch Building. A grey limestone band, built into the red brick façade, had the name carved on it in large letters. It was centered between two fair sized second story windows. Below the windows, a place known as 'Finnerty's.' A location with a long bar where one could stand around plenty of food and drink a large beer, as they built a huge sandwich to go with it. A bar with durable tables and comfortable chairs to sit at when the double-decker was done. At age fourteen and up to the time it burned to the ground in 1879, when he was forty, Enoch thought Finnerty's was heaven and there it stood.

He stared at the building for a long time and recalled all the times he was in the bar, the upstairs apartment, and the law office across the hall. He remembered the apartment had the window with the nice red velvet curtains and was where Miss Chiffon got her start. Who, on one occasion tried to entice Ezra, Enos, Brooks and him to her place. It was right after they delivered a five-hundred pound safe to the lawyer's office across the hall. She worked for the lawyer and the services she could provide them would be in lieu of payment.

He remembered, it wasn't that they weren't interested, it was they were very busy and unfortunately had a long list of different priorities at the time. Enoch told her to tell the lawyer they'd be back in the morning and to have their money ready. Which she did and they were paid. Enoch told her in such a manner that he and his brothers remained on friendly terms with Miss Chiffon throughout the years. They never backed away from the fact they knew her and were friends. In return she let her prominent customers know that, unlike them, the Mast brothers were never clients of her business.

As perfect a place as Enoch tried to make Finnerty's, it also, came to him, the setup he and his brothers had with the bar was less than admirable. It was one of several watering holes the Mast brothers paid in advance to keep their father in order for the family business to survive. It struck Enoch how he and his brothers didn't care what happened to their father in these places, until a bad episode would take place, and their attitude would change drastically from what they thought they believed.

Miss Chiffon, and the lawyer, probably hadn't forgotten the savage beating Enoch and his brothers gave a strong young bartender for roughing up their father one day when he got out of hand. It was bad enough they had to manipulate their father, through his alcoholism, in order to survive, but for someone else to mistreat him was unacceptable. The Mast brothers made it ironically apparent no other person on the planet would ever be allowed the privilege to abuse their father, but them. The recollections, both good and bad, caused Enoch to sighed to himself, "Here it is and all I can recall is it was as bad as it was good." After he said it, he wondered what it was like inside and who might be in it. He wanted to go inside, but was afraid.

*****

A voice rang out, "From a son of Molly McGuire," followed by a fast and furious slap to the back of Enoch's head. It jolted him, but was painless. It wasn't the slap, that astonished Enoch, but the voice. It came from his brother Enos, who in the blink of an eye, stood face to face, with Enoch and totally overwhelmed him. Enos sudden appearance left Enoch speechless. It was the reaction Enos wanted and he started, "Look at the two of us meeting up at Finnerty's," and quickly added, "He's not in there," to let Enoch know he knew his thoughts.

Enos covered almost every event that took place between them in a modest amount of time. Every word he spoke was the perfect term to use to get what he meant across in the minimum amount of time, with maximum clarity. He made it easy to return to where they last crossed paths, the time he ran off with the crazy Irish woman for the coal fields of Pennsylvania. The two moved in their conversation like a team of oxen and effortlessly ploughed through their lives; no stone left unturned. In the course of what was said, Enos let Enoch know he was right about the Pinkerton's

Eventually Enoch brought up Marsden and Enos chuckled, "Everyone here has a 'Royal Roy Marsden,' mine was Amos Amspoker." His reply again left Enoch speechless and Enos laughed, and added. "Yeah – I know!" It provided Enos the opportunity to tell Enoch, "It was right after he dropped a bunch of us Molly McGuire's off in Erie, Pennsylvania." Enos explained how he had robbed a mine and had plenty of money and led a group of miners from West Virginia to Cleveland, from there they headed to the mines in Pennsylvania. He told Enoch they all got out of town in the nick of time, the local authorities and an army of Pinkertons in Cleveland got wind of them and were about to track them down.

Enos explained, "We were one step ahead of them on the docks but soon to be cornered. Luckily, I ran into Amos and we put a deal together. Amos Amspoker and the crew of the *Balltara* saved our lives, he piloted us one-hundred-two miles, one late November, when no one would go out on the lake, he got us to Erie, Pa. safe and sound, took less than a day, did it in about seven hours, in rough waters.

It was perfect, the authorities had the train stations and roads covered, but not the ports – they didn't think anyone would try to escape by the lake at that time of the year." Enos continued, "That's what we did and it went smooth and fast and we slipped into Pennsylvania unnoticed with enough time to raise a lot of hell before we eventually got caught and they stringed us up. Enos continued, "Turned out the Balltara made it to Erie and Amos should've spent the night but he turned right around and headed back to Cleveland. They got caught in a god-awful gale that night and it killed every one of them." Enos ended, "You'll like Amos and won't Jenny be surprised when she finds out about what happened!"

Eventually Enoch's voice returned and the questions he had were non-stop and on rapid fire. Enos smiled and told Enoch it would take some time for him to figure out where he was and what was going on. He let him know it was no different for him when he arrived, he was just as confused. Most of all Enos let Enoch know he wasn't going to explain everything to him at once as to where he was, and who was there, or how it all worked. Enos told Enoch he would let him in on two surprises about to come his way before he would leave him.

They began to walk and Enos assured Enoch they'd meet up again, but it wouldn't be soon. He used an inside joke he believed Enoch would understand to explain, "Look, you're in a big place with a lot of souls – time doesn't exist here, you can never run out of time in whatever you pursue, it makes a big difference. For some it's a hard adjustment, they find they are a slave to time and when freed, can't change and go crazy. You know what I mean? Those who can't adjust disappear. Most take to the situation naturally, like a great weight, that was always on them, has been lifted off them. Besides I'll know who you'll catch up with and look at the compass on your tombstone what direction to take to catch up with you."

Enos said nothing more and led Enoch to the first surprise. They found themselves on the shore of a lake and he let what was off in the distance captivate Enoch's attention. They came upon two people and Enoch saw and heard, for real, what he had once dreamed. There in the same color and sound, Brooks and Mary Irene sat on a beach below a crystal blue sky. By Emmet, the horse, and the stately split hickory buggy. Only Mary Irene is doing all the talking and it's about a book she held in her hand and had just finished. Brooks Mast is the one listening, smiling and nodding his head. There they were sitting, talking like normal people, both waiting for him on a beautiful beach. It was so vivid and clear and real.

Enoch began to rush toward them and Enos grabbed his arm and stopped him. "Wait! Like you they just arrived – some things have to happen before you can meet up with anyone here, same with them! There's a protocol." Enos clarified what he said and told

Enoch the second surprise. Enoch was informed guardian angels set the protocol, once it is completed the soul can move about their new realm.

Enos let Enoch know he knew Marsden well, that like Marsden, he too was a guardian angel, and it was a long story for another day, as to how it came about. He informed him Marsden would be the one to set Enoch's protocol, and as Enoch was probably aware, Marsden liked the procedure where the soul attends their funeral and informs the bereaved about the person they've come to mourn.

He also let Enoch know, not only would he attend his own funeral; he would do so as a woman. One who bore a strong family resemblance, who would cast no shadow. The scripture would be read, according to the twenty-fifth Chapter of Mathew, verses thirty-five through forty. A verse often read to them by their mother, well known to Enoch and his brothers. A soloist would sing the negro spiritual Deep River, words from three good friends said, a burial, followed by a wake and photographs. Enoch caught very little of what was said after he was told he would be a woman, to lost in the thought, to ask any questions.

He was also told; he would see Jenny and she would see him but they wouldn't speak. They would talk to all but not each other. He would recognize her but the strong family resemblance wouldn't be enough for her to recognize him. Jenny would search for a man, not a woman. She would never find who she looked for, who she believed would show and the disappointment didn't leave her eyes.

Enoch's protocol came to pass just as Enos said and he moved on down the road. The funeral, an event, Jenny would dream about from time to time. Each episode with their own set of circumstances, each outcome noteworthy in its own way.

*****

It was close to five, maybe six months, after Enoch's funeral, Ezra, Seth and Simon Mast, met in Laramie, Wyoming, to plan their future. They spent little time there, within a day or so of their arrival they saddled up and headed two-hundred ninety-nine miles north and arrived in Deadwood, South Dakota ten days later. The trip gave them time to talk about the war in Europe. Their herds had never been larger and their bet was the demand for beef was about to go through the roof. As bad as it sounded, the war was a once in a lifetime opportunity for them. Earlier in the year they had discussed taking a trip to Cleveland, but what happen June twenty-eighth in Europe completely overshadowed what took place in Cleveland on the same day and any thought of any early return to Enoch's.

They were ready to negotiate a per head price with the brokers and talk boxcars with the railways, in Laramie, Deadwood, and Abilene, to sell all their cattle from the *Bar Z, Saddle Ridge*, and *Shadow Run*, and from there on out to just sit on their land. They were totally motivated to get their cattle to the stockyards in Chicago and for their herds to be the first to arrive in the Spring. The market never looked better and was the one to go out on. The one where there wouldn't be enough time to spend all they would make on the deal. The one that would keep them comfortable for the rest of their life's.

Before they would leave Deadwood, they would check on a large barb wire order, placed through Solomon Star associates with the Cleveland, Ohio location of American Hardware Manufacturing Corporation. It was way overdue. All their ranches needed the wire and they were aware the War in Europe might consume their order.

As a matter of record a telegram would be sent to AHMC by the associates, it would explain their customer had put down a third of the price quoted, and that either a firm date of arrival be given, or their money refunded in full. From the time AHMC received the wire, they had twenty-four hours to comply. Implied within the telegram, if they didn't reply with a date or the refund, they would be in for a most unpleasant experience.

*****

All were told: the brokers, the railways, and the associates, for the next few days, the Ohio Trio could be found at the Bullock Hotel. It was only moments after they checked in, that they ran into Pearce Buckwell in the lobby. He was from back home, and had served with Ezra and Enos in the Ohio 29th Infantry. Pearce had never met Seth and Simon, it didn't matter, both had heard his name more than once over the years, it wasn't hard and didn't take long for them to make his acquaintance.

They had their bags sent to their rooms and the four headed for the hotel casino, found a table and began to drink. Seth and Simon listened to Ezra and Pearce tell war stories until Pearce, out of nowhere, told them he had killed a pimp for Miss Chiffon back in Cleveland and she told him to get out of town for a while. He decided to head west. In the middle of his story of how he wound up in Deadwood, he made another sharp turn, again totally unexpected, and gave his condolences to them on the passing of Enoch Mast, Ezra's brother and Seth and Simon's father. He thought they knew and soon found out they had no idea Enoch was gone.

From that point on the three peppered him with questions he couldn't answer. All Pearce could tell them was he caught the death notice in the Plain Dealer and saw the hearse in the middle of a crowd on its way to Lake View Cemetery. He told them the word on the street was - Enoch Mast was in it.

Eventually Pearce grew tired of all their questions. He pushed his chair from the table, gave them a wink, smiled and left it at that. Pearce thanked them for the drinks, got up, tipped his hat and moved on. Ezra, Seth and Simon, in a state of shock, were unable to return a smile or tip of the hat. Pearce Buckwell wasn't offended, he paid it no mind; aware he had stunned them with the news.

*****

After the encounter with Pearce Buckwell all the Ohio Trio's plans went on hold for a while. The first heavy snow in Cleveland was on the ground once they returned to their plans and put them into motion. All three ranches had their instructions. The Ohio Trio would set up and complete the details of their sale in Chicago.

They left Chicago for Cleveland after all the particulars of the contracts were met and the documents signed. They wired ahead to rent a buggy that could hold three passengers and their baggage. It was to be at the railway station upon their arrival. It was there at midnight and it took them almost no time to load and leave the station and head to Enoch's

It was close to one in the morning when first, Hilda and then Jenny, heard the muffled sounds of the horse's hoofs as they moved through the snow headed towards the stable/garage. From what they saw out their window, they had just enough time to grab Enoch's Colt Single action Peacemaker pistol and find a place to hide in the stable/garage before the buggy would enter it.

It came to Jenny, as they took up a good position in the hayloft, it had to be Enoch's brother and two sons she thought out loud. Hilda was about to ask Jenny if that was the case why were they hiding? But before she could the Ohio Trio came through the doors of a place they knew so well.

They began to light the lanterns and as they did, came upon, and were struck by the presence of the 1912 Runabout. More than its presence - it had its own area, with tools and parts. Their reaction was one of distain and the three began a strange conversation on how gas stations and mechanics had started to replace and endanger livery stables and blacksmiths. The intensity of their conversation evolved into a debate over if they should wake the house or wait till morning to bring up what they found, as they made fun of the pickup no different than Enoch once did at Jesse O'Dell's expense.

They decided they wouldn't wait, and once their horse was bedded down in the stall next to Emmett, their bags off the buggy, some horse-blankets thrown on some clean straw for their beds, they made their move. The whole time they talked about what they would say to Enoch, Cap and Mary Irene. Their decision to move on the house at such a late hour put them in a good mood to stir the pot over what they found.

Jenny and Hilda found the three to be humorous, in a strange and dangerous way. Jenny decided they were harmless enough for the two of them to come out of hiding. They caught the Ohio Trio off guard as they jumped down from the eight-foot-high hay loft and were able to cut them off from the doors. They literally got the drop on the Ohio Trio, which was very rare, and the Trio was equally as embarrassed as they were surprised. Two women stopped them in their tracks. They were surprised to the point they each ripped open their winter coats and went for their large caliber, well holstered hand guns. They stopped short of the draw, stunned they were face to face with two women.

Jenny spoke first, "We also have a gun," as she moved the hand that held the pistol from behind her light blue housecoat. She held the Colt Peace Maker in her right hand, cocked and loaded, but never pointed it at them. Both sides retreated into silence and just stared at each other.

*****

Jenny had a presence about her, she was alluring in many ways and her capabilities became apparent after one listened to her. She seized the opportunity to speak first. She introduced herself, "I am Jenny Amspoker and I have a lot to tell you, bear with me." She told them she had the information they wanted but it would be hard to explain.

The Ohio Trio knew nothing about her. For all they knew, she could be someone put there to take advantage of them and fleece the family. They had been out west too long and developed a suspicious nature about strangers they ran into, until that stranger was able to prove themselves to them, which for most wasn't an easy task.

She knew it was just a question of time before she'd be asked where Brooks and Mary Irene were. As the trio began to ask questions, Jenny made a plea, "Wait till morning." She added, "It's very late let me show you to your rooms.". Without missing a beat, she began to talk about a breakfast of ham and eggs, hash browns, toast, butter, jelly, pancakes, maple syrup, and fresh coffee. The approach held their attention. She informed them that it would be late morning, it would be what some call a 'brunch.' A brunch would give them time to rest and wash up for all the questions they had about her and Hilda, and she and Hilda had about the Trio. She told them; she wouldn't have them stay in the stables. As they moved towards the house, she concluded none had any idea why Brooks and Mary Irene were not there. She knew their whereabouts would be the first topic at brunch and she wasn't too far off.

*****

Brunch took on a very businesslike atmosphere. To set the tone Ezra took the fresh cut flowers off the table and put them on the kitchen counter. As Hilda brought the food, Ezra, Seth, and Simon began to ask Jenny pointed questions that required little more

290

than a 'yes' or 'no' answer as they began to eat. Questions drawn on the information they got from Pearce Buckwell. Questions were also directed at Hilda and they looked for any slip ups from the two, where one answered 'no' and the other 'yes' to the same question.

Another line of questions concerned relatives. Jenny and Hilda were asked if they were a relation? A relative they may have heard about but never met. The Trio had a long list of such people. The people Ezra, Simon, and Seth asked about they called 'Mom Relatives.' They knew their mother, and grandmother, grew up in an orphanage. She never saw herself alone in the world, anyone she got to know, in the children's home, became a brother or sister. The Trio had over a dozen names to throw at the two. Jenny and Hilda answered "No," to all of them.

Finally, the question Jenny and Hilda waited for came, "Where are Cap and Mary Irene?" The way it was asked put some steam behind the words Ezra used that would severely burn someone if what was asked wasn't answered the right way. Jenny replied, "I believe they're with Enoch, they disappeared the day he died, June twenty-eighth, 1914, and I'll tell you all I know about their disappearance and his death."

She told Ezra, Simon and Seth why he went to the Lasbrith estate and how their brother, and father, found his way to the Lasbrith ballroom and took it over. She told them everything, from the moment he entered the kitchen, to the moment they carried him out of the ballroom. She told them all what took place and what happened afterward. She told them of the characters involved and the parts they played. She told them all she could.

It was the driving lessons that had the most impact on the Ohio Trio, and from them they learned what Enoch had left her. As she went on about the lessons it became clear how the Ford

Runabout found its way to the stable and why the stable was turning into a garage.

Because the lessons were no longer on Enoch's property, but hers, she would show them the documents. It didn't shock the Trio it disgruntled and agitated them. If they weren't angry over the revelation, they were anger's closest neighbor. The reality was they already had three ranches and didn't want another property. They actually weren't troubled by the situation but felt they should act upset.

Jenny's pace of what she said, and the rhythm of her words was able to ease their reaction and mood and allowed her to speak, without interruption, for long periods of time. She wisely used what Enoch told her about his mother to her advantage and reminded them of the *Parable of the Vineyard* found in the book of Matthew, twentieth chapter, eighth verse. She told them, "You know the one your mother and grandmother read to you about how the world isn't a fair place."

It jolted Ezra, as all the times they'd go back and forth over the scripture, as they loaded the wagons, came back to him, clear as day. It hit Seth and Simon also, they were no strangers to the scriptures their grandmother would quote. After Jenny covered this part of what she told them, she became no different than a close relative one should listen to. She told them the scripture used at Enoch's funeral, the spiritual they sang, and who gave the eulogies. To where Ezra, Seth and Simon felt they were at the service.

A small box of photographs was brought out. They were of the wake that followed the service. The Ohio Trio knew two out of three people in the photos, and there were a lot of people in the pictures. They all made their comments until one photo left them speechless.

The picture had ten people in it and was taken with Lake Erie in the background. The angle of the sun, at the time of day it was taken, produced nine shadows for ten people on the beach. The person without the shadow was a woman with a strong family resemblance. Ezra was the first to point out the missing shadow and resemblance. It went unnoticed by Jenny until that moment. She gasped when she caught what Ezra noticed, "She's him! The one person from my dream I never got a chance to talk to. There he is – it's never what you expect!"

*****

There was much more to the story, but it ended there for the stonemason and his boss. The wood was gone, the fire was out, and the warmth faded. The boss stood up, headed for the lavatory and the "voice of the past" was gone forever. Had the two known what triggered the 'voice' they would have stayed much longer. As it turned out, the dawn was at hand, and both thought home and bed a better place to be and went their separate ways.

They said little to each other, their minds occupied by all they had heard. They waved more than talked as they left the shop; the boss went one way and the stonemason another. The snow was deep and gave them the opportunity to think about something other than all the voice had told them until they got home. There in the warmth of their homes the story of Enoch's ballroom would return and never leave.

The stonemason pulled up the collar of his coat to fend off the cold, he checked its inside breast pocket for the envelope more than once. As he walked, he thought about all he was going to tell his wife. How He knew how the missing Hardin Lasbrith died, and where John Brown got the idea about Harpers Ferry, who J D Rockefeller's substitute was in the Civil War, and who convinced Teddy Roosevelt to return to public service. He'd tell her who was behind the Wooton desks, and all the other mysteries he knew. Finally, he would tell her it's the incidental people who make great men what they are, the Enoch Mast's of the world and their brothers, sisters, wives and children and the times they went through. And when he arrived at home, he told his wife everything.

The boss had a shorter distance to cover and no one to tell how he spent the night. He thought back on the Client, the one who told him the past always surrenders its secrets to fate, and wondered if they would ever cross paths again…